UNSUNG

Not All Heroes Wear Kits

UNSUNG

Behind the Scenes With Sport's Hidden Stars

Alexis James

First published by Pitch Publishing, 2022

Pitch Publishing
9 Donnington Park,
85 Birdham Road,
Chichester,
West Sussex,
PO20 7AJ
www.pitchpublishing.co.uk
info@pitchpublishing.co.uk

A CIP catalogue record is available for this book
from the British Library.

ISBN 978 1 80150 141 5

Typesetting and origination by Pitch Publishing
Printed and bound in India by Replika Press Pvt. Ltd.

Contents

To my dad. And to Riz.

May your song always be sung

– Bob Dylan, 'Forever Young'

Introduction

THE SEED for this book was planted in 2018 in the spectacular leafy surrounds of Le Golf National, Paris. It was day two of the Ryder Cup and I was nursing a rotten hangover in the freezing 5am queues. As the sun began to peep over the green hills and golden dunes of the Albatross course, a distant hum caught my attention. A battalion of greenkeepers driving ride-on mowers was plotting a path to the imposing grandstand nicknamed 'Le Monstre'. Clipped to each vehicle was the blue flag of Europe, fluttering in the morning breeze. It was a rousing sight. And for us lucky, bleary-eyed attendees it was a sign that the Ryder Cup had begun. But for those two dozen ground staff, alive and alert, it had started many years ago.

Before I arrived in France, I had written about these guardians of the fairway. I had interviewed Ryder Cup course superintendents past and present, including Steve Chappell. He was in charge at Gleneagles in 2014, and he told me the story behind one of its most memorable moments.

On the final day, Europe's Justin Rose had skewed left off the tee and into the gorse on the 13th hole. Watching on, Chappell couldn't believe it. Months prior, he had intended to remove those very bushes. But he was prevented from doing so by European captain Paul McGinley. The skipper had reasoned that, at over 300 yards from the tee, it was more likely to be the big-hitting Americans who would be caught in the trap.

Instead, it was Rose who had been swatted. His American opponent Hunter Mahan sensed a chance to increase his lead and halt the surging Europeans. But while McGinley hadn't expected his guys to be in the shrub, he had been meticulous enough to note the yardage during his pre-tournament recces. With his captain's insight to hand, Rose did the rest. His recovery to within a foot of the pin became one of the defining moments of the tournament.

A birdie clawed back Mahan's lead and, with Europe 10-6 ahead, extinguished any faint American hopes. Rose smiled at the camera and quipped, 'There's a bit of Seve for you.' He was right, it was a shot that the great Ballesteros himself would have been delighted with. The Scottish crowd cheered. The commentators gushed. And one relieved superintendent had experienced that moment like no other fan on the planet.

So as I watched the sprightly troop of greenkeepers fizz their way around lush Parisian lawns, I felt their pride. Admittedly, the Latin Quarter mojitos may have had a lingering effect on my sensibilities. But I also appreciated the years of toil that went towards laying the foundations on which golf's greats could showcase their brilliance.

Throughout sport, there are hundreds of decisions made and actions taken by peripheral figures just like Steve

Chappell. They help shape the moments that become TV montages, history-book chapters, and lifelong memories. It is their stories that I intend to tell over the following 12 chapters.

The number feels apt. In football, the 12th man is a term that describes a crowd whose commitment has compelled their team to victory. In cricket, the 12th man is the poor sap who hasn't quite made the field but could be needed at any moment. Many of those featured in these pages will relate to both descriptions. Some of the roles go way back in history. Some are recent creations born of sport's increasing professionalism. All are now indispensable.

Although they often occupy the same room, track, or pitch as the biggest names in sport, the characters described here are more relatable. They look like us, live like us, and have flaws like us. They are not the media-savvy operators that modern sportspeople are. With some understandable exceptions, they are unguarded, honest, and thrilled to be able to share the tales they rarely get to tell.

Although this began as a 2020 lockdown project, I didn't want the pandemic to dominate every word. It is something we have all lived through but it will not define us. Nonetheless, there are chapters where Covid-19's unwelcome spectre is unavoidable. Several I spoke to even played an integral part in sport's resilient fightback.

Restrictions prevented me from personally visiting all of those featured, though I am grateful to the many who did welcome me to their homes and places of work when permitted. To those I only met over Zoom, I sincerely hope that I have managed to do your story justice.

And to the reader, I also hope that I have been able to relay the pride that these people take in their work and the ways in which they are integral to their sport. If so, then maybe the next time you attend or watch a sporting event, you'll have a hair-raising moment like the one I experienced in Paris. Only without the cold sweats.

You'll look beyond the headlines and behind the athletes. For there is where you'll see the people who power them. For every Lewis Hamilton there is a pit mechanic priming his car. For every Emma Raducanu there is a performance chef fuelling her goals. For every Harry Kane there are ground staff perfecting his stage. And for every Usain Bolt there is an athletics starter launching his first steps to greatness.

While its biggest stars and household names enjoy the glory, tucked away amid sport's small print and voiceless under its fanfare is a band of unsung heroes rarely acknowledged, let alone championed. Too often these tireless facilitators and hidden organisers are only noticed when they make an error. The feats are reserved for the athletes, while those behind the scenes are only ever attributed to the disasters. This book is a humble attempt to change that.

Alexis James, April 2022

1

START ME UP: Athletics Starters

*The sound of gunfire is the precursor to every
great sprint in athletics history. Yet those
pulling the trigger are much more than a
hired gun. Meet the volunteer officials whose
strict codes on rule-keeping can break as many
dreams as they make – for even the world's
most famous athletes.*

It All Starts with a Bang

'ON YOUR MARKS'

At the 2009 World Athletics Championships in
Berlin, the field for the 100m final included the fastest
man in history. He smiled at the camera and produced his
famous pose before accepting the invitation to his blocks.
His nervous rivals were beholden to superstition. They
jumped on the spot, fiddled with jewellery, sipped water,
and prayed.

'SET'

Over 50,000 fans at the Olympiastadion held their
breath, and their phones. They were anticipating the new

world record that a global audience of 95 million were about to witness. The sprinters were poised. The world now waited on one man.

His name was Alan.

BANG!

You may not have heard of Alan Bell, but you've almost certainly heard his gun. Now in his 70s, he remains the highest-ranked chief starter in the UK and one of the most experienced in the world. As well as the World Championships he has fired the starting pistol at the Olympics, the Commonwealth Games, the World Indoor Championships, and the European Championships. It makes him the only international starter to have officiated at every major athletics meeting. And it means that when Usain Bolt cemented his greatness in Berlin, Alan had the best seat in the house.

'That night will probably be the greatest moment of my life, with the exception of the birth of my kids,' he told me when we first chatted in January 2021. 'You fire a gun at the World Championship Final, which is not a bad bonus in itself, and the big fella from Jamaica creates history. And nobody has been anywhere near since.'

Hanging on the wall of his study is the certificate that displays Bolt's name and the astonishing time of 9.58 seconds. As starter, Alan's signature also appears on there. He was keen to point out that without it, the record would not have been ratified. 'That's my 17th world record,' he said, before pointing to another framed memento from the night. It was Bolt's warm-up vest. 'My son tells me it should be on eBay. I've suggested over my dead body!'

A former high jumper who represented England at amateur level in the early 1970s, Alan was forced to retire in his mid-20s when he ruptured the achilles tendon in his take-off foot. 'I'm a knackered athlete,' he boomed in a Geordie baritone as loud as his gun. As a member of North Shields Polytechnic Club, he was invited to help out at a youth track meet. He agreed, expecting to judge the high jump. Instead, club secretary and local bank manager John Kennedy opened a briefcase and handed him a pair of pistols. Alan chuckled at the memory. 'I looked at him and said, "Mr Kennedy, I haven't got a bloody clue how to do that!" He said, "Don't worry, the kids won't know." And I did it.'

Alan was in his 45th season, in 17 of which he had featured on World Athletics's (formerly the IAAF) elite list of officials. Serendipity has played a big part in his ascent. A shortage of starters in his native north-east meant that only days after firing John Kennedy's gun, he was sitting the required exam in the kitchen of another club official. The region's renown as a host to top-level athletics, spearheaded by Olympic long-distance runner Brendan Foster and centred around Gateshead International Stadium, also came at the perfect time for Alan. He had regular exposure to high-profile events in the 1970s and '80s. 'Sometimes ambition plays no part in what happens to you. Sometimes it's just good fortune and opportunity,' he said, before adding that he occasionally bumps into Foster for a 'beer and a cry over Newcastle United'.

Some of Alan's earliest experiences at elite meetings were in Gateshead's call room, where athletes are checked to ensure they're abiding by competition regulations. It's here where they have their bags searched, their spikes checked, their bib numbers distributed, and any non-conforming logos covered with tape. 'Believe me, we used to find some really dodgy stuff in the bags,' said Alan. He described on one occasion being grabbed by the testicles and pinned to the wall after finding a vial in a Russian shot putter's bag. 'I have to be careful with naming some of them,' he added. More in hope than expectation, I told him he couldn't be sued if the athletes were now dead. 'Chances are they will be if they were taking as much as we found,' came Alan's deadpan response.

Originally a PE teacher at Benfield School in Newcastle, where he taught a young footballer by the name of Steve Bruce, Alan became a school inspector before moving into the job that would dovetail perfectly with his voluntary role as a starter. As international development director at the Youth Sport Trust, he worked with the Ministry of Sport to implement programmes all over the world in the build-up to London 2012. The recruitment process for the role saw him interviewed by Baroness Sue Campbell, a day after he oversaw seven false starts in a single 110m hurdles race at the European Cup.

One of the most powerful figures in UK Sport began their encounter with the question, 'Were you the idiot doing the starting at Gateshead yesterday?' Even for someone familiar with explosive starts, it caught Alan by surprise. But it proved to be the beginning of a fruitful relationship and he has since visited over 70 countries combining his developmental work and his role in athletics.

Now retired from the former, the latter keeps his passport well thumbed. He told me he is planning a six-day trip to Finland for the national championships, having opted against two weeks in Nairobi for the World Under-20 event. When I asked if I might be able to shadow him at a forthcoming meeting, he suggested we meet a bit closer to home. 'People think, "Wow, you started a big race in Berlin." But the skill of starting that race is perfected at the Tyneside Track League in Gateshead or the National Junior League in Birmingham.' And so we arranged to reconvene at a Division 1 meeting of the North East Youth Development League.

The Slowest 100m Race in History

'I did not move!' shouted Jon Drummond. And then he didn't move. He lay on the track, with his hands behind his head, and the 2003 World Championships in Paris descended into a French farce. Baffled officials resorted to waving flimsy, print-at-home red cards, but they were like aircraft marshals on a deserted runway. They adjudged that Drummond, along with Jamaican Asafa Powell, had jumped the gun in heat two of this highly anticipated 100m quarter-final. It was the second false start of the race, following Dwight Thomas's overeager hamstrings the first time around. As per a controversial new rule, one false start would see the entire field cautioned, regardless of who committed the offence. Any sprinter beating the trigger thereafter would be instantly eliminated.

It was a rule as unpopular with the public as it was with the athletes, and a furious Drummond found himself with a stadium of allies. With the video replays on the big screen appearing inconclusive, the whistling French crowd – never shy about sticking fingers up to the establishment – appeared to be backing the American. Frantic officials in red caps scattered like the laser target from a drunken sniper. Unlike the baying mob, they had proof of the unfair advantage. Starting-block sensor readings showed that Drummond had moved 0.052 seconds after the gun and Powell 0.086. Anything below 0.100 seconds is judged to be beyond the limit of human reflexes and is penalised accordingly.

Finally, after 15 minutes of acting like a sulking toddler insisting he hadn't fed his greens to the dog, Drummond pulled down his top and strutted off. His eyes were bulging, his head was shaking, and his bottom lip was quivering. But the drama continued. As the American whipped up a frenzied crowd, a word from a mischievous US official appeared to persuade the Olympic gold medallist to return to his blocks. Skinsuit back on, Drummond duly obliged, shaking the hands of his perplexed rivals and leaving beleaguered officials to begin the unenviable process of evicting him all over again.

Meanwhile, Powell, who had accepted the decision without the petulance, also felt emboldened to return. The crowd cheered and the athletes recommenced their warm-ups while stern men in beige suits joined their hapless tracksuited colleagues. The decision was made to postpone the race, and run the two remaining quarter-final heats instead. The sprinters walked off to a chorus of Gallic jeers.

When the six remaining entrants were eventually able to return minus the offending duo, Drummond was pictured on the big screen. He was weeping in the arms of his coach at the nearby practice track. The irate Parisians continued to pull for their guy, and, like Drummond, they refused to take their orders when a forlorn starter pleaded for silence.

Eventually, Ato Boldon crossed the line in first place, 51 minutes after the race should have been run. The new false-start rule had been intended to reduce delays and keep television networks sweet. Instead, with the schedule in disarray and advertisers puce with rage, the Stade de France had become the scene of the slowest race in 100m history. Commentating for the BBC, USA track legend Michael Johnson set aside any sympathy for a former team-mate and reflected the ire of his producers. '[Drummond] knows the rules, and the IAAF should have something in place for this kind of situation,' he said. 'If somebody won't go off, they should be escorted off by security. He has disrupted the entire competition. The rules work. The problem is what we do when we have an idiot athlete on the track. It is very distasteful. He should be penalised for embarrassing the sport.'

Lamine Diack, IAAF president and later jailed for corruption in 2020, felt that the incident had brought shame on the sport. Sat next to Olympics chief Jacques Rogge, he had witnessed the whole charade from the stands and he was particularly frustrated with starters who appeared tame and toothless.

Privately, Diack and the IAAF vowed that local officials would no longer be trusted to start races at major meetings. It was time to introduce an elite group of international starters who could handle troublemakers like Drummond. And they knew exactly where to start.

Local Heroes

It was a sunny July morning in Morpeth when I pulled into the King Edward VI school. A friendly car park attendant told me where I would find Alan, and I discovered later that this helpful chap was none other than Jim Alder, the marathon runner who won Commonwealth Games gold in Kingston in 1966. Alder was given the honour of carrying the Olympic flame through Northumberland in 2012. Still engaging and sprightly in his 80s, he remained the club president for Morpeth Harriers. He pointed me to a small, pebble-dashed storage building, situated just behind the hammer and discus cage.

As I made my way over the field, there was a nervous buzz of activity as the athletes, all aged between 13 and 17, exchanged excited chatter. One father chided his daughter for not stretching her calves, while a mother scrambled for safety pins. Half a dozen officials placed hurdles out on the track. I found Alan and his two colleagues sitting on a bench, reading through the timetable for the day. Alan stood up to hand me a copy, and I instantly understood why the IAAF thought of him when drawing up a list of elite starters. He's 6ft 3in, with closely shaved grey hair, and his voice is even louder in the flesh. He didn't strike me as the type who would have too many issues with stroppy sprinters.

He towered over the two gentlemen next to him, who he introduced as Micky and Malcolm. Malcolm Dewell was 63 and a highly experienced national starter. He had worked alongside Alan for many years, including at the London Olympics in 2012. Micky was Michael Baker, a relative newcomer to the role. Wearing dark sunglasses that seemed to be hermetically sealed to his face, he was keen to make the next step up from regional level. 'It's important that the likes of Malcolm and I come here to support the local guys and bring on the next generation of officials,' said Alan. 'And Micky is the next generation. He's a young lad.' Micky was 61.

The three of them were finalising where they would stand for each race. Ensuring clear visibility of each lane was the challenge, but it wasn't the only consideration. They also needed to keep an eye out for objects falling out of the sky. 'At this level that's not a big issue, as the kids might only throw the hammer 20m,' said Alan. 'But if this was a major meeting, it'd be going out 70m. You keep more than an eye out for it, believe me.' Malcolm's silver watch reflected in the sun as he pointed to the sky. 'It comes down like a bomb,' he said.

The two seasoned pros were in white polo shirts, meaning they would be acting as starter's assistants. They were to make sure that all competitors were where they should be before the chief starter set them off. That would be Micky, as he racked up some valuable experience and advice from his distinguished peers. As is standard for the role, he was wearing a red polo shirt and red cap. He also had an additional item of kit in the form of a luminous yellow sleeve slipped on to his right arm. Either there's a niche company making standalone glow-in-the-dark sleeves, or there's a trove of one-armed steward jackets discarded somewhere. I kept that thought to myself and asked instead about their guns.

Alan was the first to draw, producing a 9mm Ruger. 'That is *the* gun. The Olympic gun. The one used in 2012,' he said. Given the lofty introduction, I was a little startled when he casually passed it to me like it was the TV remote. I reluctantly took it in soft hands as if I had just been given a maternity-ward baby. If it wasn't already apparent that I'm as comfortable with a gun as a sheep is with a skateboard, I went on to reveal my ignorance in full when I asked to take a picture of it. Alan and Malcolm closed their eyes and shook their heads in sombre unison. 'It's fine taking a photograph of somebody using it, but not the gun itself, because people then know ...' Alan didn't finish his sentence, but I got the gist.

They may only be permitted the use of blank ammunition, but that doesn't exclude starters from the intense security checks that come with owning a firearm in the UK. In order to qualify for a gun licence, and to pass the renewal every five years, local police may search their house, write to their doctor, access their medical records, and request character references. They also reserve the right to conduct spot checks at any time, to ensure the gun and ammunition are correctly and securely stored. Starters even get asked if they're happy in life.

Courtesy of a farming background in Teesside, Malcolm has been around guns all his life. He remembered one particularly dramatic visit from Cleveland Police as part of strict checks following the 1987 Hungerford

Massacre. 'The firearms team arrived – all of them – in a Range Rover. They were in full SWAT suits, holding AK47s, parked right on my drive.' An incredulous Malcolm shuffled them into his house before any curtains began twitching, and took them to the attic where he stored his gun case. Despite it being mounted to an internal wall and reinforced with high-tensile steel plates, they adjudged the box to be deficient. 'They said the heads of the bolts on the outside needed to be welded. And they took all my guns away until I did it.'

Alan's first gun was a muzzle-loaded, black powder, sawn-off shotgun registered in 1877. Passed down to him from within the athletics community, it was the only licensed gun of its kind in the UK. Alan would occasionally fire it to launch large outdoor events such as the Great North Run. That was until he received a letter from Northumbria Police saying they had received a complaint from a member of the public. He reluctantly surrendered the weapon to his local police station, unwilling to risk losing a gun licence that doubles as his passport to the sporting elite.

Given that close attention from law enforcement is one of the more unexpected aspects of the role, it's little wonder that there are fewer than 100 starters in the UK authorised to carry firearms. Micky, a former local club runner whose involvement in officiating began when he responded to an email titled 'does anybody want to fire a gun?', is constantly awaiting a visit from his local force: 'I live in Newcastle, where they'll hold up the corner shop for anything. Every time I see a story in *The Chronicle* I expect a knock on the door.'

Rather than examples of meddlesome bureaucracy, I told them that I found their stories reassuring. They nodded their heads, rather unconvincingly. Suddenly there was a sharp toot of a horn that made me jump, indicating that a competitor was about to throw the hammer. Alan's radio crackled, and it was time for us to take our places at the start line for the opening race – the under-13s 70m hurdles.

As Malcolm and Alan trundled off to collect the runners, Micky entered the combination on the trigger locks of his two 9mm Smith & Wesson pistols. A lanyard and whistle hung around his neck as he loaded both guns, one for starting and the other for recall in the case of a false start. 'Before I did this I'd never held a gun. I was like you,' he added, miming his right arm flopping under the weight. 'I know nothing about guns, I didn't want to know anything about guns. If we could do this another way, I wouldn't have them. But that's the way it is.'

Micky may one day get his wish. Starters at national and international events use the latest electric guns provided by the likes of Seiko or Omega. But at that moment he stepped up on to the platform, called the hurdlers to their marks, and pulled the trigger. I jumped. It was to be the first of over 60 races that he would commence.

The day was in full swing. The sun was shining, accompanied by a breeze that carried every noise for miles. The honk of the horn, the crack of the gun, Alan's thundering voice. Parents, no longer permitted to stand at the finish line, attempted to make up for their relocation by cheering even louder from behind a Covid perimeter at the side of the track.

As Alan and Malcolm lined up runner after runner, I told them I was impressed by the level of organisation and sophistication at such a junior level. The guns, the hurdles, the walkie-talkies; some kids even brought their own starting blocks. It was certainly a step up from jumpers for goalposts. But it was the high level of officials that really set it apart from, say, a junior football or rugby match. And while teaching kids the rules enforced at the elite level was a key reason for Alan to attend, there were moments where exceptions were made. 'If a kid goes early here, Micky won't disqualify them,' said Alan. 'He'll take them aside and have a word. That's part of the process.'

It's a process that could well mean a future British medallist was among us. Malcolm recalled seeing a young Richard Kilty break records as a ten-year-old in Middlesbrough, 22 years before he would make his Olympic debut in Tokyo. And on the weekend that Joy Eze claimed a bronze medal in the 100m of the European Under-20 Championships in Finland, Alan vividly remembered the first time he saw her at Gateshead International Stadium, flying past kids two years older than her.

But while the competitors in Morpeth may have represented the next generation, the officials, to put it bluntly, did not. Alan told me that he remained the only level-five international starter in the country. Below him were 41 starters at level four – including Malcolm – who are qualified to start top national events. Of this number, only four were under 60. It turned out Alan wasn't joking when he said that Micky, a level-three starter, was among the youngest on the scene.

'If we held the Olympic Games tomorrow, we would still have the best start team in the world on duty,' said Alan. 'But if we were to hold it in five years' time, I'm not sure we'd even get a start team good enough. We're trying really hard to recruit new officials. The dilemma is you don't suddenly go from this level to the Olympic Games. It took me 20 years.'

Malcolm chimed in, 'This is where an athletics meet differs drastically from a game of rugby or football, where only one to three officials are required. At a meeting like this, there'll be between 20 to 30 officials. At a Diamond League, it'll be up to 100. What's going to happen in ten years' time? Alan won't be carrying firearms around when he's 80. It's quite worrying really.'

Mr Anonymous

Just weeks after Jon Drummond's trackside tantrum, Alan received a letter from the IAAF, inviting him and his wife to the headquarters in Monaco. He had been headhunted, along with six other respected officials from around the world, to form a new elite class of international starters.

Unbeknown to him, Alan had been assessed during the 2003 World Indoor Championships in Birmingham. The assessors were particularly impressed by the confident manner in which he had dealt with Britain's Allyn Condon, who had refused to leave the track after being disqualified in the 200m final.

'I'm 6ft 3in and 14st. Within my portfolio of characteristics, I do know how to intimidate,' explained Alan. 'I just got into his face, very quietly, knowing it was on international television. And said, "You're going to leave the track, or we're going to have a situation where you are going to be the joke of international athletics." He looked at me and realised I wasn't kidding. And he left the track.'

Alan told me that the UK's officiating was the envy of the world, knowing every trick in the book to ensure things run smoothly. 'If someone kicks off about a false start the officials here become intimidatory and surround them to say "leave now". And what's become an interesting strategy is, if it's a big strapping bloke kicking off mouthing and swearing, we send a woman to deal with it. It's amazing how that works.'

His adept handling of the tricky situation in Birmingham, combined with Drummond's shenanigans in France five months later, saw Alan swiftly promoted from a dependable national starter to a formidable presence on the international scene. The IAAF tasked Alan and his peers to develop protocols for the conduct of an international starter, who would be appointed to manage the entire start process for major meetings around the world. Wary of stepping on the toes of experienced local starters, and given the scope of his day job with the Youth Sport Trust, Alan persuaded the IAAF to take a more developmental approach. He argued that they should aim to raise the standards of existing start teams. To this day he remains the lead trainer for international starters.

Ahead of the Olympics in Tokyo, Alan made three trips to Japan to train and mentor the local starters.

He teaches the fundamentals one must adhere to in order to become a starter of pedigree. Somewhat incongruously, for a man holding a gun in public, the main intention is to go unnoticed. To be, as Alan described it, 'Mr Anonymous'. Given that starters are usually out of camera shot, he insisted that he is never happier than when he returns from an event and his friends say they didn't see him on television. 'If they see me, it's usually because something's gone wrong.'

To prove Alan's point, Malcolm told a story from the 2020 Glasgow Indoor Grand Prix. Ahead of the women's 400m the electric starting system malfunctioned, leaving the athletes rooted to their blocks after the trigger had been pulled. As a frantic Seiko technician struggled to fix the device, antsy TV producers directed their camera operators to show the viewers the source of the hold-up. As the commentators speculated on the problem, the live coverage cut to the starter. It was Malcolm.

Relief came in the shape of Swedish sensation Armand Duplantis, who was on the verge of a new pole vault world record. When the cameras turned to Duplantis, Malcolm made a dash for his car in search of his pistols. On his return he warned the athletes that he was reverting to real guns, and managed to start the race the old-fashioned way. Meanwhile, the young Swede had jumped 6.18m and broken the world record.

Malcolm remembered his phone being inundated with cruel texts from friends at the rugby club, but a more satisfying memory is of an unlikely source of gratitude for the gun glitch. 'Duplantis came over to me after the race,' said Malcolm. 'And he said, "Hey man, thanks for holding up that race." I said, "Think nothing of it, bonny lad!"'

Studying the idiosyncrasies of each athlete before they take to their blocks is another of Alan's golden tips. This allows starters to spot when showmanship crosses the line into gamesmanship. Usain Bolt's crowd-pleasing theatrics were known worldwide. But it was up to Alan to know the pre-race traits of the entire field, whether that be kissing crucifixes, closing eyes, exhaling loudly, or simply hanging back. That way, he could ensure that the race would be won via feats of athleticism rather than by unsporting tricks of the mind. 'There's a game that they often play of psyching each other out. But they also have their own idiosyncratic preparation,' explained Alan. 'And part of what I have to judge is, are they playing games? Or are they doing what's natural?'

Alan used the example of 1992 Olympic gold medallist Linford Christie, still the fastest male sprinter Britain has ever produced. He described Christie's tendency to remain completely unmoved after starter's orders, while his rivals made straight for their blocks. A starter sticking rigidly to the rule book may have been tempted to caution Christie for delaying. But Alan had seen it all before. 'If you're an inexperienced starter, you could warn him for not following the instruction. But over time you realise that when everyone else has gone forward and is getting ready, Linford then zoomed forward, went straight down, and he was the first one ready. It's about studying the athletes.'

On another occasion, at the 2014 European Championships in Zurich, French athlete Cindy Billaud was among the favourites in the 100m hurdles. Lining up in lane seven ahead of the first semi-final, Billaud chewed gum ferociously but hadn't taken a single step forward almost ten seconds after Alan had called 'on your marks'. He concluded that her actions had disrupted the field, and called for the athletes to stand up.

As the athletes walked back behind their blocks confused as to what had happened, what followed was a rare chance for Alan to go off-script. Viewers watching all over Europe heard the jarring combination of an authoritative Geordie voice, at an athletics meet in Switzerland, speaking French.

Still out of shot, Alan could be heard sternly telling the athletes, 'Will you all respond to the instructions when given immediately', before leaving no doubt as to who he was directing his comment to by adding, 'Comprenez-vous, mademoiselle?' A sheepish Billaud raised her hand in apology, and Alan delivered a decisive 'merci'. The athlete smirked like a mischievous schoolgirl but she had no hesitation in taking her mark at the second time of asking. Steve Cram, commentating on proceedings for the BBC, found the time to quip, 'Well, that's Alan Bell. I don't know if that's posh Geordie, or poor French.' Billaud comfortably won the heat and went on to claim a silver medal.

As Alan reflected on his patchy bilingualism worthy of a role as Eurovision Song Contest host, he said it was another example of discretion trumping Draconian. 'There are purists that say I shouldn't have done that. They'll say that I should have shown a yellow card because she's supposed to know the rules. I'm not about that. In that situation, I wanted to impose my standards. But more importantly, I wanted the other athletes to understand. I'm fair to everybody. So they all got the message.'

'Fair' is the word that Alan repeats more than any other when talking about his career in athletics, and it's one that underpins his ethos as a starter. He prides himself on a reputation for being consistent and, as he puts it, 'scrupulously fair'. Even if that requires making unpopular decisions. At the 2021 British Championships, which also double as the Olympic trials, Alan disqualified top contender Zharnel Hughes in the 100m final. Hughes was the 2018 European Champion and such is his class that only one British male has clocked a quicker time than his personal best of 9.91. That's his coach, Linford Christie. After the race, Alan was summoned to the competition director's room.

'I went in, and Linford shook my hand and said hello. And Zharnel started with, "That would never have been a false start in America." I said, "No, probably not. They would have said the gun didn't work properly, or there was something wrong with the false-start equipment. Or an athlete farted and set you off," and Linford burst out laughing.'

Hughes's point wasn't entirely wide of the mark, and Alan knows of occasions where big-name runners have been given leeway at high-profile national meets elsewhere in the world. But it wasn't going to happen on his watch.

'I said, "Listen, three starters saw you go, the reaction time on the machine says you went under the gun time, the waveform – which shows where an athlete has applied pressure on the blocks – is conclusive. I dare say the slow-motion on television will show you went early. You false-started. Leave it.'

Hughes was nevertheless selected to represent Team GB at the Olympics in Tokyo a month later. Although impressive in the 100m heats and in with a genuine chance of a medal, he would be disqualified in the final. For a false start.

A Separate Life

It was past 4pm in Morpeth and while the sun was still shining, there was a noticeable dip in the energy on the school track. Patient parents glanced at their watches, fatigued athletes rubbed cramping calves, and even the horn sounded tired. But the volunteer officials remained brimming with vigour, none more so than Alan.

He radioed in a request for water bottles, only to be told there were none left. 'Any chance you can bring a tap?' came his reply. A discus thrower requested permission to cross the track, and Alan asked if he was running the 10k. No smile, or any emotion, was forthcoming. 'Sorry, I'm an acquired taste,' said Alan, before telling the lad about the common sand-removing tricks athletes would try in a bid to make the discus lighter. 'It's called cheating,' he said.

Later on, when there was a delay in proceedings, he kept a group of 300m runners entertained by quizzing them on call-room rules, letting them guess whose kit would fall foul of the censors due to excessive logos. It led to a story about the time he came across East German shot putter Udo Beyer, a haystack of a man whose rule-breaking Adidas gear could only be covered with industrial quantities of black tape.

Teenagers are a notoriously tough crowd, but these athletes were either heart-warmingly polite or genuinely interested. And Alan isn't short of a tale. He shared the story of him being the first to congratulate Jessica Ennis moments after she won her World Championship gold in Berlin ('She sees me and she's beaming, and I just said, "Oh Jess, give a Geordie a cuddle!"'). There was another about him becoming good friends with Greg Rutherford due to the fact that the configuration of an athletics track has Alan standing by the long-jump pit when starting the 200m.

And there was the time he witnessed David Rudisha produce one of the most breathtaking displays ever seen on a track, at the London Stadium in 2012. 'I've started many great races. But I don't think I've ever seen an athlete dominate an event so gracefully,' said Alan. 'Bolt won many races through sheer raw power. But Rudisha was just remarkable to watch. And because it was the 800m, I had the advantage of being able to stay and watch it as he came around twice, and crossed the finish line where I'd started it from. So I was able to soak it in. It was just awesome.'

Alan offered to retire following the London Olympics, admitting that he cried following its culmination. The tears were a mix of relief and overwhelming pride, and stepping down following the rare privilege of officiating at a home Games felt like the right moment. But UK Athletics and the IAAF didn't agree. And on a day when he was wearing an Adidas polo displaying a logo for the 2015 World Relays event held in the Bahamas, it was clear that it wasn't only the kids he was infusing with aspirations.

'I'll never get to where Alan's been because I started off too late,' said Micky, as he reloaded his guns for the final races of the day. 'But if I can get to level four and get to a few national meetings …' As Micky's mind wandered, Alan and Malcolm could be heard in the distance, managing the unenviable task of corralling six teams of four for the relays.

I asked Micky why there aren't more people gunning to be the next Alan Bell. Sure, it's an unpaid gig. But an international starter gets to travel the world in business class, stay in the best hotels, and has a chance to stand on the doorstep of sporting history. Then there are the associated perks that Alan has enjoyed, like being asked to start events like the Great North Run alongside people like Sir Bobby Robson, and TV appearances on shows like *Superstars* and *A League of Their Own*, where David Walliams tried to grab Alan's gun.

Micky thought it might have something to do with people staying fitter for longer, and competing rather than officiating. It's certainly a more palatable and less cynical theory than the one many of his fellow volunteers subscribed to; that young people are no longer willing to give up their time for free.

As the final relay concluded and the clock ticked on towards 5pm, I joined the queue of athletes and parents making their way to the car park. Behind me a handful of officials remained, collecting the hurdles and equipment to be placed into storage. Most of them had been here since 10am. I was reminded of one of the first things Alan told me when I asked him what it takes to do his job at the highest level. 'You'll have gathered that I'm a pretty verbose individual,' he began. 'My personality is gregarious, I like being with people. I love my sport. I've made absolutely no money from it at all. It probably cost me my first marriage, if the truth be known, in terms of living a separate life.'

As I said goodbye to the three starters, one of the 300m runners that Alan had entertained earlier walked past him and said thanks. 'That's the other nice thing,' said Alan. 'The thank yous.'

Blunting Bolt

Two years after his stunning world record in the Olympiastadion, Usain Bolt was once again lining up in the 100m final of the World Athletics Championships. This time the venue was Daegu Stadium, built for the football World Cup in South Korea in 2002. On a sultry August evening, the Jamaican was facing an almost entirely different field to that which he destroyed in 2009. Other than Bolt, only one man, Daniel Bailey of Antigua and Barbuda, had returned from that historic night in Berlin. Actually, make that two. For Alan Bell was once again the man with the bang.

The false-start rule had again been tweaked. A year before the World Championships, the IAAF voted to remove any clemency for a race's first offender. It was felt that this privilege was being abused in an attempt to stifle fast-starting sprinters. Those slower out of the blocks could deliberately false-start and put the entire field under pressure. Now there would be no doubt and no margin for error. Anyone who false-started was out.

With the now obligatory pre-race theatre over, all eight finalists took to their blocks with minimal fuss. Daegu, like Berlin, was expectant. This city wanted its own page in history. A hush descended. Enter Alan, stage right. 'You might find this hard to believe,' said Alan, 'but I take no notice of who's in the race. That's irrelevant. You've got eight bodies, end of.'

Instead, Alan is in his own zone, deep in focus. 'I've got the best 30-second concentration span in the world. Outside that 30 seconds, I'm all over the place. But I think it's important to be able to switch on and switch off.' Only once he deems the time right does he summon the athletes. Contrary to what one might expect, given the pressures of television scheduling and the allocation of seven-minute slots for each 100m race, the intricate pauses between commands are for the starter to dictate in the moment. There is no standardised time between the word 'set' and the pulling of the trigger. It is an instinctive call based on the race, and the occasion.

'The real skill in my job is to wait until everybody is at the pinnacle of their set position. When you're happy that they've all had that opportunity to set and concentrate, you pull the trigger. There can't be a prescribed time,' said Alan. 'The chemistry between the nine people involved – eight athletes and the person with the gun – is unique to that event. It has to be entirely based upon what I see, and the judgement of readiness based on my experience. At a major event, between saying "set" and pulling the trigger, I'm holding my breath. Because I'm praying I don't have to pull the other trigger.'

In Daegu, Alan's prayers went unheeded. The dreaded beep sounded in his headphones and he instantly fired his recall gun. Although he already knew who was at fault, he waited for the computer printout before confirming the reason for the crowd's anguish. It showed that the athlete in lane five had moved 0.104 seconds before the gun had even fired. It was as clear a false start as one could see at the highest level. And no one was more aware than the offending athlete himself, having already removed his vest and with his head in his hands. It was Bolt.

While the crowd squealed in disbelief, the media made hay. 'Within a millisecond there must have been 150 cameramen on the track looking to milk his embarrassment,' thundered Alan. 'I've got to know him quite well as a human being, and he's a resolute and determined character. But he's also a really decent guy, and he didn't deserve that. So I said to the Koreans to get him off the track and put him somewhere that a camera can't get to him. Let him have his remorse.'

Alan was then put under pressure from Korean TV to get the race back under way. 'I said no chance. There are seven people out there now, who think they can win a gold medal. And I'm going to give them every chance to compose themselves again.' An unimpressed floor manager insisted that Alan recommence the race immediately. 'He went apeshit. He's in my face, and he's getting it in the ear from the director upstairs. So I turned to him and said, "Here, you start the race", and I handed him the guns. And of course, he just looked at me. And I said, "We wait."'

Bolt's training partner and fellow Jamaican Yohan Blake was the ultimate beneficiary, becoming the youngest ever 100m world champion at 21 years old. But for Alan, the story didn't end there. As he did at the end of every day of competition, he had arranged to meet his wife Lesley in the VIP area before heading back to their hotel. Lesley is a level-three athletics official.

On this occasion, he sensed something wasn't quite right as soon as he arrived. 'I'm walking up to row Z and I see that Lesley's looking at me with a face like thunder. And I'm thinking, "She knows I had no choice, I had to disqualify the guy." And then I suddenly realise. She's sitting with Usain's mam and dad. She'd met them earlier in the week, and they were just sitting and chatting. I thought, "Oh my God."'

As Alan made the tentative walk over, Mrs Bolt stood up to greet him. 'Usain got his mam's genes, believe me. I thought she was going to let rip at me. And you know, she was fantastic. All she said to me was, "He made a mistake." That put me at ease. I said, "I hope he can get it out of his system ready for the 200m." And she just looked at me and said, "He'll be ready." They were great with me.

He's obviously got a lot of that collectedness and stability from his family.'

Six days later, Alan's recall gun stayed silent for the 200m final. As the slowest runner out of the blocks, the false start in the 100m final had clearly had an effect on Bolt. But he powered around the bend as only he could and he comfortably took gold. 'I made a mistake but I came back to show the world that I'm still the best,' said a relieved world champion afterwards.

Alan admitted that disqualifying Bolt was the lowest moment of his starting career. 'Not because it was him, at all. But because I was having to disqualify an athlete in the final of the World Championships. It could have been any of them,' he said. 'But, like all of the people in that final, they'll have worked for 15 years just to be there, and it's sad that you have to apply the rule.'

I asked if, with an expectant crowd engulfing him, an anxious Korean production team on his shoulder, and the world's media having already written the script, there wasn't a small part of him tempted to let this generation's greatest athlete continue. He responded without a moment's hesitation. 'The circumstances were very difficult. But that was the easiest decision I've ever had to make.'

2

FUEL SELL: Performance Chefs

Football and rugby club canteens no longer resemble primary school dinner halls as the influence of performance chefs has fundamentally changed the perception of diet in professional sport. Find out exactly how these culinary virtuosos have raised the bar by embedding themselves within the daily routines of the best sportsmen and women.

Serving Superstition

'Oi chef! What the fuck is this shit?' Omar Meziane removed his denim jacket as he began reciting some of the memorable feedback he had received during his first camps as England chef. His Persian spinach soup hadn't gone down well with goalkeeper Joe Hart, who had made his feelings abundantly clear to a packed canteen of players and coaching staff. I winced, but Omar, shaven-headed and with a neatly trimmed beard, was now relaxed enough to laugh about the experience. He was less so at the time.

Hart's critique had followed Dele Alli's panic about the absence of Weetabix on the pre-match menu. Omar was told that he would simply *have* to source some. They were in Vilnius, Lithuania. 'I was running around this city in a taxi trying to find Weetabix,' remembered Omar, sat in the sun-drenched office of his meal-delivery business. 'The only thing that I could find was this very bizarre Lithuanian brand.' Omar did what all good performance chefs do to keep their clients happy. He fibbed. 'I couldn't serve it to him in the box because he'd know. That will screw with his head, and if we lose, it will be my fault. I ended up unpacking it and putting it in a bowl. He was like, "Thanks very much."'

On another occasion, Omar was instructed by England's nutritionists to replace the post-game fried chicken with a healthier selection. Only no one had warned the players. 'I'm stood in the middle of the room and Joe Hart, again, gets his plate and just shouts right at me behind the buffet, "Chef! No healthy food after a fucking game!" Then he slams his plate down and walks out.'

Omar joined Gareth Southgate's England setup in 2017, following a World Cup-winning summer with the country's under-20s team in South Korea. His gold medal is a prized possession at home but he soon found that it counted for little with the senior team. With a CV that includes Great Britain's Olympic rowers, England's cricket team, and Premiership rugby clubs Wasps and Harlequins, Omar wasn't new to catering for the sporting elite. But after just a few days' cooking for the Three Lions he wondered if he had bitten off more than he could chew.

'Those first two camps were brutal. Players were just looking at me like I was just completely out of place. I didn't understand them. I didn't understand the type of food that they like to eat. Getting home after that second camp, I said to my wife, "I physically and mentally cannot do it. I don't know how to feed them."'

With most international matches taking place on an evening, a travelling performance chef will preside over four meals a day for a squad of athletes capable of burning through 5,000 daily calories. Omar sets his alarm for 4am to give him enough time to prepare the kitchen with local chefs that he has usually only met the day before. He communicates with them in a patchwork of languages that he has picked up during his travels. Once breakfast is over, there are around 45 minutes to get started on post-training lunch, before moving to the high-carb pre-match offering just two hours later.

After waiting until the last player has eaten (usually an unhurried Jadon Sancho, it turns out), he has just minutes to pack his utensils and ingredients before accompanying the team to the game. Omar's final task for the day is to recharge a ravenous squad with a post-match feast. He is finally able to remove his food-flecked apron at around midnight. 'There is no getting it wrong on matchday,' he said.

As stressful as it sounds and despite his daunting start, Omar did return for England duty. Drawn in by the addictive buzz of a matchday, he was also reluctant to turn down another call-up to represent his country – one that had been personally made by Southgate himself.

Eventually, thanks to some comprehensive note-taking that involved jotting down every request, quirk, and criticism, things began to fall into place. Whether it was Alli's Weetabix or Harry Maguire's Cajun turkey wraps, Omar's notepad became a bible of personalised culinary cravings. 'It was only really on that third camp that I understood what a group of footballers want to eat, how they want to eat, and so I was able to construct menus around all of their wants, needs, and desires.'

Omar swiftly learned that even England's top footballers are creatures of habit. And when it comes to matchday, slaves to superstition. 'It has to be seamless, it has to be perfect. We cannot run out of anything. Because God forbid that Eric Dier didn't have his piece of sea bass pre-match, or Jordan Pickford didn't have his piece of salmon, or the pasta station was too slow. As soon as the pre-match is done the boys become ultra relaxed. There's this calmness about everything.'

The chef settled in well enough to earn his spot on the plane to Russia in 2018. For the second successive summer he would be responsible for fuelling an England side aiming for World Cup success. Like a 19th-century Antarctic explorer, that meant planning a menu that would last for up to 60 days. But while Ernest Shackleton may have packed tins of sardines, cases of whisky, and jars of marmalade, Omar's suitcase was brimming with boxes of Alpen, bottles of Robinson's cordial, and bars of Aero mint chocolate (for post-game milkshakes).

Six months ahead of England's opening match, a pre-tournament recce to the base camp of Repino, a small town outside of St Petersburg, allowed Omar to meet the in-house chefs, scope out the kitchen, and find out what key ingredients he could source while out there.

While his fundamental purpose was to produce meals that would allow the team to perform to the best of their abilities, Omar also wanted to introduce local cuisine into the mix. It was a bold strategy during confined tournament conditions where home comforts can provide solace. But for the same reason, Omar saw it as a vital way to showcase alternative cultures to young footballers who enjoy more luxury but fewer freedoms than the majority of travellers their age. 'It's about trying to broaden horizons very gently. So we wanted to include simple things like borscht soup whilst in Russia. We wanted to include the dumplings. And on the last night, we drank our body weights in vodka as well.'

That final night came further along than many had expected, but unfortunately not far enough that Omar's 60-day blueprint was fully utilised. After galvanising the fans back home with spirited performances, England were narrowly defeated by Croatia in the semi-final.

Although there would be no second medal for Omar he had memories to cherish more than gold, such as boarding the team bus with the rest of the squad. 'I had to pinch myself. We drove down this Russian street where there were thousands of people cheering. It gets quite emotional. It's every schoolboy's dream. And then you drive into the stadium and walk straight into the dressing room,' he said. Speaking to me a few weeks before the European Championships, where England would fall just one tantalising step short of victory, it was a feeling he was yet to exhaust. 'At Wembley, it's still incredibly breathtaking to walk out of that tunnel and on to the pitch. They're treasured moments. I realise the privileged position I am in.'

French Kerosene

Enter the canteen kitchen of any top-level sports team in the UK and it's very likely that you'll find a toiling performance chef working up a sweat over sizzling griddles and bubbling pans. Yet this was a role that barely existed even 15 years ago when those kitchens were more likely to have been populated by the equivalent of a school dinner lady. That the job of a performance chef exists at all is down to a nutritional revolution sparked by influential figureheads who recognised that what we eat and how we perform are not mutually exclusive factors.

Omar, a classically trained chef who once listed the Spice Girls among his private clients, was considering quitting the industry before the offer at London Wasps in 2010. A keen rugby and football fan, he decided to see if his knowledge and skillset would transfer to the relentless world of sport. He has been in demand ever since. 'I got into this completely by accident 15 years ago, and the revolution of food and nutrition, and the importance it now plays in teams, has just come on in leaps and bounds,' said Omar. 'It's no longer seen as something of a luxury. It's now a necessity.'

The seeds of English football's nutritional awakening were sewn in 1996, following the arrival of a gangly

Frenchman with circle specs. Legend has it that the *Evening Standard*'s bulletin boards read 'Arsène who?' on the day that Monsieur Wenger was announced as the new manager at Highbury. When he left north London 22 years later, his influence had fundamentally changed the game.

His bold methods were initially derided by established figures in the game, who wondered just what one of the country's oldest clubs could learn from an unexceptional footballer who had most recently managed in Japan. Wenger didn't waste any time in showing them, dictating that immediate changes be made to the club's dietary habits before a ball had been kicked.

Alcohol was banned from the players' lounge, while salt and sugar were removed from the canteen. The menu was completely re-written to exclude red meat, eggs, and chips, replaced by chicken, fish, and boiled vegetables inspired by Wenger's time in Asia. Chocolate bars would no longer be handed out on the team bus. Even cups of tea were forbidden. Under the direction of biologist Yann Rougier, players were given vitamin supplements and advised to chew their food for 30 seconds to aid digestion. Vice-chairman David Dein called it the 'Evian-broccoli' diet. It was a shock to a traditional system, and Wenger had picked the most challenging club in England to implement it.

Sodden beer mats and empty shot glasses summed up Arsenal's notorious Tuesday Club. A weekly pub crawl led by captain Tony Adams would feature a cast of the club's most experienced players, including Paul Merson, Steve Bould, Lee Dixon, and Ray Parlour. They would drink until the early hours, off the leash until training resumed on Thursday morning.

But an entrenched booze culture hadn't prevented the Gunners from winning multiple trophies under George Graham, and many doubted that Wenger's philosophy would be welcomed by the old guard. But instead of replacing them with his own acolytes, the Frenchman sought instead to convert. Within two years a reinvented Arsenal were league and cup double winners, and it was predominantly the older players – grateful for their lengthening careers – who became evangelical about Wenger's dietary and training demands. Speaking in 2011, Lee Dixon said, 'I am now convinced that his way is the only way, in the modern game. It might sound hypocritical, having been part of the drinking at Arsenal in my early years, but I am sure it does you no good.'

In an interview with *FourFourTwo* in 2007, Wenger reflected on those first days in charge: 'I always find it stupid that a player can practise the whole week then spoil his game because he eats something silly 24 hours before. I remember my first day at Arsenal when we were travelling to Blackburn and the players were at the back of the bus chanting, "We want our Mars bars!" They used to eat them before the game but I took them away. Sure it doesn't guarantee you win the football game but it means the guy with a sensitive liver doesn't have his preparations ruined. Food is like kerosene. If you put the wrong one in your car, it's not as quick as it should be.'

Wenger's focus on diet and nutrition led to a host of imitators as other English clubs tried to replicate his success. In a sport where training exercises can take weeks and months to take effect on the pitch, it is no longer unusual for a new manager to target the canteen for overnight changes. When Pep Guardiola arrived at Manchester City in 2016, he took pizza off the menu and told his squad that any player deemed overweight would not be allowed to join in with training.

The trend continues today. There is over a decade's age difference between Antonio Conte and Steven Gerrard, and their playing careers – 19 years in Italy compared to 17 years in England – shared very few cultural similarities. Yet when they were both announced as Premier League managers in November 2021, their Wenger-esque opening decree was almost word-for-word identical. Conte got rid of ketchup and mayonnaise from Tottenham Hotspur's training ground, while Gerrard added fizzy drinks, puddings, and hot chocolate to the list of Aston Villa's contraband. No doubt delighting the tabloids with his foodie pun, Gerrard stated, 'There's a lot of ingredients to get into my starting XI and the players will find that out. You've got to have the right mentality and go above and beyond basically, strive to be elite and be the best version of yourself.'

At around the same time that Arsène Wenger was espousing the benefits of a clean diet, rugby union was finding its feet as a professional sport. And being the best version of yourself was an ethos that Clive Woodward implemented from the day he was appointed England coach in 1997. Just two years after the sport had been professionalised, Woodward saw fitness as the way to succeed in a new era. In his first tour of the southern hemisphere, he watched on embarrassed as New Zealand, Australia, and South Africa inflicted heavy trouncing after trouncing. Woodward later wrote in his *Daily Mail* column, 'I realised we were stuck in the amateur era in terms of our fitness. There was only one player this didn't apply to – Josh Lewsey. He was ahead of everyone else in terms of fitness and physique.'

Lewsey, who would play at full-back, centre, and wing during a glittering ten-year England career, owed his condition to his previous role as an officer in the British Army. But in 1998, Lewsey's Spartan physique was so unique that Woodward asked the player to remove his shirt during a team meeting. This, the coach affirmed, was the standard he now expected his team to strive for.

To help them, Woodward employed fitness coach Dave Reddin and nutritionist Adam Carey, who didn't just implement a new nutrition programme but also delivered a seminar for players' spouses and families to ensure it was being adhered to at home. Whenever the squad travelled away from their Pennyhill Park training facilities, Woodward made sure to bring the in-house chef with them.

Five years later, a taut and toned England side lined up for the 2003 World Cup in a new skin-tight Nike kit (designed by Rob Warner, featured in the chapter on kit designers). Woodward was satisfied that his team were now the fittest, fastest, and most powerful team in world rugby. And when they lifted the Webb Ellis Cup in Australia, they proved him entirely correct.

Just Not Cricket

The Lewsey physique is no longer an outlier in international rugby but largely the norm. Rugby players are not only faster and fitter than they were during the amateur era, but at an average of two stone heavier, they're also much stronger. And performance chefs like Omar, who spent three years at Wasps and almost five at Harlequins, have been a crucial factor in this cultivation of titans.

'Jesus, those boys eat. They're short training days, but you're feeding them twice as much as I ever have done with any other sport,' said Omar, who released a recipe book with former Wasps and England flanker James Haskell in 2018. In rugby, Omar's days would start even earlier than in football. The extra hours were needed to knock up the amount of food required for the likes of 18st prop Joe Marler and 17st former England captain Chris Robshaw.

When I asked Omar about the difference between dishing up for footballers and rugby players, only one word sufficed. 'Quantity,' he said, gazing off into the distance and shaking his head in disbelief. 'I look back on it now and think, how did I manage to put that amount of food out? At that point, it was just me. It was really unbelievable. But a great group of people. Rugby is ahead of most sports in terms of their understanding of performance nutrition.'

If Omar was quick to praise rugby for being receptive to this relatively new field of expertise, he did so knowing that other sports hadn't always been immediately convinced of the benefits he could provide. In 2013 he encountered some high-profile resistance that still rankles to this day.

Ahead of the winter Ashes tour in Australia, he was asked to consult on the menus for England's cricket squad. Although he wouldn't be travelling with them, he would come up with the recipes that captain Alistair Cook and co. would eat while away.

At first he was showered with praise, from the Sunday papers to breakfast TV. 'There was this big write-up on the new menus that were going to power England to victory in the Ashes,' he said. 'And then a friend of mine sent me a link to a *Good Morning Australia* clip, where Marco Pierre White and the Australia *MasterChef* judges were cooking my recipes, talking about how this was the future of sports food. The praise that those menus got was incredible. Until it was a complete whitewash.'

Although they had soundly defeated the Aussies on home soil only two months prior, England contrived to lose the series 5-0. It was only the third whitewash in Ashes history. Omar's menu was no longer flavour of the month. When driving back home one night, he tuned in to BBC Radio 5 Live just as cricket pundits were dissecting England's disastrous tour. His voice lowered as he described finding himself an unexpected scapegoat. 'Freddie Flintoff was on and said, "Well, in my day it was lagers, pies, and chips. And it seemed to serve us well. Let's get rid of all this crap. Nothing else has changed, it was just the food. That would suggest the boys weren't happy and they were starving. And they didn't play."' Upon hearing this searing review from a player who wasn't even with the squad, Omar stopped driving. 'I pulled the car over and had a little cry. I was like, "It's my fault!"'

But it would be unfair to single out a generation of cricketers as the only naysayers of new-age sporting cuisine. Despite Wenger's influence, convincing footballers and managers has not always been an easy task either. In 2007, new England manager Fabio Capello requested that his players follow a Mediterranean diet in a bid to improve their fitness. When this was put to Spurs boss Harry Redknapp, his response hinted at a prevailing sentiment in the game. 'If you can't pass the ball properly, a bowl of pasta's not going to make that much difference,' he chirped.

I asked Omar if there were still cynics within the game. 'Absolutely. At the very highest levels of sport in the United Kingdom,' he said. 'And I think those people are very naturally gifted athletes, that don't really have to worry too much. Their bodies naturally adapt to training loads, they're able to take more than most people, they can push through any pain. I think they're just very naturally adapted to being able to deal with it.'

There's no better example of this than Lionel Messi, a generational talent who was able to consistently perform at a world-class level despite his less-than-wholesome diet. Messi's sweet tooth was conditioned from a young age when his academy coach at Newell's Old Boys would offer him Argentinian *alfajores* cookies every time he scored. Another South American delicacy known as *milanese* – an admittedly sumptuous shallow-fried, breadcrumb-coated slab of beef – and pizza formed the basis of Messi's staple diet, washed down with can after can of fizzy soda.

But in 2014, aged 27, Messi was noticed vomiting regularly on the pitch. It prompted his manager, that man again Pep Guardiola, to remove all vending machines from Barcelona's training ground. He also assigned his star player a personal nutritionist. Italian Giuliano Poser was the man tasked with fuelling the seven-time Ballon d'Or winner.

Out went pizzas, red meat, and sweets, and in came a strict regime centred around lean protein, whole grains, olive oil, fruit, and vegetables. Cans of soda would be replaced by water or the caffeine-rich yerba maté tea. Catch any pre-match coverage of a La Liga game and you're almost certain to see a footballer emerging from the team bus supping the hot drink from a *bombilla* straw.

Messi's vomiting soon stopped, and the following season he played 11 more games and scored 17 more goals. In a 2018 interview with Argentinian television, Messi confirmed his dietary transformation: 'I ate badly for many years: chocolates, *alfajores*, fizzy drinks, and everything. That is what made me throw up during games. Now I look after myself better. I eat fish, meat, salads. Everything is organised and taken care of.'

That concept of taking care of sportspeople, and their diets, has since reached new levels. For while performance chefs like Omar are able to dictate what a player eats while on club or country duty, making sure they don't slip into bad habits when at home is a trickier proposition. Or, rather, it used to be.

Nando's, Haribo, and Pop Tarts

'We're almost like spies. Or plastic surgeons. Or prostitutes.' Rachel Muse certainly has a unique way of explaining the job of a private performance chef. I did my best to stifle a snort while she added some vital context. 'We can talk about what we do, but we can't talk about who we do it for.' Salisbury-based Rachel runs a business that places performance chefs into the homes of athletes. When we spoke it was February 2022, and she was headed to the north-east to introduce one of her 16 chefs to a recently signed Newcastle United footballer.

It was pretty clear that I wouldn't be finding out which of the Toon Army's five January signings it was. For there's a reason she has called her company Discreet and Delicious, and it's because she values the first trait as much as the second. 'I always say when I'm training people that we wouldn't be stealing cushions from people's houses. So we can't be taking pieces of information out either.'

Although it varies from client to client, private chefs typically cater for a footballer's evening meal, with breakfast and lunch usually provided at the training ground. A chef will arrive two hours prior to service and then depart an hour after. Contrasting with chefs like Omar who serve up squad meals at a hotel or training ground, the private chef prepares a menu focused on a single client's requirements, freshly cooked and served in the athlete's home.

'If you're working for a team, it's much more complicated because you've got to deal with all these food preferences, all these different macro requests from the nutritionist,' said Rachel, who has catered for tennis, rugby, swimming, and Formula One athletes but is now predominantly working with footballers. 'We've only got to please two people, the nutritionist on this side and the player on that side. And we're the link between the two. It's been very successful because it takes away the nutritionist's sneaking suspicion that they're not being listened to.'

Rachel said that without private chefs many young footballers will resort to Nando's, Haribo, Pop Tarts, or, 'if they're really adventurous, Crunchy Nut Corn Flakes. Possibly with milk if they've got any in, but more likely no milk.' I found myself snorting again, but Rachel insisted she wasn't joking. Of course, there'll be thousands of 20-somethings all over the country without milk in their fridge, living on their own for the first time and surviving on the sort of junk food that their mothers warned them about. But there's something a little comical about imagining these wealthy global superstars sharing the diet of an overdraft-stretching student.

In these cases, Rachel encourages a 'softly, softly' informative approach that isn't dissimilar to Omar's aim to serve local dishes when on the road. 'You can't go in being all Gordon Ramsay,' said Rachel, banging the table so fiercely her reading glasses almost fell off her head. 'With nutrition, you're much better off with a lot of little subtle nudges, rather than bombarding people and saying, "You're doing it all wrong, you've got to stop that." Because most of us are doing it all wrong.'

Even when revealing that she was once asked if a lentil was an animal, Rachel was careful not to be condescending to her clients. Instead, she acknowledged that it was only normal for young footballers who have invested most of their youth kicking a ball to have missed out on some life lessons. 'That was a great investment of their time because they end up playing for their country, and being financially secure. So what if they don't know what a lentil is?'

Some of Rachel's fondest memories are of cooking dishes that have been requested by players who wish to be reminded of home or family. Sometimes this involves daunting phone calls to players' mothers in search of recipes, while other times it requires some creative thinking. One player requested a marble cake like his late grandmother used to make. 'I made it for them, and it was like their granny had come back to life. It was really quite freaky. But it's lovely to be able to do that.' Rachel also remembered a British player whose mother was from the Caribbean. 'Food is culture and culture is food. For him, food at home was curried goat and festival dumplings. But something like lasagne was pushing the envelope a bit. Because that's what his perspectives were. That's great because you learn so much from that.'

Being in a footballer's home for several hours of every day sees private chefs forge close bonds with their clients. Rachel, who had previously worked in the mania of hotel kitchens, believed that working in this more intimate setting was the toughest part of the job. Particularly with older players, when there is often a spouse and family tucking in too, she equated the social dynamic to be more akin to a nanny than a chef. 'You do see the family right up close and personal. You learn how a family interacts, what their little shorthands are, their little in-jokes, and the fact that they're always going to be late for a flight.'

Establishing boundaries is therefore a crucial part of the job. Rachel has been in the same room when players scream at their mothers and has been asked for her opinion in family arguments. She is also used to seeing clients walk around in just their underpants. Conversely, she has been asked to sit and eat with families, handed drinks at house parties, and even offered the use of a villa in the south of France. On each occasion, she has politely refused.

I told her she had shown admirable restraint. 'Because once you cross that line, you can't uncross it,' she said, twiddling with the scrunchie wrapped around her right wrist. 'You have to respect people for being individuals. It's not for you to help them or hinder them from getting in and out of their messes. Even though you desperately want to say something like, "Why don't you just put your keys by the front door?"'

Good Cop, Bad Cop

One player who I did know counted among Rachel's clientele was the Manchester City and England star Phil Foden. Not because Rachel let anything slip but because Foden had revealed it himself in an article for *The Telegraph*. When City discovered that the midfielder had recurring low iron levels, a Discreet and Delicious private chef was hired to work with Foden and club nutritionist Tom Parry. The youngster was receptive to the change in diet, which centred around meals rich in Omega-3 like salmon and soy. Plenty of other players require a little more coercion.

Rachel shared an anonymous case study of a player 'from somewhere which we all joke about as having a poor diet'. After being brought up in a sporty household where mealtimes simply meant shovelling calories, the player was now finding his body was no longer as receptive to his veggie-free fare and late-evening indulgence in crisps and beer. 'They are mid-to-late 20s, and it's all starting to catch up with them. And their club is annoyed.' And so Rachel got the call.

But being persuaded to eat more greens is not the only reason that some players are reluctant to do so. 'Culturally, for them, that's far too weird, because they came from an environment where there wasn't a lot of money. And it's like, "Why are you wasting your money on that?" That's what some people have to fight against in their own families.' It's true that the service does not come cheap. When Swansea's Jonjo Shelvey advertised for a private chef to cater for him and his family in 2015, the listing went viral due to the £65,000 salary on offer.

When Rachel's mystery player reluctantly agreed, she began the process of working with the club's nutritionist. This integral relationship is one that she described as like that between an architect and a master builder. Working closely with the athlete to target specific aims, like improving stamina or building strength, a nutritionist will map out a day-by-day timetable known as a periodised nutrition plan.

For footballers, this revolves around matchdays. In the example Rachel showed me, the day prior to the game prioritised fuelling up with an evening meal of white meat, comprising 100g of carbs, 30g of protein, and 15g of fat. By contrast, the day after was focused more on recovery and permitted red meat, only 50g of carbs, 50g of protein, and 25g of fat. But an unenthused footballer is more likely to be able to translate hieroglyphics than transform this guidance from the page and on to a plate. And so the importance of the performance chef as a nutritionist's conduit begins to emerge.

Omar's long-time collaborator is Michael Naylor, a nutritionist he has worked with since they first met at Wasps. Omar told me that the unpopular decision to do away with England's post-match feast was Naylor's. 'I've never let Mike forget that. Never,' he said, only half-jokingly. While seamless collaboration between chef and nutritionist is not always guaranteed, the pair have combined so successfully that they even went into business together. 'We've developed somewhat of a symbiotic relationship,' said Omar. 'Neither of us could excel at what we do without the other. He does all the boring stuff and the science. And then I do all the fun stuff, bringing the ice cream and my wit, and it works really well together. We've become almost expert now at playing good cop, bad cop.'

For Rachel's part, she said she had a very good relationship with most of the nutritionists she works with. Though she couldn't help a quip at their expense: 'The joke is if you put four economists in a room, you'll get five different opinions. And it's rather like that with nutritionists, in that they've all studied different things for their masters and doctorates and they've all got their own take on it. Because it's still a new science. The knowledge is growing. And so it's still somewhat in flux.'

To get across just how closely the two roles work together, Rachel put me in touch with Kate Shilland, a sports nutritionist who formed part of Emma Raducanu's team ahead of the teenager's astonishing US Open success in 2021. Now working at Crystal Palace, Kate also counts swimmers, triathletes, ultra-runners, rugby players, and boxers among her regular clients. 'Nutrition is a key part of the training process,' said Kate. 'It's not just something that you add on or you wing. It's part of your kit. Like you wouldn't forget to put your shin pads or your boots in your kit bag, actually don't forget to put in your drink and your snack for after. That informs how well you train. Because you can't get out if you haven't put in.'

As we spoke, I noticed Kate was wearing a Fan Dance hoody. The 24km march over Pen Y Fan, the highest mountain in the Brecon Beacons, is so gruelling a task that it is used in selection for the SAS. A beaming Kate told me she had just won the latest winter edition. She felt it was vital that she could practise what she preached. 'You get the buy-in if you look like you live that lifestyle also. And I think it then helps you understand the mindset of the athletes you're working with.'

Just like those athletes, she insisted that eating better improves her own performance, too. 'To be an elite athlete, you need to be an elite eater. But actually, to be an elite coach or an elite nutritionist, we also need to be elite eaters. We need to make sure that we're fuelling ourselves to do the best job that we can do for them.' Kate advises players to eat a pre-match meal of around 60 per cent carbs but to keep slow-digesting fats to a minimum. Oh, and go easy on the fibre, too. 'Because, for obvious reasons, you don't want any mishaps on the pitch.'

By and large, however, Kate is wary of giving general advice. 'It's what works for you. Some people can eat a three-course meal and then go out and train half an hour later. Some people need three hours to digest.' The presence of a performance chef makes Kate's 'one size fits one' nutritional message easier to land. 'That relationship between nutritionist and chef is really important. We can be like, "These are the things they need, now you can make that taste really great." And that's a really key role.'

But given that it is ultimately the player footing the bill, performance chefs will only bang the nutritionist's drum for so long. Rachel advises all of her chefs to cooperate rather than dictate. Which can mean taking a less stringent approach to nutritionists. And football managers. Which prompted me to ask about Conte and Gerrard's take on condiments. 'Why ban anything, because it makes it exciting doesn't it?' said Rachel, before talking me through the process of making homemade ketchup with reduced sugar. If a player insists on eating lasagne on a designated low-carb day, Rachel will suggest replacing the pasta sheets with courgettes. 'Then when they're eating it, it does feel like a lasagne,' she said. 'Ultimately, if somebody wants something, they're going to get it. You're much better off giving it to them in the freshest, healthiest, most organic way possible.'

Rachel showed me a phone snap of a meal she dished up for her problem player. He had insisted on pie and chips one evening. The chips were cut from fresh potatoes, skin left on, and cooked in the oven. Or as Rachel described it, 'Cooking the way that my grandmother would have done. Forget that fast food exists.' The only pastry on the 'pie' was a disc that was no bigger than a coaster. 'So you get the ceiling of pie. And your brain goes, "Tick, I've had a pie." You haven't had a pie, you've had a big stew with some grated vegetables in, and a little disc of pastry on the top,' said Rachel.

It's the sort of compromise that will convince the player they are getting what they want, while also keeping the nutritionist onside. Rachel's tactics with fussy eaters will sound very familiar to anyone whose toddler sees a carrot as a javelin. And as every stressed parent swiftly learns, the key to winning the war is accepting that you won't win every battle. 'If you can even make a ten per cent difference in what they're doing, then that's helpful,' said Rachel. 'Then if they buy into that ten per cent, maybe you can push for 15 per cent.'

Rachel's anonymous player lost three kilos in his first three weeks. The weight dropped off so suddenly that he initially struggled to adapt in training, finding that he was no longer able to shoulder team-mates off the ball as robustly as before. Once he had adapted to his reduced bulk, his club found that he was not only sharper on the pitch but quicker in post-match recovery. Just like with Arsenal's Tuesday Club 20 years earlier, witnessing such tangible benefits can prove to be quite the revelation. 'You can put something in front of them that they enjoy eating, that is changing their performance, and they're like, "Oh wow that's witchcraft",' said Rachel, waving her arms with a magician's flourish.

Nourishing the Soul

A frequently misunderstood aspect of feeding athletes is the difference between performance food and health food. Provide an office worker with the periodised nutrition plan of an elite rugby player and there's a good chance they'll need a bigger chair within months. Take a Rice Krispies cereal bar. For an athlete it wouldn't be recommended as a daily snack, but its high sugar content means that it would make a sound half-time option. 'It's not about good or bad food,' insisted Kate. 'It's about when's the right time, and the right amount to have it in.'

Omar also made the distinction between the two. 'I believe there's a difference between health food and the food that I cook. Although the two kind of go hand in hand – if you're eating well, you will perform better – but the food that I cook for sports associations and clubs is there to enhance their performance.'

One of the reasons that Omar works so well with Naylor is because they share a philosophy on nourishing the soul as well as the body.

And this was the reason that the decision to change England's post-match banquet – including cheeseburgers, pizzas, and fried calamari alongside the beloved fried chicken – was swiftly reversed. Ultimately, Joe Hart's criticism wasn't without justification. 'It can do one of two things,' said Omar, counting on his hands. 'One, it's about putting good fuel back into them because they've just run around for 90 minutes. But two, if you've just won it becomes a celebration and a bit of a treat. But also if you've lost it becomes that bit of a morale-lifter. Food at that point when you lose a game becomes the most important thing in the world.'

During his time in Antarctica, Shackleton wrote in his diaries, 'The meals were the bright beacons in those cold and stormy days. The glow of warmth and comfort produced by the food and drink made optimists of us all.' Omar sees his servings as offering a similar moment of escape: 'In a lot of sports I have worked in, it's the one moment of each day where a coach is not shouting and screaming at them. They're not being stuck with needles or having strapping put on them. It's almost this euphoric moment of "I can be a human being again". I've learned the importance that food plays on their mental states.'

The restaurant in which Omar cooked for the British Olympic rowing team was seen as a haven to the likes of Katherine Grainger, Pete Reed, and Andrew Triggs-Hodge. It was only there that they could enjoy a rare 20 minutes of peace. Not only were they being fed delicious and wholesome food, but it was likely to be the only time at work when they could avoid talking shop. Even at the highest level, there is a place for comfort food. 'A lot of the boys at Harlequins want to eat slow-cooked pork belly, they want ribs, they want chips,' said Omar, as my stomach began to rumble. 'And I think there's a time and a place for it. One of the big things that I always do in any role that I've had is to try and offer a balance between quinoa and kale, and Scotch eggs or fried chicken. We don't demonise any foods.'

Omar has noticed that the level of nutritional knowledge possessed by the typical athlete has increased dramatically during his time as a performance chef. Cristiano Ronaldo is, of course, the poster boy when it comes to footballers attaining peak physical fitness, with a religious adherence to chicken and broccoli helping him become a living, flexing proof that the Josh Lewsey triangle is no longer limited to rugby. Manchester United reserve goalkeeper Lee Grant revealed that when the Portuguese superstar returned to Old Trafford in 2021, the rest of the squad followed his lead in leaving the lunchtime desserts untouched.

Others in the game, such as Chris Smalling, Fabian Delph, Jack Wilshere, and Jermain Defoe, have found significant benefits from switching to veganism, a further sign that players are prepared to make fundamental changes to their eating habits in order to progress their careers. Boxer Anthony Joshua, F1 champion Lewis Hamilton, and Olympic cyclist Lizzie Deignan are other examples of British athletes who have reached the top of their sports while pursuing a plant-based diet. And, in a comment which would likely prompt a wry smile from Omar, cricketer James Anderson admitted in 2019 that he'd consider a vegan lifestyle if it meant prolonging his career. This, after all, was a man once described by former team-mate Graeme Swann as having 'the worst diet of any professional athlete I know'.

And so Omar's clientele is now more demanding, but also more appreciative. 'You have to be at the very top of your game and you have to be able to answer questions that 15 years ago nobody really cared about.' He singled out one club in particular whose players demonstrate an informed approach to what goes on their plate on England duty. 'The work that Liverpool put into their performance, nutrition, and the education that they do around that is truly unbelievable. That's down to the manager being passionate about it, and down to the nutritionist being desperately passionate about it.'

At Crystal Palace, Kate puts on a regular cooking school for the youth players in the hope that they pick up the culinary basics that many of those from the generation above missed out on. In 2021, the Palace academy Christmas dinner was cooked by the under-18s team. 'It's not just telling them "eat this, eat that",' said Kate. 'That's not doing my job properly. I need them to understand why so they can make long-term good choices. The business model for a good nutritionist is actually crap because you want your clients not to really need you.'

In truth, neither Kate, Rachel, nor Omar will be worried about their immediate employment opportunities. Compare today's Premier League managers to their equivalents from a decade ago and you'll notice an altogether more body-conscious collective, increasingly likely to espouse the views of nutritionists and appreciate the skills of performance chefs. The services of Discreet and Delicious have never been as in demand as they are today.

'It's like an arms race,' said Rachel, who was scouting for more Newcastle-based private chefs in anticipation of increased demand. 'Even if what we do only has a one per cent difference in performance, if you're playing 38 matches in the league and you win just one of those matches because you're a tiny bit fitter, that's worth it.' She told me that when she first started working with footballers, she would break the ice – and horrify nutritionists – by introducing herself to the players as a drug dealer. 'Jokingly I used to say I'm dealing performance-enhancing drugs. They'd say, "What?!" But the performance-enhancing drug I have is legal. It's called food.'

3

FIX UP LOOK SHARP:
Formula One Mechanics

The average pit stop now takes less than three seconds. Should a pit crew be on screen for longer than that, it's usually because something's gone wrong. Yet outside of these wince-and-you'll-miss-it moments is where you'll discover the real talents of a Formula One mechanic, tasked with fine-tuning the finest margin in sport.

Baptism of Fire

It had been 28 seconds. To those in the pit lane staring at the blazing inferno, it had felt like 28 minutes. The car was split in two but only the rear could be seen, smouldering on the trackside sand. The front had been swallowed by the crash barriers, engulfed in flames. It included the driver's cockpit. And the driver.

It was November 2020 and Romain Grosjean's race had ended less than half a minute into the Bahrain Grand Prix. The Frenchman had wanted to follow the line of his team-mate Kevin Magnussen, who had found a route around the congestion in turn three. But he hadn't spotted the driver in his blind spot. Daniil Kvyat's emerging Alpha Tauri clipped Grosjean's right rear wheel, sending the Haas car hurtling off the track at a 45-degree angle. Back at the paddock, the engineers heard only one word before the radio cut out. 'Fuck!'

Grosjean hit the triple-guardrail barrier at 119mph. On impact he experienced 67G, a force that meant his 11st frame weighed 737st at the instant he hit the barrier. As red flags waved and all cars returned to silent pit lanes, the driver was yet to emerge from the flames. Hidden amid the fireball was a man's desperate battle to save his life.

Mercifully, Grosjean had remained conscious. But despite being able to undo his belt, his left foot was trapped between the mangled chassis and the brake pedal. With the heat increasing and the flames testing the resistance of his race suit, Grosjean briefly accepted his fate. Then he raged against it.

As the gloves on his hands began to char, he wrenched his foot from his laced boot and wrestled his way out. As he emerged from the wreckage under a shower of extinguishing foam, he insisted on walking to the ambulance. In the pit lane, hugs were exchanged and tears were wiped away. Grosjean had escaped with only a broken foot and burned hands.

The spectacular crash and miracle escape made headline news. For viewers, it was an enthralling story with a happy ending. For F1 officials it was a vindication of their divisive safety protocols, including the much-maligned titanium halo bar. But for Haas's chief mechanic, it was a problem to solve. Matthew Scott took his team to the crash scene to help clear the car. Or what remained of it.

'It was like an aeroplane crash, there were bits everywhere,' he said, adding that some debris would be found 100m away. Some, like the bits buried into the ground under the barrier, wouldn't be uncovered until days later. 'The car had been converted to its component pieces. It was one of the worst things I've ever seen.'

At that point there remained a real and present danger in the form of the car's 800V battery, which had been at full charge only moments earlier. 'They're lethal anyway, but the battery had split open,' recalled Matt. 'It was hanging there, sizzling away. We've got protocols in place, but no one ever thought that we'd be having to move half a burned-out battery.' They slipped on protective gloves and rubber overshoe wellies and then placed fireproof matting on the ground. 'We insulated it. Then someone had to take the responsibility of cutting through those battery cables.'

All eyes landed on the chief mechanic. And so, like a regurgitated Hollywood action script, he knelt down, hoped for the best, and cut through the battery's wires. 'You don't know what's going to happen. You've got the protective gear on, you know it should work, but there's still that …' he said, a grimace replacing the end of his sentence. 'People don't realise we dragged the battery out and it stayed in the middle of that field behind the car for two days because it was unsafe to move. The next day, we had to walk a salt bath over to try and deionise it. There are all kinds of stuff like that you need to consider with the technology we've got.'

I was speaking to Matt while he showed me around Haas's base in Banbury, Oxfordshire. Due to traffic jams caused by a multi-car collision on the M1, I had arrived an hour and a half late. To my relief, Matt was as unruffled as one might expect for a guy who regularly has to pick up the pieces following a car crash.

When I arrived at the warehouse that once housed the short-lived Marussia F1 team, framed mementoes hung on the lobby walls. Alongside signs forbidding photography were race-worn helmets, overalls, gloves, and a pair of Grosjean's black and white boots. Just like the one that failed to re-emerge from the Bahrain bonfire. It was an instant reminder of what happened to this team just nine months before my visit. It will go down as one of the most remarkable incidents in Formula One history.

With his mechanics hard at work behind him, Matt admitted the crash was an emotional time for the team, which is one of the youngest in Formula One. Founded by American Gene Haas, they made their F1 debut in 2016 with Grosjean at the wheel. Their operation, which is spread over sites in the USA and Italy as well as the UK, is on a much smaller scale than most of their track rivals. Their budget works out at less than a third of what the podium regulars are spending. But their gritty make-do attitude has previously defied the odds, and in 2018 they finished fifth in the constructors' championship.

Their low-cost approach sees Haas outsourcing processes that are traditionally done in-house. Many of their key components, including the engine and gearbox, come from Ferrari. With many still working from home, the warehouse was mainly occupied by Matt's crew of mechanics, along with a logistics team who ensure that hundreds of parts arrive where and when they should, by air, land, and sea. 'People refer to race cars as being an item, when actually it's a collection of many items that all come together on a Thursday night, ready for Friday morning. Then it's the driver's tool to make him go around the track as fast as possible,' said Matt, gently pulling his face mask back over his nose.

Bespectacled, softly spoken, and analytical, Matt isn't the archetypal tea-slurping, oil-coated, potty-mouthed mechanic. But he is a typical Formula One mechanic. He hasn't got where he is by conducting stellar MOTs at his local Nissan garage, but by embedding himself within the world of junior racing from as soon as he could open a toolbox. He calls his work a vocation rather than a career. 'I'd say, certainly over the last few years, it's become less of a bobble hat, garage-dweller environment. The generations change, and Formula One itself is changing. It's not necessarily about grease monkeys going racing and drinking beer. It's now about technology. And the fact that you're doing professional sport on an international scale.'

That's not to say that his team is populated by Silicon Valley-style nerd bros. Matt's voice could only just be heard over a sound system booming out dance tracks, with an intermittent backing chorus of cackles and F-bombs. A long workbench split the garage down the middle, with the mechanics tweaking a skeletal chassis on either side of the divide.

For the 2021 season, the popular pairing of Grosjean and Magnussen had been replaced by two rookies. The names of their successors, Mick Schumacher and Nikita Mazepin, were printed in bold blue and red lettering on the pristine white walls of the garage. Schumacher is the son of German F1 legend Michael. Mazepin is the son of Dmitry, the owner of the fertiliser company who had helped to plug some of Haas's financial holes. The team's new Russian colour scheme suggested that a seat in the car wasn't the only condition of the deal.

This was a season of transition for Haas, and it was showing. It was late August and after 11 races they were bottom of the pile. Neither driver had a point to their name. Their budget-defying fifth-place finish felt a long way off.

On the Road

The job of a Formula One mechanic remains an attractive one to those interested in motorsport. Even the potential dangers don't seem to put many off. When Haas advertised for a number-two mechanic position just after Grosjean's horror crash, Matt had to wade through over 800 applications. Only 20 had any genuine credentials, with the rest populated by F1 fans keen on a jolly. From the outside, it's easy to see why.

The 2021 season was made up of 22 races, with Bahrain, Azerbaijan, Mexico, Brazil, and Saudi Arabia among the far-flung venues. Jet-setting mechanics are among the first on the scene on a Tuesday, helping the 'truckies' construct F1's famed pop-up garages. But, despite the perception, there's very little time to explore the surroundings. As the guys responsible for putting away the toys post-race, the mechanics will also be the last to leave. Usually they clock off late into the night on Sunday, long after the drivers, engineers, media, and fans have departed to enjoy the host city's hospitality. The post-race pack-up is one of the least enjoyable aspects of the job, like cleaning up after a house party when the guests have gone for a morning fry-up.

Marc 'Elvis' Priestley was just 22 when he got his dream job as a mechanic for McLaren. 'Everybody assumes you're at a year-round party. Whilst there was definitely some truth in that in the early days, it's certainly not the case today,' he said, citing the example of Monaco which, despite its associated decadence and luxury, is one of the toughest weeks of the year for a mechanic. With it being one of the older circuits, staff are forced to work within tight confines and, because of the track's higher profile, there is an endless stream of sponsors touring the garage and pit lane.

'The grid is the most tightly packed you've ever seen, so our working environment is much harder,' added Marc, who was speaking to me ahead of filming a new series of *Wheeler Dealers*, one of several presenting roles he has landed since leaving Formula One. 'The perception is that you're one of these people lying on the back of a yacht. Obviously, that isn't the case. And equally, in terms of travelling around the world. I guess a lot like many business travellers, it's never as glamorous as people back home might think.'

Mechanics spend close to 200 days a year on the road. Along with the physical toll that it can take on their bodies, the mental wrench of being away from families and loved ones for so long explains why the majority are sprightly souls on the right side of 40. Given the nature of the F1 travelling circus, it's to be expected that friendships develop between teams, and socialising with rivals is no longer frowned upon as it once was. But there remains a strict omertà when it comes to discussing the car. Chat about football, discuss the hotel perks, or exchange tips on the best takeaways in the area. But under no circumstances should you talk shop. Like any business that derives an edge from its technology, that tech must be protected at all costs. Mechanics are told to treat the car like it is their bonus.

'You sign the equivalent of the Official Secrets Act, so you're contractually obliged not to give anything away,' said Marc. 'But even without that, there's a very clear understanding when you work for a Formula One team that no matter what your role you're all working for the same cause. For your car to win or to get the best result you can. And the only way you do that is by maximising everything you have. So the last thing anybody wants to do is go and share any advantage you have because it risks compromising your chances on a Sunday.'

It has become more difficult for teams to keep new components hidden from prying eyes. Photographers are specifically employed to snap rival cars the moment they leave the garage, while in 2020 Racing Point were fined for using 3D scanners to reverse-engineer Mercedes's brake ducts. The use of scanning equipment has since been banned by the FIA. For everything else, ingenuity is encouraged. It has even been known for some mechanics to squirt syringes of water at any snapper who comes too close.

Marc spoke of the time Adrian Newey, one of the sport's most revered car designers, came up with a novel idea to hide a new bargeboard situated behind the McLaren's front wing. The design had reaped some promising results in the wind tunnel, and Newey was keen for it to go unnoticed before it got to the track. 'What normally happens is we create some massively extravagant cover to sit over the wing. And you'd have to be working underneath this little cover to make sure nobody could get pictures. It was horrendously difficult to do your job.'

But going to such efforts would often prove counterintuitive, highlighting to rivals the sections of the car that had been tweaked. It gave photographers clues as to where they should pounce the moment the guard was dropped. So, on this occasion, Newey dared his mechanics to try a different approach.

'He said, "I want everybody to put all of that effort into shielding the *rear* wing of the car." Which was exactly the same as it had been the race before,' remembered Marc, still marvelling at the audacity of it. 'We were forming human shields around it, putting covers over it, going to great lengths. And nobody took a blind bit of notice of the front wing, because everyone was convinced there was something at the rear of the car that we were hiding. Those fun and games definitely happen. The secrecy is a huge part of it.'

The quirky dynamics within Formula One mean that rivalries aren't only generated between teams. Quite often a driver's most intense duel will be with the guy wearing the same colours, driving the same car, serviced in the same pit box. Each driver will have their own allocated batch of mechanics who work on their car for large chunks of the week before merging together on a race weekend. There will be a number-one mechanic, accountable for the entire car as well as overseeing the engine and fuel cell. They will be joined by a front-end mechanic, responsible for everything from the driver's seat to the nose cone, a rear-end mechanic, managing the gearbox and everything behind it, and a fourth floating mechanic mucking in wherever required. The same four roles are repeated on the second car, with all personnel reporting to the chief. And so the competitive cordiality between drivers can often permeate through to those building the cars. It does, occasionally, result in a ripple of discord throughout the garage.

Marc saw this happen first-hand at McLaren in 2007, during a headline-generating spat between team-mates Lewis Hamilton and Fernando Alonso. 'We probably had the two best drivers that year, and we almost certainly had the best car. But the main reason we didn't win any championships was because, right from the very top, the two drivers fell out,' said Marc. He described how the breakdown of their relationship was mirrored in a fractured garage, as the two teams of mechanics closed quarters around their own driver. 'We ended up with this great big divide down the middle of the garage, which is a hugely unhealthy way of operating as a team. Because you're splitting your resource in half essentially.'

The knock-on effect of the fall-out was that the mechanics on either side of the garage began to see each other as enemies, rather than team-mates. 'You stop sharing things with the other side, which is one of your most valuable resources as a Formula One team. You start making decisions that will get one up over the guy on the other side. Rather than maximising the team results,' said Marc.

At Haas, although Grosjean and Magnussen seemed to get on, they had an unwelcome history of running into each other on the track. 'We had troubles in 2019 with the two of them. It wasn't easy. We had some problems with the car, which made it difficult for the drivers to drive. And their frustrations were highlighted in the fact they kept running into each other,' remembered Matt, who maintained that it didn't create fault lines in his team.

In fact, for an outfit that hasn't enjoyed much recent success against other cars, Matt reckoned that any intra-team rivalry could only be a good thing. 'For sure there's a competitive edge across the workshop floor,' he said, glancing over as Mazepin's mechanics worked on the fuel cell. 'I think if you took that away, that would make it a poorer sport. It'd certainly give people less incentive to work within the team. Because it relies on competitiveness as a sport to get these people to do these long hours.'

Pit of the Stomach

Every mechanic in F1 has been trained to use a wrench like a young wizard with a phoenix-feather wand, so there's a peculiarity that their main renown is for an egg-timer task that requires no expertise in the workings of a car. For 99 per cent of a race weekend Formula One mechanics are behind closed garage doors, stripping, building, maintaining, mending, and optimising a machine that can travel at 200mph. For barely two seconds of it, they are changing its tyres in front of a global audience of 100 million viewers. And it is in this sideshow role, rather than the job they're actually qualified for, that they are at their most visible, under the most pressure, and asked about most of all.

At the 2019 Brazilian Grand Prix, Red Bull's mechanics took the pit stop to new levels, recording the fastest in the sport's history. And it needed everything, and everyone, to go to plan. In a muggy São Paulo pit box, a 20-strong crew held their breath and watched through helmet visors as a 145kg racing car darted towards them at 50mph. Thankfully for them, that car was blessed with laser-like guidance in the shape of Max Verstappen. One of the finest Formula One drivers of his generation stopped within a centimetre of where he needed to. It meant that nobody needed to adjust a single sinew from where they were poised. In the pit lane, movement is time. And time is the enemy.

Without a moment's hesitation, four tyre gunners attacked the wheel nuts with pneumatic Paoli impact wrenches delivering 10,000 rotations per minute. It's a device so advanced that they're not privy to the tech contained within it. At that moment, all they needed to know was to get in and out as quick as they could. The tyres were removed and replaced before the gunners zeroed in again to secure them in place.

Quicker than the time it takes most of us to put on a seatbelt, the car was back on the track with four new tyres. It took precisely 1.82 seconds. More importantly for Red Bull, the next time the crew saw their flying Dutchman he was showering in champagne. Verstappen took the chequered flag by less than a tenth of a second.

The fine margins involved mean that when things do go wrong, the consequences can be dire. In 2016, having started in pole position, Red Bull's Daniel Ricciardo led in Monaco before coming into the pits for a regulation tyre change. Only he arrived before his new super softs could emerge from the cramped subterranean garage that Marc warned about earlier. Ricciardo stewed as the wheels well and truly came off his car and his race. It took 15 long seconds before they could be replaced, after which he had relinquished the lead to eventual winner Lewis Hamilton.

In 2021, Mercedes's Valtteri Bottas pitted in second place but never re-emerged from the pit lane. The impact wrench was applied at a slight angle, shredding the thread of the nut. The tyre was eventually removed 44 hours later back at Mercedes's factory in Brackley.

And while refuelling was banned in 2010 to make stops safer, members of a pit crew are only ever a misstep away from losing more than just race points. When Grosjean, then at Lotus, overshot his box at the 2015 Spanish Grand

Prix, the unfortunate front jack operator demonstrated why it is the most daunting role in the pit lane. The car careered into the jack, flinging the mechanic half a metre in the air. Thankfully, his only injury became clear to everyone watching when the cameras returned to find him with an icepack over his groin. His colleagues found it more amusing than he did.

It can be a lot worse. Like in 2018, when Kimi Räikkönen was incorrectly given the signal to leave before his rear left wheel had been replaced. The Finn drove off with a Ferrari mechanic standing in the path of the wheel. A stricken Francesco Cigarini would require surgery on a double leg fracture.

This daunting mix of jeopardy and consequence means that even a Fonzie-like ability to repair an engine blindfolded is no guarantee for a successful career in a Formula One garage. Mechanics who wilt in the pit lane heat are as useful as a hiccupping surgeon.

Marc vividly remembers his first pit stop. It was at the Australian Grand Prix in Melbourne in 2002: 'The pressure was something that nobody can really train for, and something I hadn't even factored into this whole scenario. It almost crippled me. I suddenly had this vision of me sitting on my sofa, watching me on telly about to have this almighty disaster in a pit stop, that I was sure was about to happen.'

As the youngest person in the garage, he was allocated one of the lesser-spotted roles, responsible for the nose cone. 'It's rare. And when I was building up to it I was really pleased it was rare, because I was suddenly terrified.'

He remembers his earpiece bursting into life only seconds after the start of the race. Kimi Räikkönen, who Marc had only seconds prior been strapping in on the grid, had been involved in an accident on turn one. He was coming into the pit for, you guessed it, a new nose cone. 'My whole world just stopped,' said Marc. 'I went into absolute blind-panic mode. Everybody else was highly trained professionals, massively experienced, and very used to dealing with these things. And there's this young kid that's just tearing around like an idiot.'

Despite shaking with the adrenaline, he managed to gather his thoughts, locate the spare nose cone, and successfully attach it to Räikkönen's damaged McLlaren. For Marc, the pit stop had been a personal success and he skipped off into the garage, elated. Only his team-mates didn't join him, and it soon became clear that there was a problem. In the crash, a piece of gravel had found its way on to Räikkönen's car seat, digging into his spine. The mechanics were furiously searching for it.

'Eventually, somebody found it and he screeched off back into the race. But the pit stop had lasted for about a minute. It may have even been McLaren's worst ever pit stop in their entire history.' Marc's high fives were left hanging as a grumpy pit crew returned to the garage cursing their luck. 'That was a proper eye-opener. It was my welcome to what it means to be part of a team,' said Marc, having learned a valuable lesson. 'One person can't make it the perfect stop. But one person can destroy it. My bit was absolutely crucial. But it was tiny. And if the whole team isn't working perfectly, you can't have the perfect pit stop.'

Over time, Marc's fear of the pit stop faded: 'It turned to an absolute love of the adrenaline rush that came with a pit stop. Knowing there are millions of fans who want your car or your driver to do well. And you feel the weight of their expectation on your shoulders when you leap out of the garage.'

Flying the Flag

Unlike Marc, Emilie Rath doesn't have a clear memory of her first pit stop as an F1 mechanic. She recalls only that the occasion made her feel nauseous: 'I felt like I was going to puke the whole time. I was so nervous, it was too much for me that race.'

In 2018 the Dane was the number-two mechanic at Force India, responsible for kitting the engine and the front wings. It wouldn't take her long to become accustomed to the pressures of race day. 'Race day is our day off,' she said, speaking to me from her Leamington Spa home. I wasn't entirely sure if she was joking. 'All we have to do is get that car on the track. Make sure that when we take the blankets off the wheels you don't cut or break anything. Once that's done, we sit down and have a sandwich. That's it for us. We would work 20 hours a day for a full week. That Sunday when you see those mechanics? They're chilled.'

Given that Emilie's responsibility in the pit stop was to remove the left rear wheels of Sergio Pérez and Esteban Ocon in under three seconds, I asked how that factored into her theory about relaxing Sundays. 'I never felt pressure at the pit stops. That to me was the calmest thing you could do. I loved that. I knew what I was doing. I've never made a mistake.'

If she felt at ease at a moment when many other mechanics felt white-knuckle terror, it's probably down to the fact that being in the pit lane was the culmination of an ambition she'd had since she was 14. 'I saw this F1 race on TV. I think it was Singapore. It was a night race and I saw these mechanics jump out in all the lights and the glam. I thought, that is what I want to do with my life.'

Emilie admitted that there weren't many teenage girls in Copenhagen with a similar dream. But she had a plan. She reached out to Ole Schack, Red Bull's front-end mechanic. Her fellow Dane responded with some advice, and then she told her parents that she wasn't going to college. Instead she was going to become an apprentice mechanic.

After completing the initial six-month course, she was due to source an apprenticeship. It would take her two years to find one. 'No one wanted a female. I was told "we don't have a shower facility", or "you could turn pregnant". Bear in mind I was 15,' she shrugged. 'I heard it all.' Undeterred, Emilie sent out more applications and bought a portable shower. 'I found one online. It's like a tube that you just put up. So it doesn't matter that you don't have the facilities. I'll bring my own.'

Eventually she was accepted at a local car dealership, and she made an instant impression. 'I'm 18. I'm blonde. I'm the first female they ever had. And the first thing I said to these guys was, "Don't get used to having me around because I'm going to become a Formula One mechanic."

Unfortunately, that made the next four years a living hell,' she said, laughing at her youthful brashness. After bolstering her CV with some weekend racing experience with (father of Kevin) Jan Magnussen's Danish touring car team, it wouldn't be long before Emilie lived up to her bold proclamation.

She moved to England to take up a role at Arden International – the team founded by Red Bull team principal Christian Horner and his dad Gary – then followed it up with seven months at Manor Racing before the F1 team went bust. When she was offered her first race-team role at Force India, it was the realisation of a ten-year journey. But she wasn't always as confident in the role as she would let on.

'I was really intimidated. I felt a bit like a fraud. In England, these guys had been working in motorsport for 15, 20 years. So who am I?' The last woman to drive in a Formula One Grand Prix was nearly half a century ago and there remains a distinct lack of female visibility off the grid too. Emilie was the only female mechanic at Force India, though composite technician Michelle Creighton and strategy engineer Bernadette Collins added what she described as a 'bit of female essence' to the team.

As the first female F1 mechanic in Denmark's history, Emilie attracted a lot of attention from back home. There were requests for interviews, and photographers made her blonde hair and blue eyes a regular focus of their lens. 'Unfortunately, that didn't play in my favour because it made it really hard to be a part of the group. I was seen as being the princess, even though something I hate is people taking pictures of me.' Emilie was torn between trying to be one of the guys while also wanting to promote her journey to others back home. 'Of course, I wanted to draw attention to how awesome it is that you can go from being a mechanic back in a little place in Denmark to being here. I wanted to do my part and promote that. On the other hand, it started to affect the way the team saw me. It's hard to have that respect when you're being looked at as a poster girl,' she sighed.

Although Formula One's dated habit of pre-race grid girls was jettisoned in the same year that Emilie made her paddock debut, it seems the sport still has a way to go to ensure that the women working within it don't feel like token figures. 'I felt a little bit of a distance between the team and myself, and I think gender had a lot to do with it. A lot of people will hate me for saying that,' said Emilie. 'But for me personally, I think it was. But I was still determined I wanted to do my year. This is everything I worked for. So fuck it, you know?'

At the end of a taxing 2018 season, Emilie opted not to stay on for another year. Instead she took a job with Mercedes. Based at the team's Brixworth plant, she spent two years working on the engines that powered the generation's most successful F1 team. It was here that she felt more at home. Although she was approached about a return to a race-team environment, she decided against it. 'Something in me said, "I think I'm done with that." My main purpose was to get to F1. I've done it, bought the t-shirt.'

It's a t-shirt that, for now at least, remains predominantly sold in men's sizes. But Emilie intends to change this.

Her new ambition is to inspire the next generation to not fear jobs like hers. After six years in England, Emilie was returning home to Denmark in 2022. Alongside her role as an ambassador for Copenhagen's technical education college, her new job involves looking after 50 interns. She is to encourage them into high-profile vocational roles, regardless of their academic abilities. Or gender. 'I want to spend my time now trying to put the word out to my country to show what you can do with a technical education.'

Refuelling

Back in Banbury, Matt pointed out one of five carbon-fibre car floors that cost £120,000. To demonstrate how quickly costs can escalate, he also showed me a handful of minuscule bespoke K-nuts that cost £30. For a single nut. Constantly scrambling for components that can't be made or repaired in-house takes its toll, but it's a lack of human resources where Matt and his crew truly feel the pinch. With around 160 employees in total, compared to a team like Mercedes with closer to 1,000, Haas have little choice but to do things differently. 'Our guys probably work harder than the Mercedes mechanics,' said Matt, within earshot of his team. 'Because they haven't got the support network. There's a lot more pressure on them to do the work themselves. If they're not there it's not going to get done.'

Whereas Mercedes, Red Bull, or Ferrari can arrive at a circuit with key elements ready to bolt straight on to the chassis, Haas's mechanics are more likely to build each individual component trackside. With those extra five or six hours saved, the bigger teams can work on aerodynamics, presentation, fitness, or pit stop practice. Matt knew that the black practice car parked in the centre of the warehouse floor wasn't used anywhere near as often as it should have been. Logistics company DHL compiles the data for every pit stop to crown the season's fastest pit crew. Haas had finished bottom for the last two years, with an average stop that was over a second slower than leaders Red Bull.

But it's not just about being quick. It's about being accurate. In the opening race of the 2018 season, Haas had both of its drivers in the top five in Australia only for ill-fitted wheels to force both out of the race. A similar pit error at the 2020 Turkish Grand Prix curtailed Magnussen's bid for a top-ten finish. 'It's something that I've highlighted that we've struggled with this year and we're trying to make some changes within our pit stop group. We perhaps don't get enough practice,' admitted Matt.

They also hadn't found the time to mend a known issue with the wheel nuts. 'That just breaks the guys' confidence, so when it becomes a pressured situation, they are automatically more careful. You tend to find you can do a pit stop in practice as quick as anybody when the onward effect of going wrong has no consequence,' he said, comparing it to practising penalties before having to do the same in front of a crowd of 60,000. 'When you're put in a race situation and there's that extra pressure, naturally, people just double check. Which slows the pit stop down. Bearing in mind you're talking tenths of a second.'

It was the mechanics' first day back following the obligatory mid-season factory shutdown. It is a mandated holiday by the FIA, the sport's governing body. It's not simply to ensure that overworked crews enjoy a fortnight's rest, but also a way to level the playing field. Matt said that two weeks without racing would normally see the bigger teams streak further ahead in terms of development and innovation. Thankfully for the likes of Haas, teams aren't allowed to so much as answer an email during the shutdown.

Matt joked that his guys had returned sunburned and hungover, but there was no time to ease them back in. They were already behind schedule due to a fuel cell glitch that had required one of the puncture-proof Kevlar bags to be shipped back to the Milton Keynes supplier for repair. The cells expand to hold the maximum allowance of 110kg of fuel (in F1, petrol is measured in mass rather than volume) and are just about malleable enough to be squeezed into the space between driver and engine. It took three straining mechanics looking like they were closing an overfilled suitcase to get it in.

The petrol tank setback meant they would be working through the night to catch up, as the next morning they would be departing for Spa ahead of the Belgium Grand Prix. It was the first of three consecutive race weekends and it promised to be a gruelling month. While there is an FIA curfew preventing teams from working on their cars on Friday evenings, it's not unheard of for mechanics to begin work in their trackside garages on Tuesday and not get to bed until Thursday.

With the mid-season vacation boost likely to wear off if results didn't improve on the track, Matt knew his biggest challenge wasn't the car. 'Performance does have a massive effect on morale. It is a negative thing to sit here at the back of the grid, and know that we're going to be at the back of the grid when we go to the next race. And the race after that. However, it's not just about that one race or that one season.'

His aim was to create a tight-knit working environment that kept his staff engaged and aspirational, in the hope that consistency will breed hard-earned success in the long run. He was confident a new budget cap set to be introduced in 2022 would reduce the delta between the teams. 'Managing the people and managing the expectations is a lot harder than working on a car. Having to try and motivate those guys, when the rewards aren't there, is very difficult.'

Dream the Same Dream

Matt suggested we leave the mechanics to their graft to take a stroll through the rest of the building. We found the bulky sea and air freight pallets, ready to be floated or flown to the late-season circuits in Asia and the Americas. For anywhere that can be reached on wheels, two giant trucks were parked outside emblazoned in crimson Haas logos that glistened in the Oxfordshire sun.

In every corner of the warehouse there were piles of magnesium alloy rims stacked like kegs in a pub cellar. Matt pointed out the logistics team, tasked with masterminding this global dot-to-dot, and mentioned that the science and performance teams would normally be housed upstairs. 'Not that we have any performance in our car,' he quipped. It was a throwaway remark meant as a joke. But, whether deliberately or subconsciously, it was uttered where his team couldn't hear. Race results must have been a source of frustration for a chief mechanic who once dreamed of becoming a race car driver. And when a general needs to rally his troops, he can't be seen frowning.

On paper, a mechanic is considered service personnel. A walking, talking driver's toolbox. But they possess a competitive edge as strong as that of the guy behind the wheel. Through the eyes of an F1 mechanic, the driver is simply the final component that allows them to realise their own ambitions. 'The most successful drivers realise it's a team sport,' said Matt, offering a glimpse into this mindset. 'They realise that the recognition has to be more than just them. They haven't built the car. They haven't designed the car. They haven't set the garage up. They haven't had the car in the wind tunnel. They don't have the models, they haven't done the science. There are a lot of people all aiming towards that one goal. A good driver understands that.'

It's no coincidence that whenever I asked about their favourite moments, mechanics talked about wins, podiums, and points in the first person, just like a driver would. They soak in every high and dwell on every low. Matt may have been experiencing more of the latter of late, but as he kept reminding his downtrodden employees, it wasn't so long ago that Haas was a Formula One success story.

He was one of the first mechanics in the door in August 2015, arriving to an empty workshop without a wheel gun or front jack in sight. He recalled hacking chunks off the gearbox in a desperate bid to get both cars out on the track. Yet, against all expectations, Romain Grosjean finished sixth in Haas's debut race in Australia. They followed it up with a fifth-place finish in the following race in Bahrain.

'Sixth in Australia was amazing. It was a bit lucky. But to actually go to Bahrain a week later and to do it on merit was a sensational feeling again. The immense amount of reward we got from doing something which no one expected was very big. It'll take a lot to beat that. In anything I do.'

Marc also remembered both extremes of the ride. At his lowest ebb he had the drama of Kimi Räikkönen crashing during the final lap of the 2005 European Grand Prix at the Nürburgring. The Finn had been challenging Fernando Alonso for the championship title. 'It looked like the front suspension, which is my bit, had just disintegrated and fallen apart,' said Marc. 'My heart sank, I thought I'd let everybody down by making a mistake on my part of the car.' It later transpired that the retirement was a result of a tyre issue, not the suspension. 'But it was at least half an hour before I got that information. And I'd sunk to the absolute depths of despair by that point. I probably smoked 20 cigarettes out the back of the garage, just feeling like I was at the world's end.'

Three years later, McLaren secured their first drivers' championship for nine years, an achievement the team has yet to repeat since. Lewis Hamilton claimed his maiden title in a dramatic final race in Brazil, pipping Ferrari's Felipe Massa by a single point. Without hesitation, Marc told me that it was his most memorable career moment. The fulfilment of his childhood reveries. 'Winning that battle with Lewis realised not only a dream for him, but it was exactly the same dream for me,' he said. 'My dream wasn't as well documented as his, but it was exactly the same. And it happened. You're not a driver, you're not the superstar of the show. You're not the team principal. You're not in the public eye. You're doing this job because you love racing, and you're competitive, and you want to win.'

In Formula One, winning has different definitions. For Haas in 2021, success simply meant not finishing bottom. As the season progressed and the gap to ninth grew larger, targets were lowered. They simply wanted their rookie drivers to earn their first points. 'There's a scale of disappointment,' explained Matt. 'Getting two cars in the points is fantastic. And it's downwards from there. But if you have to do an unplanned stop because you've got a flat tyre or damaged nose, and yet you do a good pit stop and still finish 15th, you can take satisfaction from that.'

Not that many people were paying attention to Haas. For the first time in 47 years, the Formula One season headed into the final race in Abu Dhabi with its two leading contenders level on points, unseparated after 21 races. In one of the most controversial moments in the sport's history, Verstappen overtook Hamilton on the last lap to claim his first championship. It came moments after the Dutchman pitted for soft tyres with just four laps to go.

Under the most intense pressure, Red Bull's mechanics were unflappable. After executing the most important tyre change of their careers, they celebrated wildly as their driver crossed the line for his first world title. Meanwhile, Haas ended the season bottom of the grid. The team hadn't recorded a single point since Grosjean's near-fatal crash. Matt may have delicately severed the wires of a searing battery that day, but the job of recharging his team was proving ever trickier.

Having spent the best part of a year telling his team not to dwell on results because 2022 would be better, he would soon run out of ways to prop up morale if the budget cap didn't provide any respite. 'I try persuading people that you're still working towards something. Every sportsperson is trying to win. But if they give up when they don't win, we'd be very short of sportspeople.'

Two months later, pre-season testing began. Every team was back on zero points, but there was an additional sense of reset in the Haas garage. They had cut ties with their Russian benefactors, and driver Nikita Mazepin followed his dad out of the door. The cars were returned to their original black, red, and white livery, and former driver Kevin Magnussen was welcomed back like a trusted old friend.

The first race of the 2022 season would take place in a neon-drenched Bahrain. Two seasons ago, this was a scene of terror and relief for the American team. This time there would be only the latter. And lots of it. The tenacious Danish driver marked his return to Formula One with a remarkable fifth-place finish.

For the first time in 526 days, Haas's mechanics were able to run to the pit wall and take in the sight of their driver, bringing home their car, with their points in the bag. 'That was a lot of fun, I enjoyed it a lot. It's so good to be back in this position,' said Magnussen. 'I've just got to say a massive well done to the team.'

4

SNOW WHISPERERS:
Winter Olympic Snowmakers

The effect of climate change is an increasing challenge for winter sports, as temperatures rise and viable venues reduce. Sochi in 2014 was the first Winter Olympic Games held in a subtropical climate, and not a single flake of natural snow was expected in Beijing in 2022. So who do host cities turn to when Mother Nature has other ideas? Meet the professional snowmakers.

The Prophet

Two months before its flame would light the cauldron at the Winter Olympics' opening ceremony in February 2014, Russian organisers arranged for the Olympic torch to pass through the remote republic of Altai. In a part of the world where traditional dress is still worn and centuries-old shamanism is still practised, the torch relay team sought to ask an unusual favour. It is one the locals are unlikely to have received before, or since. For there, in a region straddling the borders of Kazakhstan, China, and Mongolia, and where the annual temperature averages a bitter -3°C, Altai shamans were asked to pray for snow.

The divine intervention was not intended for Altai's effortlessly frosty capital town of Gorno-Altaysk, but for the Olympic host city of Sochi, 5,000km away on the Black Sea coast. Before being awarded the Games, Sochi's main renown was as a tourist hotspot for Russians to flee the cold weather. With a subtropical climate the beach resort had been a favourite summer retreat among the country's elite, including two men not known for their sunny dispositions, Joseph Stalin and Vladimir Putin.

In contrast to the 85 days of snow in Russia's southern Siberian hinterlands, Sochi experienced only two snow days in 2013, producing less than a centimetre in total. The average temperature in February was 10°C, making it the warmest city in Russia. Following several cancelled test events due to a lack of snow, Russia's organising committee president Dmitry Chernyshenko was ready to try anything to ensure the conditions were suitable for the biggest winter sports event on the planet. The shamans were happy to help.

Sure enough, on TV at least, the Games in Sochi looked exactly as a Winter Olympics is expected to look, draped in a gleaming white fluffy blanket. Was it down to a shamanistic miracle? No. Of course it wasn't. Just as in Vancouver four years earlier, and in Pyeongchang and Beijing since, Sochi made use of a banquet of exhaustive and costly techniques that diminished Mother Nature's authority. After all, why pray to God, when you can simply play God?

One of the first recruits following any successful Winter Olympics bid is that of a prophet. This Olympic soothsayer need not consult tea leaves, crystal balls, or even the stars. Instead they should be a wizard with a weather vane. In 2010, Chris Doyle was the in-house prophet of the Vancouver Olympics. Or, to give him his official title, chief meteorologist. 'It took years off my life,' he said, before explaining why he now regularly wears a cap. 'All my hair fell out. I think that's a pretty common experience for people involved with Games development. But I loved the pace, the excitement and the novelty of doing work we really knew could be used to make a difference.'

Within weeks of Vancouver winning the bid in 2003, Chris and his team were meeting John Furlong, CEO of the city's Olympic organising committee. It proved to be the start of a breathless seven-year project. Chris was responsible for planning the entire weather operation, implementing technology, collecting data, and training a team of forecasters for each outdoor venue. He brought in leading scientists from Canada and the USA to develop the world's most advanced high-resolution weather models.

With little existing weather information from the mountain venues, Chris prioritised putting equipment in place to ensure they had several seasons of data to work from by the time the Games began. But forecasting for the Olympics is not the same as advising Canadians on whether they need to pack an umbrella. 'When forecasting for huge areas as we have in Canada, we're looking at regions of thousands of square kilometres,' he said. 'But venue forecasts for the Olympics are to a very specific sports-weather threshold. Things like visibility and the intensity of the precipitation that falls on a very small location.' Chris's unenviable task was equivalent to asking Carol Kirkwood or Tomasz Schafernaker to predict the weather for your back garden.

But as any forecaster knows, the trickiest part of their role is not collecting data, nor even interpreting it. It's being able to communicate their findings to those of us who don't know our cumulus from our nimbostratus, from the public watching on TV to the decision makers at the Olympic Games. And that responsibility, as the key bridge between the forecasting team and the executive committee, fell on the shoulders of its chief meteorologist. 'They wouldn't wait for the weather to happen to make a decision,' said Chris. 'They would look to us and say, "What's going to happen?" and make a decision beforehand. And that's exactly how it worked.'

Chris, who would travel to Russia, South Korea, and China to provide consultation to Vancouver's successors, remembered his team's forecasts influenced several key decisions at the Games. From using wind readings to set the start times for the ski jump, to completely overhauling the Paralympics schedule to prevent the high-speed events from clashing with days of poor visibility. 'That was very rewarding because we could see we were making a real substantive contribution to the Games with our forecasts. Not with observed weather, which is the way decisions were made in the past.'

As gratifying as some elements of his role were, it also meant casting Chris as the messenger of doom on more than one occasion. The city's famous Whistler resort brought few concerns thanks to its high altitude. But organisers were sweating on the snow status of Cypress Mountain, where the freestyle skiing and snowboarding were due to take place.

Just north of central Vancouver, not only was Cypress at a lower altitude but Chris's forecast suggested that it could be affected by El Niño, an irregular climate phenomenon born in the Pacific Ocean. Its warming effect in Vancouver would be significant. 'It was expected, although we hoped to be wrong,' said Chris, who found himself in the strange situation where if he was right he would be unpopular, and if he was wrong he would be out of a job. It turned out to be the former. 'Just as we forecast, El Niño conditions did arrive early in the spring of 2010. And in January, the month prior to the opening ceremonies, we basically watched the Cypress venue melt away.'

As a precaution, Vancouver closed the Cypress Mountain resort to the public and called Chris into an executive committee meeting to provide the latest forecasts. He remembered delivering the news they didn't want to hear. 'I said, "I'm sorry to say that we don't see any appreciable cooling in the near future and very little chance of extra snow before the opening ceremony." [CEO John Furlong] said, "OK, I'm really sorry to hear that." Once they had the information from us then they executed their own contingency plan. The organising committee was ready. They had the forecast in hand and they knew who to call.'

Mother Nature, Agitator

Combatting adverse weather conditions at the Winter Olympics is far from a new battle. In fact, barely a Games has gone by without Mother Nature making her mark. At the second edition, in 1928, Switzerland's Alpine town of St Moritz saw the opening ceremony gatecrashed by a violent blizzard. Although it damaged the open-air stadium and made parading 400 athletes from 25 competing nations nigh on impossible, it wouldn't be long before its accompanying white blanket would be much missed. Just days later, a warm and dry foehn wind emerging from the Albula Alps saw temperatures rise dramatically, causing major disruption to the schedule.

When competitors set off at first light in the 50km cross-country ski, the crisp morning air was freezing. By midday the foehn's balmy influence saw the mercury rocketing towards 25°C, with a granite-like Per-Erik Hedlund the only skier able to handle the freakish conditions. The Swede finished 13 minutes ahead of an exhausted and bewildered field.

The unexpected heat saw a number of events postponed. The bobsleigh competition was cut from four runs to two, while the precarious melting surface resulted in the 10,000m speed-skating event being cancelled completely. The Argentinian contingent, the first southern hemisphere nation to compete at the Winter Olympics, must have wondered why they had bothered to forgo their airy alpargatas in favour of bulky boots.

But the unseasonable weather did not deter the hosts, as St Moritz put its experience as a longstanding ski resort to savvy use. The figure skating was moved indoors to the Kulm Hotel ice rink while horse-drawn sledges were used for transportation around the venues.

Despite the setbacks and delays, the Games were a success. A 15-year-old Norwegian figure skater by the name of Sonja Henie became the youngest ever Olympic champion, a record that would stand for over 70 years. The skeleton, a death wish on a tea tray, made its Olympic debut on the ice track considered the birthplace of the sport, the Cresta Run. And the spectacular Olympiaschanze ski jump was unveiled as the world's highest. It remained in use for 80 years.

Showing admirable composure, flexibility, and stubborn resolve, St Moritz cut steps in the ice for its successors to follow. Four years later, Lake Placid shrugged off the heat, not to mention the raised eyebrows of the bemused Europeans, by bussing in snow from over the border in Canada. The military was involved at both Cortina d'Ampezzo in 1956 and Innsbruck in 1964, drafted in to haul snow from nearby mountains. In the case of the latter, snowfall was so meagre that it required the Austrian army to carve 20,000 ice bricks to form the bobsleigh run and hand-pack 40,000 cubic meters of snow into the Alpine skiing routes.

By the time the Olympic flame returned to Lake Placid in 1980, its organisers didn't need to knock on Canada's door like a red-faced neighbour in need of loo roll. Instead, machines producing snow were in place for the first time. The use of technology at the Games grew exponentially alongside its increasing prominence, popularity, and cost.

It wouldn't be long before the IOC felt it was time for its winter showpiece to go it alone.

Rather than taking place in the same year as its higher-profile summer cousin, from 1994 the quadrennial event would become a primetime entity in its own right. Everything that comes with such a status would soon follow. Multibillion-dollar TV deals, unyielding advertising commitments, ambitious venue constructions, lavish opening ceremonies, and the scrutiny of millions watching worldwide. It meant St Moritz's legacy of stubborn resolve would be needed more than ever. But there was no longer much room for its other two traits from 1928: composure and flexibility.

A modern Winter Olympic Games simply does not entertain the possibility of postponements or cancellations for problematic weather. These days, when the Games begin, no blizzard, drought, or heatwave can stop them. But to beat Mother Nature at her own game, you need the brightest and most innovative minds in the business.

The Conjurers

'Are you a skier or snowboarder?'

Joe Vanderkelen began our conversation with the question I feared may crop up. Joe is the president of SMI Snowmakers, a company whose video ads include the promise to 'extend your snow season with or without Mother Nature's permission'.

I sheepishly replied that I had never been skiing or snowboarding, feeling as though I had just told Paul McCartney that I'd never listened to the Beatles. I followed up with a mumble about being intrigued by the things we don't see at a Winter Olympics, but by that point, Joe had jumped in to curtail my cringe. 'Oh come on!' he shouted, but with a beaming smile that suggested I wasn't in too much trouble. 'Well that's incredible that you would be aware and astute enough to think about that,' he added, demonstrating the sort of midwestern charm that could sell coal to Newcastle. Or, as it turns out, snow to Colorado.

As the architects behind some of the most recent Winter Olympics, SMI's promos also claim, 'World-class sporting events are hosted not where the snow could be, but where it will be.' The bold pronouncements come with a track record. From Sarajevo to Salt Lake, Calgary to Pyeongchang, much of the white canvas on which Olympic athletes have made history hasn't come from the heavens, but from machines built in Michigan, USA.

Joe was wearing a cornflower blue short-sleeved shirt, his thick grey hair was combed over to one side, and his teeth were as white as the snow he produces from thin air. He was sat in an unremarkable office room dotted with family portraits, and if not for a glimpse of the Olympic rings in a frame on the back wall he could quite easily have been mistaken for the cheery IBM salesman that he once was.

Instead, he's now nearly 30 years into a role he reluctantly took on aged 31 following the death of his father. Jim Vanderkelen first indulged in his love for winter sports by producing ski boots. But sensing which way the wind was blowing, Jim averted his attention to what lay underfoot and founded SMI in 1974. Based out of the back of a small carpet company, their debut product was the SnowStream 320. It was the first mass-produced snow machine that didn't require compressed air. Released to little fanfare, the first years of the company were slow going. But Jim would eventually have his day in the snow.

In 1984 the company got the nod to help out at the Winter Olympics in Sarajevo. It was a small-scale remit, providing half a dozen machines for a single slope, but it was a significant step forward for the business. Over 40 years on and the 320 has been replaced by sophisticated fan guns that resemble jumbo-jet engines. They have names like PoleCat, Puma, and Wizzard. They bring a whole new meaning to the quip 'Sun's out, guns out.' Like most tech these days, they can even be operated via smartphone. But the underlying principles of snowmaking remain the same. 'Snowmaking involves a lot of water,' explained Joe. 'Compressed air mixing in a small nozzle with water droplets creates what we call ice seeds, and those ice seeds will then nucleate the bulk water, blowing it out as the cold environment freezes those small water droplets.'

Joe's sales experience combined with a mechanical engineering degree means that he has a welcome knack of explaining complex scientific processes in layman-proof bitesize chunks. His narrative technique even extends to a priest-like ability to swear without cursing. At one point he described himself as a 'hard-working mother-fletcher'.

He told me that, depending on the model of gun, the fans can distribute the snow from anything between ten and 60 metres, providing the hang time required for freezing. Then there are the lower-energy stick guns, which are placed higher above the surface and use the natural wind in place of a fan.

Crucially, the machines are able to produce snow that is no different to the frozen water that falls naturally from the clouds. So don't, whatever you do, make the mistake of calling it artificial snow. At least not in front of Joe. 'One of my biggest pet peeves is when people call it artificial snow. It's not artificial snow. I like to say it's machine-made snow,' he insisted. Whatever you want to call what emerges from these guns, it comes out looking and behaving exactly like two-week-old natural snow. 'Natural snow sometimes takes hours or days to form as it's going through the sky. We're forming that snow crystal in somewhere between three and 15 seconds.'

Joe's first experience of a Winter Olympics was in Calgary in 1988, but his first Games as company president came at Salt Lake City in 2002. He was working on the steep freestyle slopes at Deer Valley. Given his expertise in sourcing and building water systems high up in the mountains, Winter Olympics organisers now have the Michigan area code saved on their speed dial. Following Chris Doyle's ominous forecasts in 2010, SMI was tasked to help out in Vancouver with 35 guns that could blanket the Cypress Hill slopes in one metre of snow in just two days.

It is a measure of how well regarded Joe's company is in Olympic circles that, four years later, even the Russians came calling. In terms of the scale of the project, the challenges of the local climate, and the immense media spotlight and scrutiny, Joe believes that making snow in Sochi was his toughest challenge yet. 'I'll never forget the first time I got off a plane in Sochi,' he said. 'As I walked out of the military airport, I saw a palm tree. I thought this will be interesting. There was nothing built. There were barely roads up on that mountain. We did huge creek crossings in tracked Russian vehicles, it was a little iffy driving around these places trying to figure out where the slopes were going, and where the water sources would go.'

SMI helped build Sochi's Rosa Khutor resort from scratch, installing more than 400 snow guns over 20 miles of slopes for the alpine, snowboard, and freestyle competitions. In order to provide the 12,000 gallons per minute of water required, they built two lakes sourced by a mountain river, fed by 35,000m of pipes. And while gravity provided some welcome help, eight megawatts of pumping power was still required to deliver the water at high pressure.

As Joe recalls, the Russians were pleased with what they got: 'A lot of the Russian leadership involved with this believed. But when we started that system, and it actually made snow, you could see them all have this huge sigh of relief.' As a thank you, they invited Joe to take in the European Cup alpine skiing finals at Sochi a year ahead of the Games. As someone who has come into regular contact with sporting VIPs such as Bode Miller and Lindsey Vonn, Joe saw it as no big thing to say hello to the event's highest-profile attendee: President Putin.

'I had VIP credentials, so I could walk around shaking hands. The Russians were really proud because there were blue skies and snow top to bottom,' said Joe. Emboldened by the textbook conditions, Joe walked over to the presidential entourage and got a metre away from the man himself before his well-meaning plan was foiled. 'One of his KGB guys said "NIET!", grabbed my arm, and pulled me off to the side. I thought, well that's probably not going to happen.'

It was estimated that 80 per cent of the snow in Sochi was machine-made. In Pyeongchang in 2018, where SMI built a brand-new lake that could store 33 million gallons of water, that number reached 98 per cent. When the Games began in Beijing in 2022, there wasn't a drop of natural snow in existence. A modern Winter Olympics is effectively hosted on a film set.

Proponents of man-made snow say that it is more durable and denser than natural snow, and so more likely to maintain its integrity for the duration of the competition. This makes it as fair for skier number one as it is for skier number 50. Athletes can move quicker on the firmly packed man-made snow, as opposed to the wind-drifted powder that is great for snowballs but unreliable on the surface.

It meant the ground crew in Pyeongchang found themselves in the paradoxical scenario of patrolling the Jeongseon Alpine Centre in the early hours of each morning, removing any unwanted slush. The same occurred in Beijing four years later, when an unexpected heavy flurry forced events like the women's freeski to be postponed. These days, even when nature does play ball, Olympic hosts kick it over the fence.

Firing Blanks

While SMI had some of their guns at work in Beijing, it was Italian firm TechnoAlpin that won the tender to oversee the main alpine venue. The additional competition in Europe may not be entirely welcomed in Michigan, but it is a sign that the market is expanding. Just as Jim Vanderkelen had predicted, business is booming for snowmakers around the world.

Joe's daughter Brooke works in sales and marketing at SMI, having become a third-generation snowmaker 'right out of diapers'. She told me that nobody in the company was kidding themselves as to why their snow guns are as in demand as ever: 'Climate change is real. It's something that's very heavily linked to snowmaking, which is becoming more popular with resorts just to ensure that they can open for their customers and provide a great experience.'

Brooke spoke about the changing gun density, which determines how far apart each machine is placed from the other, 'Instead of having snow machines that are 100 to 150 metres apart from each other, they're going to 20 to 50 metres apart. You're getting snow guns that are closer and closer. That has been a trend that we've been seeing in this industry.'

Joe was at pains to point out that while snow-making requires vast quantities of water – it takes over 280,000l to cover an area of 200ft in six inches of snow – it is more efficiently used than in other water-reliant industries. 'One of our company mantras from day one was to have energy-efficient snowmaking,' he said, his merry demeanour unchanged despite the thornier topic. 'Snowmaking is really one of the most efficient water users because we take that water and we put it out on the slopes, then it melts and it goes back into the water supply where we took it from. So we return 85 per cent to 90 per cent of the water we use. Whereas a bottled-water plant, a beer plant, or in industrial processing, they're 100 per cent water users.'

Yet while SMI and other snowmakers are turning to automation in a bid to improve the efficiency of their machines, there's no getting away from the fact that snowmaking requires high levels of energy. Especially when pumping vast quantities of water uphill. The cost of snow production typically accounts for over half of all annual energy consumption at resorts that regularly use snowmaking machines.

But that isn't the only polar bear in the room when it comes to snowmaking. For it turns out that these snowmaking guns tend to fire blanks when the temperature rises above zero. 'People think you can make snow in any temperature,' said Joe. 'But we generally have to be below freezing, depending on a combination of temperature and relative humidity.' It's a fact that Joe wishes was more widely known, especially when he's fielding phone calls from doting parents wanting a winter wonderland for little Johnny's birthday. 'They'll think you can take a house faucet and power a snowmaking system. They'll ask us to bring a snowmaking machine over for their kid's party. It'll be the middle of July, in Michigan. Well no, actually, we can't.'

It means increasing the number of guns is not always the answer to a melting ski slope. And as cheery as Joe is in recounting his experiences at the Games, hitches and glitches did and do occur, despite advanced snowmaking capabilities. In Vancouver, the hosts found that no matter how many snow guns they had in their holster, nature was still the quickest to draw.

Weatherman Chris Doyle could only watch as his troubling forecast played out just as he had predicted, with temperatures too high to create snow. 'We couldn't make snow during the month of January,' he said. 'We made the decision to remediate the venue at Cypress Mountain after the amount of snow stockpiled at the top was inadequate to match the melt-off.'

The committee took inspiration from its historic predecessors and brought in snow by any means possible. Helicopters transported buckets from nearby peaks, while over 300 dump trucks drove 150km west to pick up snow from inland provincial parks. Bales of straw were used to bulk up bare slopes, while canisters of carbon dioxide were inserted into the freestyle jumps to act as internal refrigeration.

Maintaining the snowpack throughout the day and night took a Herculean effort behind the scenes, recalling the Austrian military operations at Innsbruck in 1964. Yet it went completely unnoticed by those watching at home. 'If you looked at the Cypress venue on TV,' said Chris, 'it looked like a winter wonderland. But if you were there in person you could see to the left and to the right – mud!'

Eternal Snowman

Mikko Martikainen introduced himself to me in his cautious, almost robotic, Finnish accent. He was speaking to me from the town of Leppävirta in eastern Finland, and rather wonderfully the first thing he showed me was that it was snowing outside of his window. For a man whose nickname is the snow whisperer, it seemed only right that it should be.

Every winter, Mikko welcomes the first sign of snow with the same routine. Wherever he is in the world, whatever the time of day, he stops what he is doing and opens a bottle of cognac. Then he puts on the same CD. 'I play Rachmaninoff Piano Concerto Number Two,' he said, miming raising a glass to the sky. 'And I salute the first drop.'

Mikko, with the granite features of a man who's spent a career below zero, described his relationship with snow as a love story. And just like any whirlwind romance, it has been responsible for hope, pain, and happiness. His early memories of a 1960s childhood in the small industrial town of Varkaus are dominated by thrills when the flurry arrived every October, and tears when the Nordic heat melted it away in May.

He would spend as much time in the snow as he could, and at just 15 he started coaching at the local alpine ski slope. By 17, he was the youngest ski instructor in Finland, and at 25 he became the country's youngest ever Olympic-level coach. 'I was too young,' he said, his face crinkled and forlorn. 'We didn't have much success.' It didn't diminish his passion for powder, and he was soon exploring other ways to satiate it. 'I tried to learn many different things about the snow. From how to handle the snow for building snow castles, to how to use snow as a secondary wastewater verification system. The only word I cared about was snow.'

Eventually Mikko's obsession would take him down the path of what he calls 'eternal snow'. A summer skiing trip to Norway's Jostedalsbreen glacier in 1978 created a yearning for year-round slopes in his own country. 'I wanted something like this in Finland, but we don't have mountains.' He never thought it would be possible until one summer's day he went on a bike ride out of town, and stumbled on a giant heap of what he calls Coca-Cola snow. 'There was a sign saying "waste snow area". This huge pile of dark snow had been collected from the streets of my small town. I thought, "Oh my God."' The concept of snow preservation would dominate Mikko's life for decades. 'I said we needed to start storing snow. And for 40 years people said, "you are mad", "you are absolutely crazy", and "this won't work".'

A dogged Mikko persevered. He applied for EU funding and moved his family north to Ruka, where he could pester one of the country's largest ski resorts with his idea of using metal sheets to insulate heaps of snow over the summer. Eventually the EU money came through, those at Ruka warmed to his idea, and the world's first mass snow depot was successfully stored throughout the summer of 2000.

Mikko stressed that his technique is not to replace snowmaking technology but to work alongside it. 'It is big brother and little brother. They are not enemies. They need each other, the whole package.' The basic idea is that 'big brother' allows resorts to stockpile during optimal snowmaking temperatures, and his younger sibling protects reserves that can be dipped into when the weather is too warm.

Thanks to Mikko, Ruka now boasts one of the longest ski seasons in Europe with over 200 days of skiing between October and June. 'This crazy idea 40 years ago has become reality, and it has been very hard work designing a concept that will also work in high mountains, in strong winds, under high ultraviolet influence, in rain, and heat.' Although once close to being declared bankrupt, Mikko's company Snow Secure now has hundreds of snow storage systems all over the world. So when he saw what was happening in Vancouver in 2010, he looked on not as an intrigued bystander, but as an innovator who believed he had the solution for future Winter Olympics.

'I was looking at the Vancouver Olympics, and saw the problems in Cypress Mountain,' he said, before letting out a mischievous chuckle. 'Then I looked at my wallet, it's empty. I had to do something, then I recognised what was coming. Sochi's next. Where is Sochi? Taxi!'

Mikko wrote to the general secretary of the International Ski Federation (FIS) to offer his services. With his ideas no longer deemed fanciful he was given a contact in Moscow, where he would deliver a hastily translated pitch. It earned him the role of snow consultant in Sochi. Over the next four years he helped amass a reserve of one million cubic metres of snow, cloaked under Mikko's signature reflective blankets. These giant shimmering molehills, looking like the set of a low-budget sci-fi film, became tourist attractions in themselves.

By reducing the dependency on snowmaking machines and doubling them as vital water storage that doesn't require expensive pumping stations, Mikko believes his patented insulation silos provide not only a cheaper option but also a more sustainable one.

His Rachmaninoff revolution is gradually gaining favour in top ski resorts. But, so far, his Sochi experience remains his only Olympic call-up, despite being invited to both South Korea and China to showcase his solution ahead of their respective Games in 2018 and 2022. In Beijing, his methods broke records by storing snow for 220 days at an average temperature of 23 degrees. He even calculated that snow storage could save $50m in water infrastructure.

'You can save a lot of money, as where you store the snow you don't need so many snowmaking ponds,' said Mikko. 'You get the legacy of the Games. You recycle the insulation, you recycle the snow. It is so ecological. But at the end of the day, they said "no thank you". And now they have a very powerful snowmaking system. Their duty is to organise the Olympics. Not to think about legacies. So it was a pity, but that's how it is.'

I sensed an undertone to what Mikko was suggesting, which I took as an invitation to speculate cynically about it potentially being very good business for those involved to spend money, rather than save it. He didn't discourage me, but wouldn't be drawn to speak candidly about it. Instead, he shrugged and said just one word, 'Politics.'

The Heat Is On

The IOC has raised more than a few eyebrows with its choice of recent Winter Olympics hosts. Sochi broke all records for the warmest Games, records that were set just four years before in Vancouver. Temperatures in Russia hit highs of 11°C in the mountains, prompting skiers to stuff snow down their suits to cool down during races.

Thermometers hit an ice-cream-melting 20°C at the coastal Olympic Park, culminating in the bizarre sight of thousands of fans turning up to watch ice hockey, skating, and curling dressed in t-shirts and shorts. At times it was warmer than the summer Olympics in London two years earlier.

While ingenuity from the likes of Joe and Mikko kept the alpine venues up to standard, the melting half-pipe came in for stinging criticism. American snowboarder Hannah Teter, a former gold and silver medallist, said the half-pipe was 'dangerous because it's crappy'. Compatriot Danny Davis labelled the same venue 'garbage', adding, 'It's a bummer to show up to an event like the Olympics and not have the quality of the half-pipe match the quality of the riders.' Shaun White, the snowboarding icon who was aiming for his third consecutive Olympic gold, also complained after falling during practice. Despite being the favourite, he would finish only fourth. And after defending women's champion Torah Bright also crashed, her coach showed typical Australian tact, saying, 'I've come to the point of being diplomatic, but it's actually very shit.'

A year later, the 2022 Games were awarded to Beijing. This was despite the fact that, in its own evaluation report, the IOC admitted that the Chinese venue 'has minimal annual snowfall', 'is becoming increasingly arid', and 'due to the lack of natural snow the look of the venue may not be aesthetically pleasing'. Yet its cold and dry climate allowed for enough snowmaking to turn a desert into a snow globe. Which was useful, given that skiing venue Zhangjiakou sat on the edge of the Gobi.

In awarding Beijing the honour of becoming the first city to host both the Summer and Winter Olympics, the IOC rejected a strong bid from Almaty. Kazakhstan's largest city put authenticity at the heart of its campaign, promising 'real snow, real winter ambience, real Winter Games' alongside its slogan, 'Keeping it real.' Despite its longstanding tradition of winter sports and the picture-perfect Ile Alatau mountain range, Almaty lost by four votes.

In January 2022, Canada's University of Waterloo updated a paper it had first released in 2014, about the future of the Winter Olympics in a warming world. Its conclusions were stark. It stated that the average high temperatures in host cities have been steadily increasing, from 0.4°C in the 1920s to 1950s, to 3.1°C between the 1960s and 1990s, to over 6.3°C in those held in the 21st century. The report emphasised that this is only partly attributable to the effects of climate change, with the IOC's willingness to award the Games to warmer locations also a key factor.

It is a habit that the IOC may soon be forced to reconsider. After applying current climate-change models to previous host locations, the report found that just one of the 21 venues would be climatically suitable to host a Winter Olympics by the end of the century. In this scenario, by 2050 the likes of Grenoble, Salt Lake City, Innsbruck, and inaugural hosts Chamonix are no longer capable of providing the conditions where even machine-made snow is able to help.

In 2026 the Olympic flame journeys to Cortina d'Ampezzo, previously a host in 1956. After that, who knows? With Vancouver among the cities mounting a bid, weatherman Chris Doyle can expect a call. So too can Joe, Brooke, and Mikko. Because in an uncertain climate, the only certainty is that the expertise provided by world-leading snowmakers is now indispensable to host cities. The men and women engaged in a quiet battle with the elements to ensure that, at least for now, the Winter Olympics continue to enthral a global audience of millions. And if all else fails? The shamans will be waiting.

5

GET SHIRTY: Football Kit Designers

Many football shirts become as iconic as the legends who wear them. But unlike the great players, Old Father Time can't age these stylish and beloved garments. Yet while the shirts may be famed, the creatives behind the designs remain cloaked in mystery. Discover the soccer sartorialists at the game's leading kit brands.

The German Kit Queen

For over a quarter of a century, Ina Franzmann had no idea that she had designed one of the most iconic shirts in football history. You'll know the one. It's got three geometric lines in black, red, and yellow, chicaning along the chest from shoulder to shoulder like volatile trendlines on Wall Street. Designed for the European Championship in 1988, Ina's West Germany kit is ageless.

It may seem like a simple arrangement compared to today's vibrant efforts. But back when international teams wore single blocks of colour with the occasional contrasting trim it was a handbrake turn away from tradition. Ina's visionary design was over 30 years old when we caught up in the spring of 2021. She is now in her 60s, but she looked younger in her white fleece hoody and with a habit of tucking her brown bob behind her ears. She seemed a little surprised that anyone wanted to talk to her, expressing her gratitude at being able to discuss a topic that she had remained quiet about for so long.

For while it's common for her kit to be referenced among the greatest ever in fan polls, it wasn't until around five years ago that she became aware of the cultural and stylistic impact that her work has had on the sport. During Euro 2016, one of her son's friends spotted an original signed 1988 shirt that Ina had lying around. To her disbelief, he then revealed a legacy to which she had been totally oblivious.

Ina, who followed in her grandfather's footsteps by completing a tailoring apprenticeship, joined Adidas in 1984. She had assumed that her popular tennis wear – produced for a teenage Steffi Graf – had been her biggest mainstream success. Learning of the lasting reverence for her football jersey came as a surprise because she had been living not only in ignorance, but also in denial.

'I got some very negative critiques, so I never mentioned the soccer shirts when I was with customers,' said Ina, who set up as a freelancer in 1990 to work on non-Adidas sports such as yoga, skiing, and basketball. 'I mentioned my tennis success, but not those designs. Because if I mentioned it to companies who worked in, say, skiwear, they'd said, "Oh my God we don't like it. It's so bold and so ugly." So I did not know about the big hype of this iconic design. I got a lot of offers because of my tennis experience, but definitely not about this famous soccer shirt.'

Company chairman Horst Dassler, son of Adidas founder Adi, was the man who employed Ina as one of only four designers at the company. It was he who encouraged his small team to introduce a more artistic approach to football. Dassler had been encouraged at how Ina's artistic flourishes had proven popular in tennis. As well as masterminding Graf's collection on the theme of 'A Star Is Born' with jagged angular lines not dissimilar to those that would appear on the German shirt, Ina designed shirts for Stefan Edberg, a six-time Grand Slam winner.

For the Swede, she moved away from a masculine, linear approach and took inspiration from the softer, surreal styles of Spanish painter Joan Miró. Edberg's initials were displayed in elegant black brushstrokes. Although tennis was a prestigious, luxury sport in which style and sophistication were natural bedfellows, Dassler felt that Ina's panache could also translate to the grittier and industrial surroundings of soccer.

Inspired by English graphic designer Neville Brody and a 1980s backdrop of synthesisers and crumbling walls, Ina set about her work. 'The graphics of this time were very loud, very bold, very visible. You always have to have a concept behind it, and these dynamic lines went up to stand for winning. I also wanted to make the players look good, accentuating the shoulders so that the body looked really strong.'

Ina now teaches at Frankfurt's Technical College of Design, and despite the esteem in which her shirt is today held there is nothing wrong with her memory. On release, the shirts were far from loved. German fans accustomed to sedate white shirts with black collars and cuffs were especially uncomfortable with the addition of distinct national colours.

More than 40 years after the end of the Second World War, the country's national psyche was still not in a place to welcome subtle patriotic gestures. 'First of all, there was a lot of criticism because Adidas used the German flag colours. Due to Germany's history, it was a certain [sensitive] point. And this very loud design also had a lot of critics,' explained Ina, who went on to say that a lot of design and art isn't appreciated in its time. Almost as if she knew I was about to mutter something trite about Vincent van Gogh, she quickly chided herself, 'I don't want to compare myself with an artist, which I'm definitely not. I'm a bloody designer. Not an artist or sculptor.'

If Ina was a little stung by the criticism at the time, then Adidas showed no such angst. Dassler remained confident that his company was on to a winner. Quite literally, in the case of those wearing it. Despite being eliminated by the Dutch (themselves advertising Adidas's bold new direction), the Germans headed to the World Cup in Italy two years later with kitbags stocked with their controversial colours.

And so, when Lothar Matthäus lifted the Jules Rimet Trophy at the Stadio Olimpico, Ina's controversial tricolour was emblazoned proudly across the captain's chest. Just a few months later, the shirt became the first to be worn by a reunified German team. The black, red, and yellow colour combination has been a feature of almost every home kit since.

A favourite among terrace-culture hipsters and five-a-side vets, the shirt continues to sell today. Adidas issued an updated replica as recently as 2018. Yet Ina remains reluctant to take all the plaudits, crediting Dassler for his faith in her vision: 'The real breakthrough always requires a brand behind the designer that has the courage and the daring to produce his or her designs. I had the [Adidas] trefoil stamped in my head.'

Thanks to Dassler's stubborn ambition and Ina's creativity, this distinctive, memorable, and highly marketable kit provided the blueprint to selling shirts in the millions. Ina, who believes the next revolution in kit design will be in sustainable fabrics, made it seem simple. But it's not easy coming up with a shirt that will resonate decades after its release, as any of today's top kit designers will attest.

Chatting Shirts

The savvy idea of selling replica kits to consumers can be traced back to British sportswear company Admiral. In 1973, Leeds United wore the first branded kits in English football. A yellow Admiral logo was stitched to the right breast of a traditional white cotton shirt with a stylish V-neck and collar. With Leeds's distinctive smiling 'LU' crest on the left breast, the shirts were a hit with the fans. The following season Admiral followed Don Revie to Wembley, agreeing to pay the Football Association

£15,000 a year in exchange for the privilege of producing England's official clobber.

Kit design, an idea that began as a visual tool for players and fans when Sheffield FC decided to wear matching flannel caps in 1857, was now a commercial enterprise with a new captive market. From the moment non-league Kettering Town printed the words 'Kettering Tyres' on the front of their red shirts in 1976, football jerseys increased their worth ten-fold by becoming advertising boards with muscular legs.

Back then, it would have been unthinkable that the garment a player was wearing could become more valuable to a club than the number of fans it attracts through the turnstiles. But that is certainly the case at most of Europe's biggest clubs today. In 2019, Real Madrid demonstrated just how lucrative this polyester real estate had become. They signed a four-year shirt sponsorship deal with Emirates worth over £200m, joining the 12-year kit manufacturing partnership with Adidas that surpassed £1bn.

But footballers haven't been forgotten in all this and, despite what some cynics might say, shirts are not uniquely channels for income. In the spirit of marginal gains, kits now come with benefits that surpass the original idea of making it easier to spot your team-mates. The job of a kit designer today is to somehow strike a balance between commercial and performance.

Two men who know all about this sartorial balancing act are Rob Warner and Craig Buglass. I met them at Vessel Studios, on a clanking industrial street near Liverpool's Stanley Docks. When I arrived, the pair were sitting behind a desk covered in football shirts and surrounded by lighting rigs. They had just finished filming a sponsored segment with kit YouTuber Chris Chats Shirts, a friendly and excitable chap who told me he had travelled all the way from Plymouth to introduce the experienced design duo to his thousands of followers.

Craig, in a bright yellow jacket that matched the colour of his Nike high-tops, was telling Chris all about the time he received a delivery of Manchester United's black away shirts. The badge and logos had all turned an unwelcome shade of grey. 'It was an absolute disaster. It was on a boat and it took ages to get from China. And there'd been some chemical reaction inside the plastic bag. It affected the launch date of the away kit. Heads rolled for that.'

After Chris departed, Rob and Craig began recording their own reviews, to be posted on Twitter to promote the Spark design agency they formed in 2016. They rifled through dozens of jerseys, assessing each in sharp two-minute bursts. They spat out terms like body mapping and overlock stitching all while pulling at hemlines and stretching the fabrics. They discussed new innovations like the Prozone tracking pouch within Hoffenheim's kit that removes the need for those ubiquitous black sports bras. A Spurs kit was described as looking like a hangover, while a Manchester City effort was said to resemble both a sandwich board and Tesco pyjamas.

Their frank views will fit in well on a social media platform that attracts heated opinions like sniffing dogs to a sodden lamp post. But unlike many keyboard critics, Craig and Rob have the track records to back up their barbs. Like Ina, they too have World Cup-winning kits on their CVs. As design director at Nike Football in the early 2000s, Craig was responsible for the 2002 Brazil shirt worn by the likes of Ronaldo, Roberto Carlos, and Rivaldo. He would later join Puma, where he met Rob, the man behind the 2006 shirt that still gives every Italian fan goosebumps.

The pair teamed up together again at Umbro when it was the home of the England kit. At Spark, their scope of work is much broader. They work with the likes of Dunhill, McLaren Automotive, and even Warner Bros, for whom they designed wearable technology for *Batman*. Although they now rarely work on football shirts, they have decanted their vast football experience into a comprehensive course for aspiring kit makers.

I was with them during the week that Newcastle United's new takeover had been announced in the autumn of 2021. As a Geordie who admitted to once mischievously designing Sunderland training kits in black and white, Craig was desperate to get his hands on a Toon Army shirt to review. Chiefly, it seemed, to plead for the return of Adidas and the retro trefoil logo that Ina spoke so fondly of.

Rob, who at 43 is seven years younger than Craig, is a diehard Aston Villa fan who wasn't quite as enthused by the news from the north-east. Instead he wanted to tell me about the time he managed to get world champions Italy to wear claret. Pitch meetings with the Italian Football Federation may have alluded to the country's red-wine heritage for the reason behind the colours of the goalkeeper and coaching kit, but Rob was happy to divulge his ulterior motives 15 years on. 'For me, it was a little inside joke that Italy won the World Cup wearing Villa colours,' he said, pointing at pictures of goalkeeper Gianluigi Buffon and manager Marcello Lippi.

The home shirt was of course Azzurri blue, and the concept was based on the Italians as comic book superheroes, with a dark blue blurring under the arms giving the effect of the players moving at high speed. Even in photos. The white away shirt took the role of the Clark Kent alter ego. 'We still had the same collar and the same material, but it had an insert blue V-neck within it,' said Rob. 'So the home kit was like their Superman outfit, and the away kit was as if they had just put a white t-shirt over their costume. I loved the story of that.'

Brimming with talismanic talents such as Francesco Totti, Andrea Pirlo, and captain Fabio Cannavaro, Italy went on to win the trophy following a final best remembered for French captain Zinedine Zidane's head-butt to the chest of Marco Materazzi. This superhero kit suddenly had its very own arch-villain, and the enraged final act of one of the game's greatest players further cemented Rob's garment into folklore.

Telling Tales

Lore is a vital part of the design process. A good story can elevate a piece of cloth to something symbolic and more marketable. Finding this narrative can be the most intrepid part of the job. When his first task at Adidas was to come up with AC Milan's 2017/18 kits, Germany-based designer James Webb travelled to northern Italy. 'Seeing the San Siro and then standing in front of the Duomo, I had to pinch myself because I couldn't believe it was actually happening,' he said. Delving into the club's history inspired a subtle change that would tap into the Rossoneri fans' 1990s nostalgia. 'They hadn't played in white shorts and socks for a number of years. It was quite a classic AC Milan kit and aesthetic. To see them playing in that again was quite humbling.'

James likens designing kits to creating album covers. As the son of a biker father from Llanelli and a musician mother from Swansea, he has a variety of influences to call upon. And while graphically kits may be departing ever further from tradition, the past remains a useful storytelling mine. James used the historic shield of Owain Glyndwr to accentuate Wales's traditional tones for the 2019 shirt. 'Growing up Welsh and being proud of my heritage, to play with the reds and the yellows of the banner really hits home. It's about delivering a story that is impactful and true to the fans. Something people can get behind.'

When designing Arsenal's 2020/21 away kit, he sought to evoke the art deco architecture of the club's former Highbury home. The slightly off-white shirt was speckled with red vein-like cracks, giving a textured look resembling the stadium's marble halls. 'It was about looking for key signifiers from Arsenal's history that really cements them as a club,' said James. 'This is a really rich moment in the club's history, one that was cherished on and off the field. There were trophies coming into the club and being celebrated. But you also saw the East Stand marble halls being crafted as well. So that was definitely a nice idea to try and link the two.'

But while individuals are encouraged to seek personal inspiration, companies like Adidas have seasonal themes to sway designers into consistent directions across the collection. The idea is to aid the process of reinvention and prevents ideas from going stale. 'The 2019 creative direction was "united by art and football",' explained James. 'Football kits had become quite vectorised and computer-generated. So the idea was to go more tactile, go back to the roots, and give a hand-crafted feeling.' It meant all nine Adidas jerseys on show at Euro 2020, including Germany, Spain, and Belgium, started life as a hand-drawn sketch.

Clubs and federations can also play their part in defining a kit's narrative, and one of the first steps for designers is to incorporate significant anniversaries or events. For 1999/2000, Nike celebrated Barcelona's centenary season with a stylish half-red, half-blue shirt. It had a large collar and the badge, logo, and dates centred in gold. Umbro helped Manchester United celebrate their own centenary in 2001 with a reversible away kit that was white on one side, gold on the other. In 2019, Brazil marked 100 years since their first Copa America win with a shirt in the nation's original home palette of blue and white. History repeated itself as the Seleção went on to win the tournament.

Sometimes design briefs can even predict a future story. After winning their first World Cup in 2010, the victorious Spanish players changed out of their match-worn away jerseys into a new version of their Adidas home kit. It meant that not only were they decked out in their traditional red in time for the trophy presentation, but there was already a gold star stitched above the badge. Assuming Nike had a similar idea for Spain's opponents, somewhere there must be two dozen discarded Dutch shirts representing an alternative reality.

Then there are the tales that turn out to be more fiction than fact. To mark Arsenal's final season at Highbury in 2005/06, Nike changed the Gunners' traditional pillar box red kit to a redcurrant colour with gold lettering, sponsor, and crest. The marketing spiel stated that burgundy red was worn by Woolwich Arsenal when they first played at Highbury in 1913. The fans lapped it up and a memorable season saw Arsène Wenger's side beat the likes of Real Madrid and Juventus on their way to the Champions League Final. Following some sleuthing from kit historians, however, it is now believed that Arsenal never actually wore that colour. Instead the photos used to illustrate Nike's campaign were digitally colourised from an original black and white photo.

And so the need to come up with a new narrative every season can see credibility stretching at the seams. When Umbro announced the new Republic of Ireland shirt in 2022, it was said to be inspired by 'the unsystematic shapes and varying sizes of the fields of our homeland'. Come again?

Given what he had told me in Liverpool about Italy's 2006 'red wine' shirts, admittedly with his tongue lodged firmly in his cheek, I asked Rob if designers are ever guilty of retrofitting a story to suit a favoured design. 'I think there's plenty of that goes on,' he said, pawing at the dozens of shirts in front of him. 'But I've always been heavy into research before I start anything. I just enjoy trying to build that provenance into what we're doing. But some stuff just comes about as a laugh.'

On that latter point, he referenced the Puma v1.06 camo boots worn by many at the 2006 World Cup. It was covered from toe to heel in a green turf graphic. 'We said, "Imagine if these boots were so quick you couldn't even see them." Well, let's print grass on them, and you won't be able to.'

Despite the occasional bit of improv, Rob insisted that, like James, he enjoys doing his homework before putting pen to paper. 'Insight and storytelling have always been central to how I would want to work,' he said, recalling how as a kid he used to Tipp-Ex over the kits in *Roy of the Rovers* magazines and draw his own designs over the top. 'I graduated from that to then Tipp-Exing out the storylines and converting it to being a bit more like *Viz*, with swearing. I used to get a pound each for selling them at school. Then my mum found them and I had to cease trading.'

Zero Distractions

Designers are allocated a budget for each kit, and they can be swallowed up in ways that aren't always apparent to the average fan. Everything you see on a shirt costs money. It's why clubs in countries where multiple sponsors are common often have the branding printed directly on to the shirt. 'Because to do it all as individual heat transfers will cost you a fortune,' said Rob. He mentioned the example of Bayern Munich, where the tradition of placing the team name across the back of the shirt automatically deducts $1 from a designer's budget. 'That spare dollar can be the difference between a V-neck and a polo collar.'

The World Cup-winning Italy shirt was one of the most expensive designs Rob had ever worked on, with laser-cut seams, a super-stretch panel across the back, and graphics that came from a collaboration with Milan-based British fashion designer Neil Barrett. 'I've made a couple of great shirts where the materials were cheap, like $3 to $4 a yard, which is about the going rate for a very good activewear t-shirt. The material that we used for the World Cup shirt was more like $15 to $16 a yard.'

The high production cost of the Italy kit wasn't simply for the purpose of spinning a good yarn. The best concepts combine storytelling with function. Can a shirt really maximise the abilities of its bearers? Rob never tires of trying to find out: 'I get my rocks off on insight. How can I solve things? Fix things? Make things better? Which pisses my wife off no end when I tell her I've found a more efficient way of loading the dishwasher.' Inspired by the man he would later go into business with, Rob's 12-nation 2006 Puma collection was designed to improve a physical trait that not all footballers are blessed with: speed.

'In 2002, Craig was working on the Nike Cool Motion stuff, and it was very much geared around performance. Exactly as you'd expect from Nike,' said Rob, referring to the two-layer Brazil shirt with a mesh base intended to wick sweat away from the body. It helped players to stay cool in the sweltering Japanese and Korean heat. Four years later, Rob wanted to do something similarly functional. 'As we got towards 2006, the brief was to get players to the ball faster,' said Rob, his gentle Brummie tones speeding up in excitement. 'We developed a material that was tested in a low-velocity wind tunnel and we created something that gave you a 70cm advantage in aerodynamics over a 30m sprint. Which is a big difference.'

Rob, who also designed Usain Bolt's gear for the Jamaican's breakthrough Olympics in 2008, said that the science drove the aesthetic. It offered the players wearing Puma a psychological advantage. 'Even the weight difference from the next lightest shirt was half a Snickers. Snickers were still quite big in 2006.' I asked him if that's what he said in pitch meetings. 'Yeah!' he responded, as if using confectionary as a measurement of weight is standard practice. 'It was like, "Would you send the players out with half a Snickers on the front of their shirt? Because that's what your opponents are going to be doing."' Rob said the equivalence was important to get the point across. 'Because if you say 70g, it doesn't really mean anything. Whereas you can imagine what half a Snickers feels like in your hand.'

Rob said the speed testing, which was done in conjunction with Manchester Metropolitan University where he had previously studied, also helped when it came to one of kit design's most contentious topics. 'Yes, it was a template. Apart from Italy away. But it was the performance solution. So the way that we sold that into the federations was, "We've tested it, this is the fastest kit in the world, your players will have a performance advantage. We can design you something different, but you'll probably get beat." It was made as simple as that.'

In a sport that has seen many performance fads over the years, from Robbie Fowler and his nasal strips to Patrick Vieira's Vicks VapoRub, I was a little dubious about some of the stated benefits. I mentioned this to Rob, and he revealed that at one stage he met with a company that could micro-encapsulate menthol into the fabric. The idea was that as the players moved, capsules in the shirt would break and give off the eucalyptus whiff. The shirts were never put into production before football moved on to its next trend. Regardless, Rob told me it's not really important whether they work or not. As long as the players believe they do then the psychological benefit outweighs any minimal physical advantage.

Take the example of goalkeeper shirts. One school of thought dictates that luminous colours will make the wearer seem more imposing. The other is that it will simply highlight an area to avoid. In the absence of any definitive evidence, goalkeepers are left to make their own call, which is likely to be based on superstition over science. 'Even if there was [evidence], ultimately players wouldn't give a shit,' said Rob. 'If they believe it's right, that's more important than whether it is or not.'

He reckoned the same applies to compression clothing. 'Most of it is just bollocks. It will facilitate some of the claims, but not anywhere near the level that is implied.

Unless it's custom-made for you and it's medical-grade compression. But you put it on under a shirt, and it's quite a nice sensation to wear,' said Rob, tugging at his tangerine jumper. 'Athletes described it as feeling locked in. They are getting more from that feeling than anything else.'

Above all else, kit designers work on the basis of zero distractions. Many fans love the look of retro collars on shirts, and an upright collar was the famous calling card of Eric Cantona, one of the Premier League's most iconic stars in the 1990s. But today's footballers find them a hindrance, which explains why only three of the 60 Premier League shirts used in the 2021/22 season featured polo collars.

Similarly, skin-tight clothing might suit the muscular builds of many of today's footballers but those with non-athletic frames may feel too self-conscious to play to the best of their ability. Recently, when tight-fitting socks designed to reduce cramps saw footballers hacking holes into them, sheepish kit makers were forced to revert to comfort over data.

'We had to factor in the psychology of the athletes that we were putting the products on,' said Rob. 'We could have been more aerodynamic by being skin-tight. But we weren't just dressing Samuel Eto'o and Rigobert Song. We were going to be dressing Tomáš Rosický and Jan Koller. Koller is 6ft 7in and Rosický is probably eight stone in his boots. It would have looked terrible. Just like Usain Bolt can run in lycra shorts, but if you're an away player showing up at Old Trafford in tight-fitting shorts, they're going to make a noise about it.'

During filming, Craig told a story from his time at Nike, when the sock designs for Barcelona and Portugal were signed off by Luís Figo. Rob remembered Roger Lemerre, the Euro 2000-winning France manager who was then in charge of Puma-sponsored Tunisia, had a similar obsession. He believed that comfortable socks were key to his team's success. At Umbro, the English FA would consult its senior players. 'It would be subject to Rio Ferdinand and those guys liking it,' said Rob. 'When I was working with Manchester City, we would speak to Joe Hart and Kyle Walker and then present to the club with the solutions based on their views.'

So I was interested to know if there were any examples of players crediting their kit as a reason behind a team's success? Rob answered my question with one of his own. 'Out of all the jackets you've ever owned, which one had the best zip?' I mulled it over for a few seconds, but my memory wasn't playing ball. 'Exactly,' said Rob, satisfied with my silence. 'Now, have you ever had a jacket with a crap zip?' and he nodded knowingly as my mind darted back to an old Superdry windbreaker. It was a perfect example of the zero distraction policy. If something is memorable, it's not always for the right reasons. 'The best feedback you'll ever get,' he said, 'is no feedback.'

From Pitch to Pitch

Brands differ in their approaches to pitching their ideas. Nike tends to present a single fully fledged idea, while Hummel goes in with several options. The levels of involvement from clubs and federations can also vary wildly. Sean Pankhurst, a freelance designer who has made kits for Nike, Kappa, and Hummel, spoke to me from his London home. 'Some clubs are more involved than others. I never did the Arsenal kit, but I heard that Arsène Wenger had a very strong opinion on what the kit could look like. Alex Ferguson wasn't involved at all. The only thing that he said was that he always wanted United to have a white kit within their away or third. And I remember at Aston Villa, Martin O'Neill wouldn't have a yellow kit. I never found out why.'

Getting club sign-off often revolves around a single influential figurehead. It's not always the manager or captain. During Arsenal's invincible season of 2003/04, their away shirt was originally meant to be grey. Perhaps recalling Manchester United's notorious 1995/96 third shirt, which was swapped at half-time in a defeat at Southampton and never worn again, Nike's choice was vetoed by the Gunners' vice-chairman David Dein. Craig reveals why in Spark's online course: 'David Dein threw the football kit at me, saying, "We're a happy club, we don't want that colour, give us our classic yellow." He made it very clear that he wanted Arsenal in the traditional colours.'

The pitching process can therefore be challenging, and draining. In 2006, Rob spent a week dashing from airport to airport to show his ideas to the federations of Italy, Senegal, Tunisia, Cameroon, and Bulgaria. The Italy presentation featured displays in baroque gold frames, resembling an art gallery. The Senegalese delegation was so pleased with the shirt's baobab tree graphic that they signed it off at Nuremberg Airport. As reigning African champions, Tunisia demanded more pomp and ceremony, and it wasn't just because of Lemerre and his socks. 'What we thought would be a couple of hours' presentation turned into an all-dayer,' said Rob. 'The president of the federation said, "You've done all this amazing stuff for Cameroon, well we are champions of Africa." And he had a point to be fair.'

For Cameroon, Rob would always present to the team. 'If the key players like Rigobert Song were into it then selling it to the federation was dead easy.' Not so easy was presenting to national legends. Rob ended his jet-setting week with a trip to visit Bulgaria national coach Hristo Stoichkov. The icon was sat with his entourage in a room fogged with cigarette smoke. 'I'd been out with the Cameroon team the night before so I was hanging out my arse,' said Rob, before explaining that a testing atmosphere was made worse when a translation error appeared on the back of the training kit. Printed in Cyrillic was the word Bulgarian, rather than Bulgaria. Thankfully for a hungover Rob, Stoichkov burst into laughter.

Cementing Rob's theory on feedback, Sean was sporting enough to tell me about the worst he has ever received. 'There's been plenty that's gone wrong, trust me. There was one I did for a Romanian team. After it was pitched to the club I spoke to the rep, and he told me, "The chairman said that was the worst football kit he's ever seen." I had to redesign it.'

Once a kit has been given the go-ahead production can begin. Materials are sought, factories are engaged, and designers are sworn to secrecy. 'The first rule of designing a football kit,' said a smirking Sean, 'is don't talk about football kits.' Sight screens, security guards, and restricted access are standard tactics employed by factories servicing the biggest teams in the world.

Unfortunately for manufacturers keen to protect their marketing campaigns, leaks are so common that websites and Twitter accounts exist purely to publish them. Although he is not always able to resist a peek himself, Sean lamented social media's disdain for delayed gratification. 'It does really bother me when I see leaks. I do feel a bit sad that people can't just keep that to themselves for a bit. They have to spray it all over the internet because they saw the new Man City kit that's not due to be launched for six months.'

His love for football kits burgeoned as a seven-year-old whose parents were reluctant to buy him the 1990 Chelsea home shirt. They feared that, like other kids his age, he would never take it off. Instead he saved three months of pocket money in order to buy the shirt himself, filling the hours of yearning by flicking straight to the adverts in *Shoot!*. Ahead of the 1994 World Cup in the USA, Sean produced a catalogue of kits covering each of the 24 teams. By the time he was 12 he was telling his school career advisor that he wanted to design football shirts. He ignored the advice that he would be better served pursuing a job in IT.

After a role designing life jackets that cemented his desire to produce performance-driven clothing, Nike came calling. He vividly remembers his first day in the office: 'I was taken into a room full of old shirts. It was like when Charlie first goes into Willy Wonka's factory. I was in awe of this room, and the amount of polyester that was in there. I was in heaven.'

Sean designed apparel for Nike for eight years before moving into rugby for Canterbury. His career highlights include designing England's kit for football's 2014 World Cup. 'I went on my stag do during the World Cup. It was brilliant to watch the game in a pub with all my mates and the team walking out in my kit. Although I have to be honest, I was pretty pissed by that point.'

Now as a freelancer working with a variety of sports brands, he retains his childhood passion even as he now knows the industry is very different to how it can be perceived. 'One of the things that really bothers me is when people think that we get our crayons out and off we pop. The vast majority of the time there is a hell of a lot of work that goes into creating something that resonates with fans, the club, and the brand.' Sean told me that juggling these three demanding stakeholders is the trickiest element of being a kit designer. He notched his Romanian experience down as an early career lesson in what happens when you try to please them all. 'It is a tremendous great big puzzle to put together.'

Ham-Fisted Sponsors

Pro designers can get frustrated by the naivety with which many fans, including the increasing number that are creating concept kits online, approach the subject of football shirts. The mocked-up alternatives are often well produced but, as Rob pointed out, few consider the production obstacles that lie in wait in the real world. 'When there's a kit launched you'll find people latch on to the concept kits and say, "Why didn't they do this?" Well, if you think of a really intricate pattern that runs across the chest and on to the sleeve, there's a seam there. So you've got to figure out printing it so that those lines all match. Then somebody in a factory has got to try and get it to line up.'

It's not just budget restrictions and the intricacies of tailoring that can give designers a headache. A mere mention of the words 'shirt sponsorship' can see the best of them break into a cold sweat. While Craig talked warmly about designing kits for a sponsorless Barcelona and said the likes of Sega and O2 were happy to agree to colour tweaks to match Arsenal's kit, Rob recalled other experiences that weren't as satisfying. 'It's difficult when you don't always know what sponsor is going to show up on a kit.' He still despairs about one experience with Lazio. 'It was always Siemens Mobile, and we knew what we could do with the colours. They were local, so they'd send a guy down to measure it and make sure it was as big as it could be, but we knew where we stood.'

When that longstanding sponsorship deal came to an end, Rob was forced to design the new kit blind. 'It was 2004 and it was the first concept I had ownership of. We did this shirt in black with little inserts in electric blue. It looked great. I was really fond of it.' Lazio announced their new sponsorship deal so late in the summer that manufacturing had already begun. It meant the new logo needed to be applied locally. It was Parmacotto, a Parma ham company founded in 1978. 'They've probably got the same logo they had when they were set up,' said Rob, still bristling at the thought. 'It's burgundy, mustard yellow, and brown. They'd just lopped it straight on the front. It looked a joke,' he seethed, adding that he was thankful Twitter wasn't around at the time.

But the chief stiflers of creativity are not sponsors, clubs, manufacturers, or even the fans. FIFA's kit guidelines run to over 100 pages, covering permitted colour combinations, number sizes, and sleeve-free zones. Knowing your way around the governing body's Byzantine regulations is what separates the professionals from the dreamers. And with Puma's reputation as a disruptive underdog brand, founded by Adi Dassler's feuding brother Rudi, Rob would regularly find himself in FIFA's crosshairs.

In the early 2000s they had made a habit of testing the boundaries, and president Sepp Blatter's patience. In 2002 the Indomitable Lions of Cameroon debuted a sleeveless shirt at the African Cup of Nations, the tournament that they would go on to win. When FIFA deemed the kits to be against their guidelines, chiefly because they couldn't display the governing body's sleeve logos, Rob's first job at Puma was to provide a fix only months before the World Cup. He considered painting the requisite branding on to the players' biceps. In the end he opted to go with a black mesh sleeve.

Two years later, Puma and Cameroon were at it again, the team turning up to the 2004 African Cup of Nations in a onesie. The shirt and shorts were stitched together into a single bodysuit featuring meshed ventilation lines parallel with the players' ribcages. The advertising campaign saw an animated Samuel Eto'o dribbling past a lion. 'The ventilation on the side had red mesh behind it and looked as if it had been clawed. It was left raw-edged. And it was all about eradicating shirt pulling,' said Rob, adding that he took inspiration for the claw marks from a *Jurassic Park 3* poster. 'It wasn't against the rules at the time.'

Blatter disagreed, handing Cameroon a $154,000 fine and docking the team six points from World Cup qualifying. The points were returned when Puma successfully appealed, but both the sleeveless and all-in-one shirts have been confined to history. Needless to say, both are now collector's items.

Feedback Is a Gift

Typical lead times for kits can be up to a year and a half. The design element takes less than two months, with the remaining 16 months being used to garner club feedback, implement changes, develop samples, and seek approval before going into production, at which point designers are usually in the midst of a new cycle working on the following season's shirts. It is common for them to have forgotten some of their work by the time it appears on its turfed canvas.

As daunting as it can be to seek approval from powerful figures like Stoichkov and Wenger, nothing can prepare a designer for launch day. It is not only the first opportunity for eager fans to see a kit that has been teased for weeks, but also the first time the accompanying story has been told. Whether it has resonated will usually be apparent long before the sales figures are compiled. If feeling brave enough, all a designer has to do is log in to social media.

Criticism comes thick and fast. A search on Twitter found the following tweets in response to the respective 2021 launches for Liverpool and Manchester United: 'who signs off on this shit?'; 'whoever is in charge of Nike design, please just go or at least get your eyes tested ffs'; 'OMG this new home shirt is hideous. The designers are rotting just like Old Trafford'; and the charmingly succinct 'that's fucking rank that'. There are hundreds of similar comments, alongside memes such as Jeff Goldblum stood by a large dinosaur stool. Some are in jest, others are really quite aggressive. 'I don't have a Facebook or Twitter account. Which is probably for the best,' James told me.

For Sean, one launch caused such a reaction that the criticism went from digital to medieval. When designing Paris Saint-Germain's kit in 2009, he dared to remove the home shirt's red band in favour of a subtle red pinstripe. French fashion designer and former club president Daniel Hechter is credited with the original look worn in 1973. But inflexible designs anchored in history are not always easy to work with. 'There's not a lot you can do with PSG. It's a bit like Ajax, it is what it is,' said Sean. 'So I wanted to try and pull the club out of that mould of just repeating the same stuff every season. The colours would still be the same, but I wanted to do something really dramatic and take off the band to push the club in a slightly different direction.'

The traditional band was alluded to via the shirt's red collar and red cuffs. The club were on board with the idea. The fans were not. 'There were protests outside the Nike store in the Champs-Élysées as the kit was released. There was shit being thrown at the store,' said Sean. I told him it can't have been human faeces, surely. 'Actual shit,' he confirmed. The French really do know how to protest.

'My name is mud in Paris. But the point is that it was the biggest-selling PSG shirt in history. And is now fondly remembered. It always helps if they do reasonably well in the kits.' Sean was right. Although it was two years before the club's transformative Qatari takeover, a mid-table PSG side won the French Cup in his design.

That's something of an uncomfortable truth when it comes to kit design. Most often, the deciding factor in whether a kit enjoys a legacy like Ina's is not the graphic design, the technical specs, nor even the narrative. It's how well the team performs in it. Who knows if Leeds's first Admiral kit would have sold as well had Revie's men not won the league that season?

One of Rob's favourite designs is Stuttgart's 110th-anniversary shirt. It featured a red V-neck collar and an oversized badge with four stars stitched above it, signifying the club's four league titles. 'I still love that shirt. Yet nobody really thinks about it, because a couple of years later they won the Bundesliga.' And so the title-winning shirt, which Rob also designed, has been etched in the club's history at the expense of the designer's preferred pick. 'I could say I love all my children equally. But I think teams winning stuff in it does make a difference.'

Minor performance innovations withstanding, there's little a designer can do about this. Alfred can give Batman a bulletproof vest, but he can't fight the Joker himself. And so, once he had found the Newcastle shirt he had been hunting for, I asked Craig about the times his hard work has been ruined for reasons beyond his control. Without hesitation, he recalled the 2002 World Cup. 'Nike had spent so much money on promoting the Netherlands,' he said, referencing the de Boer brothers, Patrick Kluivert, and Edgar Davids. 'They turned Davids into a superstar overnight. So much was housed around them. And then they didn't bloody qualify. The amount of money [Nike] lost was massive. I don't think I've ever met a Dutch person who thinks those kits are good.'

In 2018 Ina was invited to the launch of Germany's World Cup shirt, which was based on her original 1988 design. She liked the new version, which copied her geometric lines, but it failed to ignite the team. Germany were eliminated in the first round, finishing bottom of their group. And so Ina's design lives on, its 21st-century tribute act failing to displace it in football's collective consciousness.

With long-term success out of their hands, the best thing a kit designer can aim for in the short term is to make a noise. Given his Parisian experience, Sean knows that more than most: 'Everyone's a critic. Everyone thinks they know how to design a football kit. You will always get people who say, "That's a load of shit", or, "That's the best thing I've ever seen." It might sound cliché, but if a kit is making people talk – good or bad – then you've done your job.'

While kit designers may breathe a sigh of relief when they receive no feedback from footballers, the opposite is true when it comes to showing the fans. To Ina, Rob, Craig, James, and Sean, a kit that fails to generate opinions is a kit that fails in its purpose.

In 2010, Rob created the Umbro England shirt with graphic designer Peter Saville. Saville, famed for his album sleeve designs for Joy Division and New Order, came up with a concept featuring the St George's cross in various colours across the shoulders. It was intended to reflect the country's diverse cultural make-up but it was destined to cause a stir. Rob remembered something that Saville told him during their collaboration. 'Peter said, "If I design something and show it to 100 people. I'd rather 50 people love it and 50 people hate it than 100 people, think it's OK. Because nobody ever bought anything because it was OK."'

6

SHADOW RACING:
Cycling Moto Pilots

In most sports, camera operators and photographers are restricted to documenting the action from the sidelines. But when it comes to cycling, those beaming back the live pictures are part of the race and along for the ride. They owe that privilege to a rare breed of skilled motorcyclists whose job it is to keep up, but keep out of the way.

Rock Stars and Rubber Ducks

It was 9.30am and I was standing with over 60 leather-clad motorcyclists at the base of Carlisle Castle ahead of stage six of the Tour of Britain. The pre-race safety briefing was under way as race regulator Andy Hawes was struggling to make himself heard over the Ed Sheeran song that was booming out from start-line speakers.

'At 63.5km we're against the one-way system in Penrith; it should be closed down by the time we get there,' shouted Hawes. The assembled crowd of police, marshals, commissaires, and moto pilots listened intently and took notes. 'More hairpins, and at 96km, I honestly don't know what is there,' Hawes continued. 'Front Street in Alston has been dug up. I don't know what that road is going to look like. Fortunately, it's ...' I lost the rest of the sentence as the DJ decided that Sheeran's ditty about first kisses on Friday nights needed to be heard by all of Cumbria.

Hawes raised his voice and bellowed out the next line. 'At 112km, you have got to be as far out to the right as you can, to make the left turn. If you're not, you will not make the left turn. DO NOT, *NOT* MAKE THAT LEFT TURN.' Perhaps a little concerned that his instructions were being lost in a cacophony of smash hits, Hawes lifted his arms like Bruce Forsyth at the London Palladium and asked the crowd, 'What have you got to do at 112km?'

'STAY RIGHT!' I responded, at the exact moment the sound system cut out. As heads turned towards me, I realised I had overestimated the enthusiasm of this bikers' chorus. I had at least caught the attention of the man I had come to meet, and he walked over smiling as the speakers came back to life. Sheeran was singing about driving at 90 down country lanes, just as Jason said hi.

Jason Jenkins has been a moto pilot since 2009 when he ferried freelance camera operator Phil Rowe around the inaugural Tour Series criterium. Based out of Caerphilly, Jason's company Media Motos is now the world's largest independent supplier of tracking vehicles. It is involved in everything from TV ads to documentaries, triathlons to marathons. He even has a business transporting vital organs between hospitals in south Wales. But as a former cyclist who competed at amateur level ('before I enjoyed my steak and Guinness too much'), cycling remains his number-one gig. He and Phil were back on board today, one of three TV motorbikes responsible for providing live footage for ITV4.

We had met for the first time a few weeks ago at the Tour Series race in Sunderland. That day, Jason was the only moto pilot filming the dizzying laps around a short but sharp city centre loop, with both the men's and women's races done in around an hour. As it was highlights only, he and Phil filmed 'the tape' that night, though it's only the terminology that hasn't caught up to the fact it was a memory card they handed in to the editors post-race.

Jason's prep in Sunderland involved a quick recce around the circuit. He consulted with the production team on where five fixed cameras should be installed and nominated crash corner. He had picked the fast downhill into a sharp left, where there was what he called street furniture. I think he meant the drain.

Sure enough, when I found the spot he was describing, the St John Ambulance was already parked and waiting. But there wasn't much detail in Jason's course notes. 'Left. Left. Left again,' he told me. 'If I get that wrong I've done something drastically wrong.' Instead, with cyclists lapping each other within minutes of the start, his toughest task would be to keep track of the race leader. 'The last thing we need is to be filming the wrong guy,' he said. He and Phil had no such issues, and even St John Ambulance had a quiet night. So Jason suggested I come along to see him at work on the Tour. An entirely different animal, he promised.

In Carlisle his pace notes were extensive and freshly scribbled on a roll of white masking tape that he had stuck to the route map lodged between his handlebars. Three exclamation marks denoted Sheeran corner at 112km. There was another sticker on his left speaker, listing the leading cyclists in the general classification. And one more on the right with those contesting the King of the Mountains title. At the base of his left wing mirror was a small red light that flickered when they were live on air.

As always, he and Phil would be Moto 1, which meant they would take the front of the race. Phil rides pillion, but he begins the race sitting with his back to Jason. He then films the head of the peloton until there is a breakaway. At that point, Jason drops in behind the leading pack and Phil spins around to face forward. This is on a moving bike doing upwards of 60mph. It's the sort of lark that Tom Cruise brags about at film premieres. 'He stands up and humps my back, pretty much,' said Jason, zipping up his leather jacket. 'We're very good friends.'

Supporting Jason was Moto 2, which starts at the back of the race before filling in at the head of the peloton following a breakaway. Lastly, Moto 3 is responsible for grabbing scenic shots, before taking up a position at the back and catching any of the ensuing carnage. 'Moto 3 is unofficially called the crash camera,' said Jason.

The 198km route from Carlisle to Gateshead would cut across the country from west to east. It's one that will be familiar to any amateur rider who has completed the popular Coast to Coast challenge. I'm no cyclist, but brimming with naivety I tried it with a few friends some years back. It was three 12-hour days of gruelling torture. The pros on the Tour of Britain, including Wout van Aert, Julian Alaphilippe, and Mark Cavendish, take just four and a half hours.

For Jason it would be 270 unblinking minutes of focus, judgement calls, expert handling, and keeping the voices in his head happy. That's not a medical issue. A small black dashboard links him to six people chirping in his ears throughout the race. As well as the TV director, he has the race director, the engineers, the Tour radio, the commentators, and, finally, his internal line with Phil. Each person is chasing their own, often mutually exclusive, objective. 'It's finding that happy medium of being far enough away that the race director's happy,' said Jason. 'But not too far away that my TV director is saying, "Get in closer, get in there!"'

Over a couple of light refreshments in the pub on the eve of every stage, Jason and his fellow moto pilots consult the roadbook that acts as a bible to members of the Tour's sizeable caravan. 'That's our life,' he said, pulling it from his tank bag. Thumbing through today's route, Jason predicted where we would see breakaways and crashes, just as he did in Sunderland. 'The race is likely to be blown to smithereens going up Hartside Pass,' he said. Hartside is the exposed seven-kilometre climb that rises to a height of over 1,900ft. I tell him I cycled up there once, and that I could never do it again. 'I could,' he said, raising his eyebrows and pointing to his motorbike. 'With an engine between my legs.'

That engine is a BMW R1200RT. It weighs 229kg and can travel at speeds of up to 140mph, though its most important feature is being able to climb steep hills at a fraction of that pace, all while having enough grunt to power the vehicle's oodles of electronic telemetry. Phil's camera links to the beanpole transmitter on the back of the bike, which beams the signal to a plane flying high enough to have a line of sight over both the start and finish lines. That signal is then returned to the media trucks at the finish line, where the dirty feed is cleaned and colourised, graphics are added, and then the commentary. Finally, an uplink truck pings the clean feed to a satellite, before the live footage appears on our TV screens. This whole process takes less than a second. I know this because Jason was eager to tell me. He was keen to emphasise that he was but a small cog in one well-oiled engine.

'We're just the rock stars that turn up two hours before the race,' he said, in his strong Welsh twang. 'You've got guys back at those trucks sleeping in hammocks, arriving 12 hours beforehand to set everything up.' With his broad shoulders, shaved head, dark shades, and black leathers, the rock star vibe rings true. Although four yellow rubber ducks wedged up against his windscreen don't exactly scream Motörhead. 'Jason didn't want you to see those,' said Phil.

'We have a running joke with our director,' explained Jason. It was all to do with the filler shots that live cycling coverage depends on during the moments when the action is one-paced. 'Two years ago we got a little plastic snake and we wrapped it up on the dashboard,' said Jason. 'And

Phil told the director we'd found a story, so he comes to us with the live feed. Then we slowly panned up to the snake on the dashboard.' Viewers would have noticed the camera shaking as Phil struggled to conceal his giggles. 'So today it's rubber ducks.'

Respect the Spandex

Bruce Draper sent me his CV, listing every sporting event where he had featured as a moto pilot. It starts with Australia's Commonwealth Bank Cycle Classic in 1994, back in the days when tape really did mean tape. And the list continues over seven pages, including the Sydney Olympics and Paralympics in 2000. The only gaps are Covid-shaped. You can be fairly sure that if you've ever watched a road event held in Australia, the pictures have come directly off the back of Bruce's bike.

Like Jason, Bruce was a cycling nut in his youth. Every day he would get up at 4.30am to train, enjoying the freedom of Sydney's deserted roads just hours before he would begin his day's work as a schoolteacher. He would race at weekends, first competing at just five years old, and eventually lining up alongside Australia's top international cyclists. It all came to an end at 35 when he was diagnosed with chronic fatigue. But it didn't entirely curtail his two-wheeled career, and swapping pedals for an engine meant that he could finally keep up with the elite. 'I was a sprinter, so I was fast. But I see some of these guys going up hills as fast as I was sprinting,' said Bruce. His red and white motorcycle helmet sat on the table behind him, below a wall poster for Sydney 2000.

Remarkably, Bruce had no experience of riding a motorcycle before a chance encounter at a wedding opened the door to his next big adventure. A former racing rival offered him the opportunity to become a marshal, providing support to the police to ensure the route is clear of traffic and obstacles. 'The next week I went out and I got my licence, got my permit, and bought myself a motorbike.' Two years later, while marshalling on his Honda VT250, camera operator Honie Farrington asked if he would step in after a no-show from her regular pilot. Twenty-five years on and the two remain Australia's go-to moto. 'In Australia, when anyone talks about one of us, it's always in conjunction with the other.'

Bruce's entry into the world of moto piloting may seem unusual, but it seems there is no standard way to become a moto pilot. While Bruce had never considered himself a biker, Jason had always had a motorbike. He too had started as a race marshal before making the step up.

Then there's the example of Luke Edwardes-Evans, a former club cyclist whose love for the sport bubbled from every sentence he uttered while sitting in his kitchen in Kent. And every sentence that he writes as a journalist, the career he opted for in order to get as close as he could to cycling's biggest events. 'Cycling is such a beautiful sport. You can walk out of your front door with your family and stand there and watch this bike race go by,' he enthused. One day, he was given the opportunity to get even closer.

On a typical morning on London's motionless roads, famed cycling photographer Graham Watson spotted Luke easing through traffic like a downstream trout. 'Graham was working on the magazine that I was also working on,' said Luke. 'He just saw me riding over-exuberantly through the traffic on Wandsworth's one-way system. And he thought, "Maybe that guy could do one of my driving jobs."'

Unlike the pilots carrying camera operators, where being able to speak the language of the TV production team is a prerequisite, Luke's role as Graham Watson's photo moto has allowed him to experience the biggest races in mainland Europe. It means Luke has been in the caravan at the Tour de France, Giro d'Italia, Vuelta a España, and the two major cobbled classics – Paris–Roubaix and the Tour of Flanders. He was also at the Olympics in London 2012 and in Rio 2016, before Watson's retirement saw Luke switch to ferrying photographers from French newspaper *L'Équipe*. 'It's not the kind of job where you wake up in the morning and say, "Yes, I'm going to take up that career." I think we all somehow get lucky. When you're behind the bunch you are basically part of the show. You get that energy, the joy that the crowd's experiencing as you're passing through it. It gets into your bones.'

Media Motos receives around four enquiries a week from applicants wanting to become moto pilots. Not all of them are interested in cycling, or marathons, or even sport. Some are professional motorcyclists and trainers. Others, particularly in the USA, come from law enforcement. Many are casual hobbyists who see it as a cushy way to get paid for riding their new motorbike.

Jason handles each application in the same way, sending everyone a pie chart that shows four equal sections of what is required. Being an expert at carrying a pillion, knowing the rules of the sport in which you're working (cycling moto pilots must be credited by the UCI), and understanding the requirements of the production are three of the slices. The final piece is simply being professional. Jason said his company can teach new recruits the nuances of each sport, and the intricacies of the media: 'But number one and number four, I can't train.'

In order to receive a licence to work as a moto pilot in France, Luke was required to undergo a training course with the French gendarmerie. 'Basically, you ride around a few cones, and they tell you how to go around a corner,' he said. 'Then they take you out on the open road and you go as fast as you can to try and drop the other guys. To show how big your balls are. It's got nothing to do with riding in a bike race.'

With over two decades of filming on Australian roads, Bruce has seen plenty of inexperienced motos come and then swiftly go. He has no doubt as to what it takes to succeed in the saddle. 'My experience has been that the best moto pilots are the ones who have been cyclists.' A peloton hurtling down winding mountain passes at full speed is like a rabid, wheezing beast. It plods and then paces. It smiles and then snarls. And when it lashes out, it is capable of overwhelming even the most experienced motorcyclist.

But those who have been part of that beast, who know how swift it can move, who can sense when it will play dead, and who can spot the signs that it is about to roar, are those who are best placed to track it. 'I can read the race,' said Jason. 'I know when somebody's about to make a jump. I see him leaning down and adjusting his shoes.' When he recognises the tells, he will inform his director just as the rider plotting his move changes his gear. 'And we'll focus on him. And there he goes.'

'People think we tootle along at 15mph, put a picnic rug down, get a baguette, take the Instamatic out, and take a couple of pictures as the race goes by,' said Luke. 'They have got no idea how fast the riders go. How crazy these kids are that ride bikes.' And it's not only the public who underestimates the speeds involved. In the early days of the Tour of California, Jason crossed the Atlantic to advise a group of police motorcyclists who were to form part of the caravan. The Americans were far from daunted by the task ahead. 'One cop said to me, "I've been riding this bike for years, you think some guy in spandex is going to overtake me?" And he almost crashed, because he couldn't corner as fast as a cyclist can. The following day he came up to me and shook my hand and said, "I get it."'

For Jason, 'getting it' meant being able to manoeuvre a bulky two-wheeled vehicle in a tight environment that it wasn't built for. 'You're expected to go up a very steep hill at six miles an hour, with an awful lot of equipment on, with a lot of crowds and noise around you. And then you're going down the descent at 65mph, being chased by 100 lunatics.'

Watching Jason live, it was noticeable how his helmet bobbed like a Weeble in a washing machine. His eyes constantly flicked between his mirrors, his head flitting side to side as if in the front row at Wimbledon. According to Bruce, moto pilots have no other option. 'You've got to be doing it constantly. Because the police will come through at 200kph [124mph] to get to a marshalling point. And you can look in your mirror, and look in the opposite direction for five seconds, and they're going past you. They're on you so quick. So you've got to be mindful of everybody that's on the circuit.'

Help Me, to Help You

Back in Carlisle, the stage was under way. I was lucky enough to be on the route with the peloton only a few minutes behind me. I may not have been on the back of a motorbike but I had the next best viewpoint sitting in the front seat of a sleek Škoda guest car. My driver was a softly spoken Scottish chap called Russell Davidson, a former Glasgow traffic cop who was used to jumping red lights. Unlike me, whose instinct every time we drove through one was to jolt upright.

Russell's career includes driving the police command vehicle at the 2014 Commonwealth Games in Glasgow before an arthritis condition saw him take early retirement. These days, when he's not helping out at cycling events as both a driver and sometimes commissaire, you'll find him inspecting roads for the council. So there can be no better pedigree for a driver as part of a Tour of Britain convoy. But by God does he take a corner at speed.

Five minutes before we departed, dozens of race marshals in high-vis jackets zoomed off one after the other, like growling orange lemmings, to begin the rolling closure of the roads. We were the next to follow, and Russell explained that we would stay ahead of the pack until a breakaway formed with a suitable gap to get in behind. Somewhat disconcertingly, Russell then asked me if I could read a map. 'Because what'll happen is if we get behind them, we'll need to try and find a way back in front,' he said. He then handed me a laminated map, including the off-race route in case we needed to play catch-up. My intention to sit back and tuck into the complimentary pastries no longer seemed quite so straightforward.

As the race began, what was immediately striking was just how many vehicles formed part of the caravan, just as Bruce had warned. In addition to the marshals and our intrepid moto pilots there were four commissaire cars, two motorbike commissaires, team cars, radio cars, press cars, timekeeping cars, neutral cars, ambulances, and police bikes buzzing around like late-summer wasps.

As we drove south through Carlisle, crowds had lined the roads to watch the cyclists amble by on the 6km neutralised start. Russell suggested I wind my window down, and as I did he began honking the car horn. Almost instantly, the hundreds gathering on the pavements, from schoolchildren with handmade banners to pensioners crumpled into camping chairs, began frantically waving and cheering. I waved back. I did so for most of the first hour, lapping up every moment of this presidential motorcade experience just as Luke had described. I was beginning to get a sense of the rock star buzz the moto pilots must enjoy.

Just as Jason predicted, things had opened up by the time the race reached the first King of the Mountains

Stood on his platform with his gun held aloft, Alan Bell can be seen in the background firing Usain Bolt to greatness at the 2009 World Championships in Berlin

Closer to home, Alan Bell (left) joins fellow athletics starters Micky Baker and Malcolm Dewell (right) at a junior athletics meeting in Morpeth in 2021.

Private performance chef Rachel Muse steers footballers away from Nandos, Pop Tarts, and Haribo by dishing up banana bread muffins and fruit.

England chef Omar Meziane (centre, eighth from left), celebrates with the World Cup-winning under-20s team in 2017. Gareth Southgate would be in touch with a senior squad call-up soon after.

Chief mechanic Matthew Scott is in the zone and hoping for a change of luck in the Haas garage. Credit: Haas F1 Team.

The clean-up job begins on what remains of Romain Grosjean's Haas car at the 2020 Bahrain Grand Prix.

Emilie Rath (right) fulfils her childhood ambitions in the pit lane during the 2018 Formula One season.

Joe VanderKelen demonstrates the worth of his snow guns at the 2018 Winter Olympics in South Korea. The background is how the Jeongseon downhill course would normally have looked. Credit: SMI

Mikko Martikainen pulls off the world's first mass snow storage test in Ruka, Finland in 2000. Credit: Esko Raty

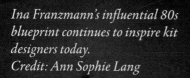

*Ina Franzmann's influential 80s
blueprint continues to inspire kit
designers today.
Credit: Ann Sophie Lang*

West Germany captain Lothar Matthaus shows off the full splendour of the iconic Ina Franzmann-designed Adidas shirt at World Cup 1990.

Designers Craig Buglass (left) and Rob Warner (right) discuss which of their World Cup-winning kits was better – Brazil 2002 or Italy 2006.
Credit: Sketch Benjamin

Moto pilot Jason Jenkins and camera operator Phil Rowe give chase at the Tour of Britain. This time without rubber ducks on board. Credit: MediaMotos intermediate sprint at Hartside Pass. There was a breakaway of seven riders with a gap of four minutes to the peloton, allowing Russell to drop off and pull in behind the leaders. I spotted Jason and Phil on Moto 1 a couple of metres to the right of the pack. Sprint legend Mark Cavendish, not known for his climbing prowess, was an unexpected but welcome inclusion in the leading pack. A TV helicopter hovered only metres above us as we drove the spaghetti roads of Hartside. As we chicaned right the view below showed the Tour caravan in full, with the peloton at its centre and all around it a vast expanse of green and yellow Cumbrian fields. Four minutes looked a hell of a long way from here.

As someone who has spent a career reaping the rewards of a well-organised lead-out train, Cavendish knew that it was far from long enough. And he didn't seem overly happy. As we got closer, he appeared to be saying something to Moto 1. Jason had previously described his relationship with the cyclists as good. He even offers them coaching on ways to boost their profile. 'If there are five or six riders in the breakaway all day, segments can be quite boring to watch,' he told me, so he advises them to interact with the camera to guarantee some coverage for themselves. And, more importantly, their mortgage-paying sponsors. Jason tells them, 'When the camera comes to you do something. Wave and say, "Hi, Mum." Take a drink. Offer a gel to the camera guy. Because you can guarantee it'll make airtime, it'll make the highlights, it'll make the sizzle reel. And it'll be replayed and replayed.' He likes to think of it as a symbiotic relationship. 'Help me, to help you,' he insists. Though I got the impression that, on this occasion, Cavendish wasn't chatting to Jason about sizzle reels.

Once we were over the climb, Russell decided that now was the time to make our way past the leaders. He awaited the nod from the commissaire, and we overtook team cars on tight two-lane country roads with an excitable human perimeter. Moto 1 slipped in behind the leaders and Russell took the invitation, turning full traffic-cop mode as he put his right foot down. I wound my window down just as Cavendish glanced right. He would have seen me gritting my teeth and holding my breath. For even with only seven cyclists on the road, that felt tight. The thought of being alongside a fast-moving peloton, when the slightest misjudgement could send dozens tumbling, made me feel a little queasy.

But Russell had timed our move to perfection, as the Tour radio broadcast an update announcing that the lead had been cut by 25 seconds. The beast was beginning to roar.

Daydreamer, Slipstreamer

'An important part of our role is to remember that we're not part of the race,' said Bruce, folding his arms. 'We're just showing everyone what's happening out on the road.' While there can be few doubts regarding the intentions of Bruce and his fellow moto pilots, there are plenty of people who disagree with his sentiment. Professor Bert Blocken of the Eindhoven University of Technology is one of them. In 2019, he used wind tunnel measurements and the Dutch national supercomputer to calculate, for the first time, the exact advantage a cyclist gets in the slipstream of a moto pilot.

He found that a motorbike riding 20m in front will reduce drag by 15 per cent, therefore increasing the speed of a cyclist by 5.4 per cent. That amounts to a time advantage of 3.3 seconds per minute. This time boost differs depending on the gap between cyclist and moto. A distance of just 4.8m would result in a 9.3-second-per-minute gain, while 50m brings that down to 1.4 seconds per minute. 'The often-heard complaint that motorcycles can influence the outcome of races is therefore justified,' concluded the professor.

At the Tour de France in 2018, an irate Tom Dumoulin accused his rival Primož Roglič of using an unfair advantage in the Slovenian's stage 19 win. 'He was flying downhill,' raged Dumoulin, 'and eventually I got dropped on a straight part just because he was on his tube and full in the slipstream of the motorbike. I was sprinting to his wheel and I couldn't get any closer. It's ridiculous really.' Dumoulin would end up finishing second behind Geraint Thomas that year, while Roglič would come in fourth. But the issue of drafting has long been a contentious one in cycling.

Professor Blocken may argue that they are not sufficient, but the UCI does have rules in place to reduce slipstream advantages. Yet while riders can be penalised for sitting behind team cars, they will encounter no trouble for enjoying the benefits afforded by neutral motorbikes. Instead, the only wrists getting slapped are those gloved in leather. 'Cyclists never get penalised for jumping on the back of the bike,' said Jason. 'The bike is always in the wrong position.'

It's a rueful point shared by both Bruce and Luke, and presumably every moto pilot on the circuit. 'I always maintain that there should be some ruling that riders who deliberately do that should be penalised,' reckoned Bruce, who remembered an American moto pilot being ordered out of the Sydney Olympics road race for riding too close to the cyclists.

Luke, too, fell foul of a Tour de France commissaire, when he contravened rules on overtaking during team time-trial stages. 'You're not allowed to overtake a team. My *L'Équipe* photographer thought we could do it. I did say, "I'm not sure we can." Maybe my French wasn't good enough. Anyway, we had the day off the next day.'

With punishments only ever directed one way, cyclists are understandably inclined to try their luck. And with the increased coverage of races, in no small part due to footage from the helicopter, it's becoming easier for authorities to spot when moto pilots commit infractions that either impede or help a rider. It means shaking off mischievous cyclists is another task to add to the moto pilot's to-do list.

'It's like putting bloody flares out in a fighter jet,' said Jason, viewing the mischievous cyclists as incoming flak. 'There are different tactics we can deploy. When we know somebody is coming over to us, we will try and flick them,' he said, using his hands to show how he whips from one side of the road to the other. 'Then maybe we'll decelerate to no longer give them any advantage.'

If that fails, a good old-fashioned shaming is the next port of call. Phil will point his camera to the ground to indicate to the director to cut away. Jason will then pull up alongside the offending cyclist and scream, 'STAY OFF THE BIKE!' A red-faced cyclist is then left to the mercy of a disapproving peloton. 'It's a tricky little dance,' concluded the Welshman.

I asked him if there are repeat offenders on the tour. Usual suspects who he is constantly trying to shake off. His answer was an unequivocal 'yep'. While he had no appetite to share names, Jason said it was a subject that is commonly discussed in moto pilot circles. The consensus was that, actually, the elite riders don't bother chasing the bike. 'It's the ones that are in the next echelon down that always jump on the back of the damn bike.' Jason believes that, in a desperate attempt to make the next level, some are instructed to do so by team bosses.

But as one of a small band of gatekeepers deciding what is shown on television, and with teams needing to get their sponsors on air, Jason has leverage when it comes to dissuading repeat offenders. 'I spoke to one of the team directors a few years back. I said, "I'm going to make it my mission that every time I see one of your riders, we'll put the camera down."'

Creative Diversions

As the breakaway headed towards the final King of the Mountains stage at Burtree Fell, the fiendish left turn at 112km was successfully negotiated by all. Race regulator Andy Hawes 1, pop prince Ed Sheeran 0. Russell pulled over for a 'comfort break' by the side of the bush-lined road. Now that we had come to a stop, it meant that we got a glimpse of the entire field. Cavendish remained part of the breakaway, who had consolidated their lead. Three minutes later and the peloton ticked by at a brisk pace that brought with it a musty isotonic waft. The cyclists were by no means hitting top speed, and a handful even got off their bikes to take a pee alongside us.

When we set off again Russell pulled in behind the bunch and I got my first experience at the tail of the caravan. It was a lot less fun than at its head. I had gone from seeming presidential to feeling like a marathon fun-runner who has lost the head of his costume. People were still looking and clapping, but there was an air of underwhelming confusion. They exchanged glances that said, 'Was that it, then?' Russell did his best with the car horn, but nobody was waving now and the air was a little despondent. I could see why Jason prefers his seat in Moto 1.

As the race reached Hexham, a torrent of rain dropped from the heavens. It didn't last long but if there's one thing moto pilots hate, it's variable weather. You can't suddenly pop the waterproofs on. You simply get wet. What's more, the peloton appeared to have lost its appetite. Until it gets hungry again, this is when moto pilots and their camera operators must get inventive. For while they may be at pains to avoid jeopardising the integrity of a race, there is no question of remaining passive. Not when so much of a stage race requires a creative spark from those covering it. Before he set off in Carlisle, cameraman Phil described a typical day as, 'Twenty minutes at the start, and 20 minutes at the end. In between, there's a vacuum.'

When I spoke to Bruce about this, he attributed it to the rise in technology. Like everyone else on the caravan, the cyclists have a live communications feed, ensuring that they're up to date with the vital statistics of a race. Previously, cyclists relied on the occasional chalkboard update.

Bruce isn't convinced that the comms are conducive to exciting racing. 'One of my pet hates is that it's become so choreographed. Because they've got radio communications, the riders don't do a terrible lot of thinking,' he said harking back to a time when an impromptu breakaway would be rewarded with the promise of stealth up the road. 'Once upon a time, if a break went away you were very lucky to find out how big the gap was. Whereas now the teams are watching it live on their car TVs. I find that a bit frustrating. I'd like to see a race where there's no team support and no radios because it would be a completely different ball game.'

Just like Jason with his rubber ducks, Bruce admitted to having taken a few steps in the past to liven things up during the mid-race lull. During one Commonwealth Bank event, Bruce entered into an in-race wager with some tiring stragglers. 'There was that much gap between the leaders and the tail-enders they might as well have been in another country. And I was bored.' Bruce dropped back to the neutral spares car and asked them for some cash. They gave him a $20 bill. 'I went up to the riders and said, "First rider at the top of Governors Hill gets $20!" Then I went ahead to the top of the hill and just stood on the side of the road. They made a dash for cash.'

Luke has also been known to inject some in-race excitement of his own, though his distraction was more of a subconscious one. At the 2018 Tour de France, he had stopped on a hairpin bend so that his passenger could take a shot focusing down on the road beneath. 'Quite often, four or five bikes will stop and all the photographers will jump off and take pictures as the bunch comes up,' explained Luke. 'As the bunch comes around the corner you jump back on.'

The risky manoeuvre leaves little room for error, with officials barking at the photo motos to get a move on as the bunch gets closer. 'We all roared away. And about a kilometre up the road another photographer came up alongside me and pointed to the back seat. I look behind me.' Luke's pillion saddle was empty. He had forgotten the photographer. 'At that moment, I just thought, "My career's over."'

Turning around against the race is a misdemeanour that will never be tolerated as part of a cycling caravan. If you're caught doing so you will be instantly sent home. So Luke had no choice but to pull over and endure an agonising ten-minute wait for his incandescent French snapper to run down and catch him up. 'He was shouting at me, "Where the effing hell were you!"' said Luke, now comfortable enough to laugh at his error. 'When I got into the press room that night all the photographers got up and clapped.'

Luke not only worked again but he has since been reunited with the same photographer. There are no hard feelings, and it's symptomatic of the bond that forms between a pilot and his passenger over a long and gruelling tour. 'I love the element of teamwork and support for each other,' said Luke. 'Even with a photographer that you may not work with very often, or you may not get on with that well, there's a real bond of trust. Because it's got to be that way.'

Meanwhile, Russell and I took a leaf out of the moto pilots' book and created our own diversion. Quite literally in this case, as we embarked on an off-route dash with the aim of returning to the front before the frantic final 50km. Russell handed me the laminated map. I pulled my phone from my pocket and opened Google Maps.

Calling the Shots

Along with the camaraderie with their passenger, a healthy element of competition helps to keep a moto pilot sharp. If the commentators are discussing Ethan Hayter's new shoes, you can be sure the moto team that gets the first close-up shot won't be shy about mentioning it in the pub that evening. And while they are primarily employed for their skill on the bike, there is a ton of professional pride in the shots that their positioning enables. Especially when they've done more than just put the bike in the right spot.

A camera operator only ever sees what's going on through a viewfinder no bigger than a casino chip, meaning the moto pilot is expected to act as the eyes and ears for everywhere outside of that small window. That brings with it directorial responsibilities too. Whether that be scouting interesting shots on the route, or spotting sights that really shouldn't be aired pre-watershed (crowd nudity 'happens a lot' according to Jason), it is quite often down to the pilot to give their camera operator the tip-off. 'I know what shot Phil wants sometimes before he knows it's coming up,' said Jason.

As for Bruce, he remembered a time at the 2010 World Championships in Melbourne when he called it just right. 'They were within the last ten kilometres of the finish and Honie [Farrington] and I were shooting the breakaway from behind. And we got on to a really long road, and I looked in the mirror. I said, "They're coming."' Honie's instincts, like those of any camera operator, would have been to turn around instantly and make sure she got the shot of the chasing peloton reeling in the pack. But Bruce had other ideas. He insisted Honie wait and keep shooting the riders in front, hugging the railings in a desperate attempt to outpace the peloton. They never had a chance. Just at the last moment, Bruce called action. 'I said, "Wait. Wait. Turn!" Honie turned around, just as they came up. And she got them coming past. I thought it was a killer shot.'

The commentary team agreed, as Paul Sherwan excitedly described the peloton's brooding emergence from the heat shimmer as a 'big black mass', while fellow commentator Phil Liggett exhaled in awe. 'A few years later I spoke to Rob Arnold, editor of *Ride Magazine*,' added Bruce, 'and he said that shot at the World Championships still gives him shivers down his spine.' Arnold had been among the crowds at the finish line watching the live feed on the big screen. 'He said when we panned around, the place just erupted. He maintains it's the best cycling moment he's ever had. Well, it was great to be part of that.'

Not all of the stories told by the moto pilots are as fondly remembered. This is, after all, a high-speed sport. And one which comes with all of the accompanying pitfalls. In 2012, Jason broke his leg when the barriers of a circuit race blew over and landed on top of him. Another time, he came inches away from ploughing head on into a car that had somehow evaded police roadblocks. In 2005 Bruce was taken out by an official car, causing Honie to suffer a broken collarbone and seven broken ribs. Then there's Luke. He even has the footage of his only crash, which occurred when he was carrying a *L'Équipe* photographer at the 2017 Tour de France.

'I was following a small group with Chris Froome in the yellow jersey over the Port de Balès, in the Alps,' he recalled, keen to show me the video. 'We were going over the top of the summit, where you've got banners and the crowds. As we crested the top of the summit, the next thing I was flying through the air and rolling along the ground. The bike slid over to the right side of the road. Me and the photographer got up and thought, "What the heck just happened?"'

It all remained a mystery until 24 hours later when amateur footage uploaded to YouTube showed the incident in full. With crowds cheering, flags waving, and drums beating, a live TV moto comes up quickly on the inside. As it overtakes, a loose camera cable wraps around Luke's handlebars, flipping the wheels from under him. Thankfully he and his photographer escaped with minor cuts and bruises, though he admitted to being somewhat shaken by the ordeal.

Given the number of high-profile incidents involving professional cyclists and convoy vehicles in recent years, including the tragic death of Belgian cyclist Antoine Demoitié at the Gent-Wevelgem classic in 2016, it's a testament to their skill, experience, and expertise that Bruce, Jason, and Luke have managed to avoid a collision with cyclists. 'Safety is always, always, always number one,' said Jason. 'The shot is secondary.'

Unwanted Attention

Thanks to Google's shrewd navigation, Russell and I made it to the Gateshead finish line ahead of the final sprint. There was disappointment among the crowd that the peloton had finally swallowed up Cavendish, but excitement that it had propelled all three Tour of Britain leaders, van Aert, Hayter, and Alaphilippe, into a thrilling finale. On a big screen in the shadow of the Angel of the North, thousands of spectators cheered the pictures beaming in from Moto 1. Jason must never get to see this reaction live. Like Bruce, the best he can hope for is that someone down the line will tell him about it. But I suspect there's a good reason why Bruce remembered that interaction with the magazine editor. Because it rarely happens.

'It's difficult sometimes when we've worked our asses off, and something goes wrong,' Jason told me before the race. 'Everybody focuses on the thing that went wrong, whether the picture broke up, or whether it was an incident with a bike. We all get tarred with the same brush. I guess it's easy for people to focus on the negatives rather than positives.'

As the race leaders bounded down the finishing straight on Durham Road, a screaming crowd banged the red advertising boards. Wout van Aert timed his final burst to perfection and crossed the line ahead of Hayter in second, and Alaphilippe in third. It was a thrilling finish, and the fact I didn't see Jason meant that he had successfully found the deviation route. Crossing the line on a moto is another sanctionable offence.

As the leading cyclists enjoyed their moment on the podium, I found Jason loading his motorbike back into his van. He would be making the 90-minute drive north to Hawick in the Scottish Borders early the next morning, ready for stage seven up to Edinburgh.

'So that's the job we do. Full on wasn't it?' he said. I asked him if he had any issues. 'We got shouted at by Mark Cavendish a couple of times,' he replied, recalling the incident from earlier. 'It's part of the job. He wanted us on the front of the breakaway. We sat behind. If we're on the front, we're obviously towing them along.' Jason had no intention of risking a day on the commissaire's naughty step in order to please the Manx Missile. 'It tarnishes our reputation.' It was the first time I had seen him a little downbeat. Maybe he was just exhausted. Or maybe he knew what was already trending on social media.

It turned out Phil's camera had picked up Cavendish shouting, 'You're helping them! What's wrong with you?' His ire was directed right down the lens. The former road world champion thought Moto 1 was unwittingly helping Tim Donovan, a general classification contender. With Donovan remaining in the breakaway, Cavendish knew that the peloton would never be too far behind. And he wasn't finished there, returning to the camera to add some context, 'For all you people at home, these motorbikes have a bearing on the race. The guys [cyclists] are sat on them.'

Jason likely knew that this talking point, rather than the exciting finish, was going to plague him and his colleagues for the next few days. I quickly changed the subject. I asked if he got his rubber ducks in the shot. He was smiling again. 'We got our ducks in,' he said, smirking as he did an impression of his director. '"Fucking hell Moto 1 you threw me under the bus again!"'

7

LOST IN TRANSLATION:
Football Interpreters

*Football may be described as a universal
language but without interpreters, its wheels
of communication would grind to a halt.
From deciphering Champions League press
conferences to tutoring reluctant foreign stars,
leading linguists reveal the high-pressure
work that goes into the game's lingua franca.*

The Pioneers

On Tuesday, 10 March 1998, Bayern Munich coach
Giovanni Trapattoni arrived at his press conference
bubbling with indignation. He pulled up a chair but he
needed a pulpit. For there would be no questions from the
media, only a tirade from a man at odds with his squad.
It had been two days since Bayern had lost 1-0 at Schalke
to stay seven points adrift of leaders Kaiserslautern. The
59-year-old was ready to dismantle the criticisms of
senior players including the out-of-favour pair of Mario
Basler and Mehmet Scholl. But Italian fury and primitive

German go together like jam in broth. It was a hot, sticky mess.

Having won the Bundesliga only the season before, the highly respected coach felt that he commanded enough respect to get his point across despite his basic German. It resulted in one of the most famous rants in football history. He began calmly but his voice began to creak like a rusty gate. His demeanour became as erratic as his grammar. He slammed his desk and, like a Bavarian Yoda who just stubbed his toe, insisted that 'a coach not an idiot is', called his players 'weak like a bottle empty', and described them as 'having without courage at words'. His three-minute performance ended with the curt line, 'I have finish.' As he stormed off, the stunned journalists felt compelled to applaud. Some of these phrases remain popular memes used by wisecracking German fans.

Though Trapattoni's commitment was undoubted and his passion unparalleled, his frantic word soup served only to portray a man at his wit's end. A manager who had lost control not only of his players but also himself. He would depart the club within three months. It would be 11 years before Bayern would appoint another foreign boss.

Trapattoni's replacement was Ottmar Hitzfeld, the manager who had brought Borussia Dortmund their first Champions League in 1997. Hailing from the town of Lörrach in south-west Germany, Hitzfeld would have little trouble conversing with the likes of *Bild*. But European media would be a different matter. This was a decorated coach who would later turn down Manchester United because he couldn't speak English. And Bayern is not a club that does embarrassment. They had no intention of repeating Trapattoni's argot invention workshop and began the hunt for an interpreter.

Over in England, football clubs had known for some time where to find such a service. English football's first professional interpreter was a Scouser by the name of George Scanlan. Scanlan was fluent in Russian, French, Arabic, and Persian, having graduated from Christ's College, Cambridge. His day job was teaching at Liverpool Polytechnic, but the rise of pan-European competitions meant that he became increasingly in demand in football circles.

His expertise was sought at the 1966 World Cup in England. As well as helping the USSR side, he chaperoned Azerbaijani official Tofiq Bahramov the night before the final. That's the man who became fondly known as the Russian linesman. There's a good chance Scanlan's charm was the reason England won the World Cup.

A trusted confidant of Bob Paisley, Bobby Robson, and Alex Ferguson, Scanlan also accompanied the likes of Liverpool, West Ham, and Aston Villa on memorable European nights. In the 1990s the gifted linguist travelled with the England football team to the World Cup in Italy, and as the Cold War came to an end he became a figurehead for the influx of eastern Europeans finding their feet in English football.

Scanlan chided a reporter for asking new Ipswich signing Sergei Baltacha if he was a communist, and became especially close to Manchester United winger Andrei Kanchelskis. So much so that when the boyhood

Everton fan discovered that Kanchelskis was set to move to Middlesbrough, Scanlan called Toffees manager Joe Royle to give him the tip-off. The Russian international ended up at Goodison Park, where he became a crowd favourite.

At Old Trafford, a tireless Scanlan was kept busy with a prodigious Frenchman by the name of Eric Cantona. He even joined the fiery forward at the police station following the kung-fu-kick incident at Selhurst Park in 1995. 'Je n'ai rien à dire' ('I have nothing to say') were the only words he needed to interpret that day.

Scanlan died in 2017 aged 82, having played an integral role when British football first began to open its arms more widely across the continent. He had become loved by players and respected by managers because, in football at least, his talents were so unique.

But before long, the game would find itself needing more George Scanlans. In 1999 Chelsea became the first British team to name a starting XI entirely made up of foreign players. Just over a year later, Bayern Munich's interpreter shifted nervously in his seat. It was Peter Clark's first press conference, and was one he remembered vividly when we caught up in March 2021.

'I had to do Bayern München against Arsenal,' said Peter, pronouncing the Bundesliga teams as they are known in Germany. Hitzfeld was sat to his right, Bayern captain Stefan Effenberg on his left, and goalkeeper Oliver Kahn nearby. Born in Germany to an English mother and an American father working for NATO, Peter had grown up idolising these greats. A former semi-professional footballer, his bilingual upbringing and sporting passion combined to put him right next to them that day. Over 250 members of the media were tuned in to Peter's every word.

'I couldn't take my glass of water, I was shaking,' he recalled. 'But then Stefan Effenberg took me aside and said, "Whatever you want to say, just say it. It's fine by me." I looked at him and said, "But I can't do that." And he gently punched me and said, "Go on, be a devil." He relaxed me. I picked up the glass of water and took a sip.'

The press conference went without a hitch and it launched Peter's distinguished career. Celtic became his first regular client, a prestigious commission that made every subsequent pitch a whole lot easier. 'Imagine you're a building contractor and your aim is to get all the building work in and around London. And your first job is Buckingham Palace,' said Peter, teasing his analogy. 'Rather than starting from the bottom up, I started from the top down. In later years I realised the advantages that made. Because everyone thought, "Well Celtic use them, why wouldn't we?"'

Rangers followed, as did Arsenal. Then in 2003 Celtic drew Bayern, Lyon, and Anderlecht in the Champions League. Peter took the opportunity to outsource the French and Belgian assignments to local interpreters. It was an idea that would catapult his business into football's big-time. For all that he attributed it to luck, it took a fair chunk of marketing acumen. 'It was pure fluke. I thought it would be nice to have branded clothing, and I made these simple jackets.' While wearing the jacket, Peter's French colleague was approached by a production manager from ITV Sport. A regular Champions League gig was the result.

Since then, Clark Football Languages (CFL) has been integral to players and managers communicating within Europe's favourite sport. Interpreting – that is, working with spoken word – accounts for around 40 per cent of their work. Translation services – involving the written word – are increasingly sought for producing web pages, press releases, and video subtitles. The company coordinates over 450 interpreters for more than 200 clubs and organisations. No matter how niche the language combination is, they will source it.

In addition to comprehensive coverage in Germany, England and Scotland, Peter established interpreting teams in Spain, Italy, France, Greece, Holland, Switzerland, and Austria. 'These international weeks are the ones where you get challenges,' he told me, just a few days before Germany were due to host North Macedonia in World Cup qualifying. 'German/Macedonian is not something that happens every day. But I've got a fantastic guy from Salzburg.'

Peter delighted in telling me about the perks of football interpreting, which included getting one of the best seats in Wembley ('You get a lovely balcony, there's food nearby, the view is great'). But he warned that for even those gifted enough to speak more than one language, interpreting is often a step too far. Unlike the days of George Scanlan, supply now outstrips demand. Like professional football, for every kid that makes it, dozens will fall short. 'To be a new football interpreter, you have really got to be special,' said Peter, running his hand through his grey hair. 'Unless you're so good, it's nigh on impossible.'

Gift of the Gab

Patrick Kendrick is a lip reader's dream. He enunciates every word and honours every syllable. Gristly consonants are treated with as much esteem as a lyrical vowel. He speaks four languages, with French, Italian, and Portuguese complementing his native English. Normally based in Milan, when we spoke he had just arrived at his in-laws' home in Naples ahead of a family wedding.

Although he has worked in Brussels as an EU-accredited interpreter and was once on the books at Peter's CFL, Patrick is something of a rarity among his peers. As well as being an accomplished conference interpreter he is also a commentator and broadcaster. He provides weekly commentary for Serie A's global feed, along with occasional Champions League reporting for BT Sport.

'The two [translating and commentating] are quite complementary,' he told me while ducking and diving between rooms and family members. 'I wanted to do both but I thought, sooner or later, one would fall by the wayside. But I seem to be juggling them quite well.' The skills required for each role feed nicely into the other. The synonyms that form part of a commentator's toolbox bolster his interpreting vocabulary, while swotting up on background detail for commentating gives him additional knowledge when interpreting. 'I remember listening back to a simultaneous interpretation I did in 2012. It was all correct but in the same sentence, I used the word "game" four or five times. If I were commentating, it will be "game" the first time, "fixture" the second time, and "encounter" the third time. I just thought we can incorporate things like that.'

Patrick likens an effective interpreter to a top referee. 'You shouldn't really notice them. Often these jobs aren't spoken about unless someone messes up. It's almost like we should be heard and not seen.' This is easy enough with simultaneous interpreting, which has the interpreter sitting in soundproof booths or, having been dragged into Covid's remote-working revolution, stuck at home on video conferencing.

The translated speech is recited in real time via a short delay known as 'décalage'. This gives the linguist around four seconds to give those words a new nationality. But because the original speech continues as they're interpreting, it requires the ability to compartmentalise listening, speaking, and note-taking, while doing all three at the same time. 'Often people don't even realise it's a person doing it. They think it's just some sort of abstract machine,' said Patrick. 'But when you're doing consecutively, you're very visible.'

Consecutive interpreting sees the linguist sitting alongside the speaker, waiting until the person has finished before relaying the entirety of what was said. This can range from a few grunted lines to eloquent soliloquies of several minutes. In this case, an interpreter is more reliant on their memory and efficient notes. They are indeed more visible, but usually only to those in the room. For the rest of us watching at home, the interpreter is rarely in the frame.

'We're always put to one side of the top table,' explained Patrick. 'I understand that. Broadcasters and photographers don't need to see this random face. Even diplomatically there are so many instances of photos that have been cropped. Then you see the original and the interpreter is whispering into the ear of Obama and Merkel. We're used to that.'

Unlike working for the EU, football interpreters need not be accredited. It's a subject of dismay for Patrick, who has an MA in Interpreting and Translating from Bath University. 'Without formal training, it's very hard to cope with the pressure and do a convincing job. It reflects very badly on the football industry as a whole. I have a lot of dealings with journalists, and I always think it's a pretty damning indictment on football interpreters that whenever I go and work, someone comes up to me and says, "Oh, you're so much better than a lot of the interpreters we get." I feel like saying, "Well, because most of the time they're not interpreters."'

Marcelo Bielsa's unforgettable four-year spell at Leeds United is a prime example. The former Argentina and Chile manager used bilingual members of his backroom staff rather than professional interpreters. It led to stilted and sometimes comical interviews that didn't always live up to the standards that Patrick and agencies like CFL attain.

Patrick's YouTube channel gives a flavour of his interpreting know-how. In one video he provides a note-taking masterclass, demonstrating a form of shorthand that blends standard practice with his own homemade cipher. Whereas formally trained interpreters are taught geopolitical abbreviations, those in football are left to come up with their own. Thankfully, sport has a natural predilection for condensing popular terms. 'You can have G and A for goals and assists,' said Patrick. 'But there are other times when it's quite abstract in its idea. Then you have to rely more on your memory.'

In his consecutive interpreting example, he uses a clip from an Antonio Conte rant when Siena manager. Conte angrily repeats the phrase 'we're talking about', says he's been 'hearing lots of bullshit from so-called football experts', then lists several players no longer at the club. Patrick's accompanying notes initially look like Turing-level encryption. But they become less mystifying as he talks through his methods.

There are arrows to the repeated phrase to avoid the need to re-write it, a drawn ear representing hearing, and BS for bullshit. 'Experts' is written in quotation marks to recall Conte's disdain. Where Patrick knows them, the players mentioned are simply initialled. He then recites Conte's entire three-minute rant just seconds after finishing his notes. It's a splendid feat of recall but a hypercritical Patrick is less than enamoured with his performance, which he recorded during the 2020 lockdown. 'I'm not massively thrilled with my display,' he concludes in the clip, 'but in this game, you only get one try.'

He has certainly improved since his first taste of interpreting in 2008. Teaching English in the southern

Italian city of Brindisi, he was asked to help out a local fair trade organisation. A visiting producer of handmade toys was visiting from India so Patrick agreed to interpret from English into Italian. 'I didn't even know the difference between *artigiano* [artisan] and *artigianale* [artisanal],' he said, adding that he even neglected to take a notepad. His amateur performance was so inept that he was swiftly replaced by a delegate. 'He was a native Italian speaker, he had booked the speaker, he knew all about his toys, and it was that much easier for him to understand what was involved because he had all of the terminologies involved in fair trade.' Patrick's chastening experience didn't stop him from applying to Bath University a year later, but he had gained a valuable lesson. An interpreter who knows little about the topic matter will quickly lose the respect of their audience. And football is not an easy language to master.

Patrick mentioned a colleague who talked of 'La Coppa d'Oro' when interpreting from Spanish into Italian. 'I was wondering what that is. Then I realised it was the Gold Cup. Which, in Italian, they call La Gold Cup.' That example may have been a minor slip but Italy's *calcio* lexicon is littered with Anglicisms that interpreters should be comfortable identifying. It dates back to the early 20th century, when the country imported coaches from England. To this day managers in Italian football – even females – are called 'mister'.

Italy also has unique terms that do not translate neatly into English. Knowing these nuances, navigating linguistic false friends, and swotting up on popular idioms are what transforms a good linguist into a great interpreter. 'In Italian, they have a word, *diffidato*. In English we have to say "one booking away from suspension". There's no other way around it,' said Patrick.

Peter offered an example from Germany, where the term for a second yellow card that precedes a red is *Ampelkarte*. It translates as 'traffic light card'. He recalled a press conference where it was interpreted literally, much to the befuddlement of the English media. 'If you're not getting someone who's a football expert you're taking a 50/50 chance it's going to be really embarrassing,' he said. On the day we spoke, he had already watched four live matches from his Surrey home. 'It's crucial. If you don't have football knowledge it's like driving a car with flat tyres. You will get caught out, you will be embarrassed, and you will lose the respect of the manager. The club will never use you again.'

The Special One

When it comes to interpreting at the top level of European football, the ability to deal with pressure is as vital as knowing your *registas* from your *mezzalas*. Having seconds to do your job while being watched by the world's media, and judged by the biggest names in the sport, can take its toll. This intensifies when those big names possess a linguistic proficiency of their own. Manchester City's Pep Guardiola and Liverpool's Jürgen Klopp are not only the two most revered Premier League managers of recent times, they are also able to impart their wisdom in a multitude of languages. So it takes a brave person to convert their English press conferences back into their native tongue. Mishaps can and will be called out.

At a 2019 Champions League press conference ahead of Liverpool's game at RB Salzburg, captain Jordan Henderson was asked how his team would approach the game as European champions. His 25-second answer included the line, 'That doesn't mean it's going to be easy.' But in German, the press was told that Liverpool would 'go easy'. A prickly Klopp was quick to scold the interpreter in his harsh Swabian dialect: 'It's shit when next to the translator sits a coach who speaks German. You should really listen. Otherwise, I can do it by myself. It's not too difficult.' The following day, after his side's 2-0 victory in Austria, Klopp apologised to the interpreter. The pair shook hands.

Peter remembered some of his own experiences with the former Borussia Dortmund boss. 'Jürgen Klopp has a tendency to take the mickey out of interpreters. This happened to me too,' said Peter. I asked whether he meant in a good or bad way. 'In his way,' was his diplomatic response, with a grin.

'If you're a German/English interpreter he's going to understand every single word you're doing, and he wants everything relayed absolutely the way he says it.' Peter interpreted for Klopp in Augsburg, where Liverpool were playing in the Europa League. The Stuttgart-born boss was in his element talking to familiar journalists. He gave Peter a mischievous glance when using a German phrase that literally translates as 'the grapes are hanging high', meaning that it will be challenging. Peter's attempt elicited a cruel roar of laughter from Klopp and the local press pack. Many inexperienced interpreters may have wilted. Peter, though, proved himself to be a good sport.

'I wasn't actually that far off. But it caused laughter in the press room. Now, if I wasn't as experienced as I was, that can really damage someone psychologically. I just stood my own ground and said, "Go on, you translate it, then." But you've got to have a lot of clout to do that. And you've got to judge if they are in a good enough mood for you to do that.'

Patrick was preparing to interview Klopp the week after we spoke. As it was for Italy's Amazon Prime output, he would also be interpreting in addition to asking the questions. And so it would be a mic, rather than a notepad, in his hand. 'If you work with Jürgen Klopp, rarely are you going to get any answer under a minute. You're relying on short-term memory.' Patrick agreed that it was more of a challenge working with multilingual managers, but tries to thrive on the occasion rather than be daunted by it. 'I do feel more pressure. But I look at it as more of an opportunity. Rather than thinking they could correct me if I slip up, I think I've got a chance to impress them.'

Patrick's showreel features a post-match interview of Pep Guardiola complimenting him, while in another clip he's snapped joshing with Klopp at a conference. But there's one manager he takes particular pride in keeping happy. 'I idolised Mourinho growing up. I've done several press conferences with him. When you get a multilingual coach like him who understands what's involved and takes time to thank you and congratulate you, that's priceless. I don't think you can really top that.'

With furrowed brows and a jet-black bouffant, José Mourinho began his career as the Portuguese voice of Bobby Robson. As interpreter first at Sporting and then Porto, Mourinho's intelligence and eye for detail saw his brief extended to compiling opposition and scout reports. When Sir Bobby was headhunted by Barcelona, he insisted his interpreter came with him. Only in Catalunya, Mourinho would also be taking training sessions. Within four years he would be appointed as manager of Benfica.

Whenever Mourinho returned to Barcelona as a visiting manager, fans taunted him by reminding him of his nickname, *'el Traductor'* – the translator. What was once a term of endearment was now laced with contempt. While many interpreters will quietly bristle at being called translators by a public not always clued up on the difference, this was not the reason that the term felt so demeaning. Barça's taunts were based on the assumption that Mourinho was under-qualified for a role as manager. A multitude of European and domestic trophies, including league titles in four different countries, has proven them wrong.

While it's not a common route into football management, it's easy to see why interpreting proved the perfect platform from which Mourinho could launch his coaching career. Linguistic nous is a huge advantage in today's global game, and the man who would christen himself the Special One has shown willingness when it comes to learning the languages of his host countries.

He has little time for any peers who don't share this dedication. Of Claudio Ranieri, he once said, 'I studied Italian five hours a day for many months to ensure I could communicate with the players, media and fans. Ranieri had been in England for five years and still struggled to say "good morning" and "good afternoon".'

Having an analytical knowledge of football has been covered above, and spending time with the best brains in the game can only improve one's understanding of the sport. After Robson left the Nou Camp, Mourinho learned much from his successor, Louis van Gaal.

And when it came to handling the pressure at the top table of one of the world's most prestigious sides? Well, it had such a negligible effect on Mourinho that he would often give his own insights to the press, extending his manager's original answer. There was also one other area of interpreting that stood him in good stead for his future gig in management. It was the perfect introduction to the ruthless nature of the beautiful game.

A Capricious Business

When former Real Betis boss Pepe Mel was appointed as West Bromwich Albion manager in January 2014, Ronan Malt received a phone call from CFL. He was studying in London, but within days he was at The Hawthorns sitting alongside the Spanish coach. The Baggies had won only seven of their 34 league games in 2013 and Mel arrived with the objective of keeping them in the Premier League. As an indicator of the expectations at the club, and an example of the tricky idioms journalists are fond of using,

Ronan remembered 'hitting the ground running' was one of the first phrases thrown at him. He went for '*empezar con el pie derecho*' (to start with the right foot).

Despite working amid the tension of a relegation battle, Ronan enjoyed his time in the Midlands. He would accompany Mel to the pre-match conferences on a Thursday before travelling with the team at the weekend. 'It was a really great experience, travelling around the country with the team. I'd go along to the games, interpreting the post-match interviews with *Match of the Day*.'

Ronan didn't set foot in the dressing room. Instead, team talks were delivered by assistant coaches Keith Downing and Dean Kiely, as Mel insisted he would only do so once his level of English was at the required level. That day never came. Despite fulfilling his brief and keeping West Brom in the league, the Spaniard left in May 2014. And so too did Ronan. 'Unfortunately, it didn't turn out to be as long as perhaps we would have liked,' Ronan said.

Job security is a rare privilege in football interpreting, such is the fickle nature of the industry in which they work. They are at the mercy of a European draw or a transfer window. Or, as in Ronan's case, a manager's success. Depending on your languages, opportunities can be scarce. Make a mistake and a second chance could be a long time coming.

In October 2019, manager Zlatko Dalić and winger Ivan Perišić were speaking to the media in Cardiff before Croatia's Euro 2020 qualifier with Wales. Six minutes in, Croatian press officer Tomislav Pacak interjected to announce that he would assume control of interpreting duties. 'If you don't mind I will translate the rest of the press conference because you are missing out pieces of information that Ivan has said,' said Pacak. The embarrassed and confused Croatian interpreter had referred to Wales manager Ryan Giggs as an active player.

It is the sort of moment that makes every interpreter's stomach churn. Danny Lane, who would regularly be seen alongside Unai Emery when the Spaniard was at Arsenal, told me that it can be difficult to recover. 'That is a big part of the nerves when you first start off. If I make a mistake, is that my relationship with this particular client over? Probably. Is my reputation in the wider sector damaged? Probably. Everybody makes mistakes on a daily basis in their work. It's just unfortunate that there's extreme scrutiny on these guys.'

Danny, who completed the same Bath University course just a year after Patrick, said the flighty nature of freelance interpreting had tempted him to reconsider his career options. With a one-year-old daughter starting nursery, he was on the hunt for a more stable role. 'I find the dependency on factors outside of my control quite difficult. The Champions League draw, the Europa League draw, who a particular club signs. As I've become more established and grown a little bit older, I'm not so comfortable with that anymore.' Just a few months after we spoke, he would join Arsenal full-time as communications manager.

After his experience with West Brom, Ronan sought a similar in-house role. He headed to the north-east to act as player liaison officer for Sunderland's Spanish-speaking contingent, with manager Gus Poyet fond of cut-price South Americans. Ronan would be there to provide 24/7 support for the likes of Santiago Vergini, Sebastián Coates, and Ricky Álvarez. Just like George Scanlan did for incoming Europeans 40 years before him, Ronan found himself opening bank accounts, negotiating rental agreements, and shopping in IKEA.

Interpreters can therefore be privy to the most personal moments in a footballer's life. Ronan once had to relay a doctor's diagnosis that a player's injury was season-ending. There were happier moments too. 'Quite an eye-opener was when a player's girlfriend was pregnant and I ended up interpreting for her antenatal classes,' he said with a timid laugh.

Traditional interpreting responsibilities remained part of his remit. He recalled the time Sunderland were thumped 8-0 at Southampton, a rout which included a spectacular volleyed own goal from centre-half Vergini. The Argentinian must have been tempted to bury himself in the sanctity of the changing room. Instead, he sought out Ronan so that he could front up. 'After the game, to his credit, he was really keen to come out and speak. That brought home how important it is really. Because Santi Vergini wouldn't have had that relationship with the Sunderland fans and the press had it not been for the interpreter. There's a satisfaction of being able to be that voice.'

Although he left the post when Dick Advocaat replaced Poyet in 2015 – proof that even full-time language roles are susceptible to football's whims – Ronan kept in touch with several of those Sunderland players. 'They were grateful to have someone there who could speak their language and help them out. You do build up that relationship.'

Boleyn Bromance

Marc Joss discovered on his first day at West Ham that his presence reassured the club's new Senegalese signing Cheikhou Kouyaté. 'I think both of us were as nervous as each other. So it was nice to help each other through it. We were both in our early 20s, and going to sit in a press room in front of journalists and cameras is a bit daunting,' said Marc, whose first job in the industry was translating Guillem Balagué's 2013 book on Lionel Messi. 'Being able to build up a rapport with players is a really nice thing. I wouldn't go so far as saying it's a bit of friendship, but you do definitely feel like you get to know them a bit.'

Marc, who speaks French, Italian, Spanish, and Portuguese, is the playful type. He giggled when he told me he runs a Nando's review website. He joked that his black curly locks made him a dead ringer for Bruno from Disney's *Encanto*. And as a long-time Arsenal fan who captions PSG press conferences, he laughed about having to write the complimentary things Mauricio Pochettino says about Spurs. But the story that gave him the most enjoyment was the time he was crowned West Ham's Hammer of the Year. Awarded in 2016 at a lavish ceremony in central London, there's even a video to prove it. Provided you conveniently crop out Frenchman Dmitri Payet stood to his left.

In front of a raucous crowd, Payet asked Marc to join him on stage to interpret his thank you speech from French into English. Marc grabbed the mic and duly obliged. 'It felt like I was West Ham's player of the year that season,' he said, beaming from ear to ear. 'It was pretty stressful as well. I was in a suit, looking as respectful as I can with this hair. It was a great moment.'

During a memorable season in which he became the first West Ham player to be named in the PFA Team of the Year since Trevor Brooking in 1978, Payet found himself in demand. At his side during every radio interview, press conference, and TV recording was his trusty interpreter. 'It was a very nice connection that we had. It got to a point where I felt like I could invite him to my wedding,' said Marc, though Payet's day job prevented him from attending. 'West Ham were playing at home on my wedding day. But as far as I'm concerned he would have come otherwise.'

Not every interaction will live up to the bromance of Marc and Dmitri. There are characters in the game who are much less endearing and aren't as grateful for the help. It will often occur with players whose nervousness with journalists spills over into their dealings with the interpreter. Most of the linguists I spoke to had experienced this but, understandably, none were keen to name the naughty parties. Except for Marc. Who must be fairly confident that Diego Costa won't read this book.

'As an Arsenal fan, I just hated watching him play because he usually scored against us. Then when I got to meet him there were a few issues. First, he was one of those who just didn't want to be there. Secondly, his actual language skills. He's native Portuguese but speaks his own brand of Spanish which has a lot of Portuguese thrown in. It was a really tricky mix. Although I speak Portuguese it's not something I am used to handling quite like that.'

To compound matters, the Chelsea striker believed he was only doing one interview. It fell to Marc to tell him there were in fact two more. 'He didn't realise. Or hadn't been told. So he was annoyed with me for telling him. That wasn't fun.'

Marriage of Convenience

The relationship between interpreters and the media can be an uneasy alliance. Journalists would prefer time alone with their subjects, without the need for a third party. Radio broadcasters in particular would rather record a player speaking in patchy English than air the articulate voice of a nameless conduit.

But there is begrudging acceptance in the press that some foreign players will not speak without their bilingual comfort blanket. Better a translated quote, than a blank page. 'At the end of the day, they're fulfilling their obligations. If that means they can speak more erudite or more confidently, then more power to them,' said Danny, who inherited his love for Spanish from parents who once lived in the Dominican Republic. 'Obviously, I have a vested interest in being there anyway, because that means I'm getting paid.'

In the case of Payet, West Ham's star would only agree to weekly media commitments if he could speak in French. Yet even when it was *France Football* or *L'Équipe* paying a visit, Marc was still asked to attend. On these occasions he wouldn't be the voice of Payet, he would be the ears of the club. 'They wanted me to be listening in just to make sure,' said Marc, of a time when his client's form had other clubs glancing through the window. 'Has he said anything about his future? Has he said he hates London? Or that he hasn't settled? They wanted to know immediately to get it under control.'

Playing the role of media muffler may not endear them to hacks on the hunt for copy. But protecting the player and the club is an unwritten part of an interpreter's job description. They develop a journalist's nose for what will make a story. Marc recalled one occasion when he knew the words coming out of his mouth would hit the back pages.

After a 3-0 victory over Andorran club FC Lusitanos in pre-season Europa League qualifiers, West Ham's post-match conference was expected to be as routine as the victory. Only visiting manager Xavi Roura had taken exception to the absence of his counterpart, Slaven Bilić. Instead, academy coach Terry Westley had taken charge. 'Bilić showed a lack of respect by not being on the bench,' Roura barked. 'It makes me sad, in a country where fair play was invented, that something like this could happen. He must have thought our team was not important for him to be present. Maybe he thought he was the Special One.'

Marc sat beside an irate Roura, knowing that it would be up to him to deliver the angry message and put smirks on the faces of a pleasantly surprised press pack. 'I was thinking, oh my God I'm about to have a fight with Slaven Bilić. And that's my job. What can I do? I have to say what this coach has said. It was a surreal moment. I knew that would become a story.' With Marc helping to get the message across, the press had their story. And Roura got his way for the second leg in Andorra. Bilić took his place in the dugout.

Marc was again joking when he said he feared the wrath of the imposing West Ham manager. Interpreters are not responsible for the words of their clients. But they are answerable should a story emerge from something the speaker didn't actually say. Errors can range in their severity. They can cause confusion, like during Maurizio Sarri's opening press conference when his statement that he wanted to add a 'pinch of quality in central midfield' was actually interpreted as 'central defence'. A minor miscommunication perhaps, but one that was likely to cause an uncomfortable few hours in the households of David Luiz and Gary Cahill. A correction was swiftly sent to the press.

At other times, misinterpretations can create unintended animosity. When Bayern manager Jupp Heynckes was said to have called Chelsea striker Didier Drogba an 'outstanding actor' ahead of the 2012 Champions League Final, it was attributed as a jibe about the Ivorian's ability to win free kicks. Bayern set about correcting the record, insisting that the word Heynckes used, *Schauspieler*, should instead have been translated as 'performer'. It was too late, and Drogba was already fielding questions about his diving. The striker refused to be baited, but the taunts were fresh in his mind when he equalised with two minutes of the final remaining, before slotting home the winning penalty.

On rare occasions a mistranslation can have serious ramifications. Like when Spanish-speaking Rangers striker Alfredo Morelos was interviewed by Sky Sports News in February 2020. 'It was very frustrating to hear the crowd screaming at me. They were saying offensive and racist words,' read the original English subtitles, after Morelos was asked about his celebration in the Old Firm match against Celtic. It was a major mistranslation, and at no point in the interview had Morelos accused Celtic fans of racism. It led to an embarrassing correction from Sky, who admitted to inaccuracies, uploaded a corrected version, and released a statement apologising to Celtic. The Hoops, meanwhile, reported Sky to media regulator Ofcom and banned their reporters. 'The use of mistranslation to convey false meaning is a dangerous form of fake news which must be condemned and sanctioned,' fumed Celtic chief executive Peter Lawwell.

Sky didn't disclose the identity of the hapless translator, but it is unlikely that a professional would have made such an error. Formal training stresses the importance of taking the utmost care in their choice of words, particularly on sensitive topics. Marc has a favourite phrase that neatly sums up his approach to avoiding unwanted attention,

'If in doubt, vague it out.' This technique is especially useful if the player has used an unusual turn of phrase or is prone to a mumble. 'If you can't get the exact thing just try to keep it safe and steer away from controversy,' said Marc. 'Our job is not to create any extra stories beyond the content itself.'

But in the madcap frenzy of a transfer window, with agents scurrying like hamsters on a wheel, even the most conscientious of linguists can be drawn into a famous Premier League trope. The scenario will be familiar to many, and it begins with a foreign footballer speaking to his native press. By the time the story is given an English lick of paint, the picture is of a player desperate for a move. The club is annoyed, a sheepish footballer pleads innocence, and the whole affair is shuffled away as a mistranslation.

From Nicolas Anelka to Romelu Lukaku, with an Alexis Sánchez and a Luis Suárez in between, the 'lost in translation' excuse is now the go-to tactic to diffuse the grumbles of a restless star. Knowing just how many of those players end up in new club colours within a year of their 'misunderstanding', fans are rarely impressed by the charade. It will prompt some to repeat a common complaint. They will argue that if a player or manager intends to work in England, then they should speak English. After all, how difficult can it be?

Old Dogs, New Languages
When Fabio Capello became England manager in 2007, Peter was asked to provide the Italian with his first English

lessons. 'I taught him for two years. He did rely on an interpreter but his English was good enough to cope with everyday stuff.' Capello was not the only former England manager that Peter dealt with. In May 2010 he was back in Germany to accompany Steve McClaren, who had just been appointed manager of Wolfsburg. 'I spent the first six weeks with him as his personal interpreter. I was with him all the time. Even in the evenings we would sit and watch World Cup games together. A lovely guy. Just a really nice, unpretentious bloke. It just didn't work out.'

While Capello displayed a much better grasp of English after four years on the job, McClaren was dismissed after just nine months, giving him barely enough time to learn to count to *zehn*. I asked Peter if having an interpreter at their beck and call meant managers were less inclined to learn the language. 'It totally varies. Learning German was not Steve McClaren's thing. To learn a language you need to dedicate time to it every day. For someone at that level, I would say two hours a day. They do not have two minutes a day. In all fairness to him, what he would have had to learn before the start of the season is just absolutely impossible.'

If a lack of capacity is an acceptable excuse for a manager to use when struggling with the lingo, it's not one that footballers can reasonably resort to. Peter had plenty of fun in the classroom with Chelsea's foreign legion, turning up at the club's Cobham training ground three times a week. 'More than half the team were my students. In a very pleasant, matey way, I had this kind of control over them so that they did do their homework and they did attend their lessons. Especially the Brazilians. They're very good at trying to sneak away,' said Peter, the memory prompting a chuckle. 'Oscar, he's a little stinker.'

But not all of the footballers were unwilling schoolboys. Peter gave a glowing review of the Spanish contingent that included César Azpilicueta and Oriol Romeu. And a star pupil that Peter proudly stated was the antithesis of how footballers are often portrayed. 'They can [learn a language] if they set their mind to it. Juan Mata is a perfect example. He wanted to learn English, he learned English. Look at his English now. I taught him for three years. We became really good friends.'

Interpreting is very often a solitary job, sat alone in booths or positioned out of shot at the far end of a table. As someone who once dreamed of becoming a pro player, Peter thrived on the moments when he could feel part of a team. And all the japery that comes along with it. 'I've gone into a dressing room of one of the major clubs in Britain, for my student to come out splinter naked and say, "I've been waiting a long time, darling." Then grab me by the balls.'

Peter also couldn't wait to tell me the story of the coach who had difficulty with personal pronouns. 'Everything was "your". Your computer, your mobile phone. The words "my", "his", "her", "our" didn't exist.' One lesson dealt with phrases to use around the house, asking the student what activity he would typically do in each room. When Peter asked about the bedroom, he was buckled in laughter at the response. 'He said, "I sleep with *your* wife." No you don't!'

Learning a new language is never a quick process, but the British press isn't renowned for its patience. Players requiring an interpreter after several years in the country can find it counts against them when times get tough. Carlos Tevez's acrimonious final years in England saw his struggles with the language mentioned in several outlets as an example of his supposed poor attitude. It was deemed that a player who had lived in the country for five years should be able to conduct at least a basic English interview.

Given their frequent media commitments, managers are judged to an even higher standard. Ronan remembers Pepe Mel feeling obliged to try his hand at the lingo even just a few weeks into the job. 'Despite the fact that I was there, he did sometimes try to answer in English where he could. He was quite conscious that if he just answered in Spanish all of the time it would look like he wasn't making an effort.'

Argentinian Mauricio Pochettino experienced the same pressure after he was named Southampton manager in 2013. He was resolute in his use of an interpreter at press conferences. At the time he explained why: 'I have an interpreter because he gives me the security that, when I have to answer complex questions, and with my complex answers, it's much better I have an interpreter to make sure nothing is misconstrued.' Leading the Saints to eighth, the club's highest league position in a decade, showed that there were few problems with getting his message across.

After 17 successful months at St Mary's he was linked to the vacant position at Tottenham. The *Daily Mail* ran a story with the headline 'Pochettino must speak English in public if he wants Tottenham job'. No source was cited nor any direct quotes used, and it could well have been read as an ultimatum from Fleet Street itself. They got their wish. On the day Pochettino was unveiled in north London *The Telegraph* wrote, 'After a year and a half of hiding behind a translator at Southampton, the Argentine vowed to address Spurs fans in their native tongue.'

Journalists often have a sneaking suspicion that their interviewee has a better command of the Queen's English than they choose to let on. It may be an unkind stretch to label this as 'hiding', but cynics may conclude that having an interpreter can be a useful barrier to probing questions. When I put that viewpoint to Peter, he confirmed that it does in fact occur. 'These guys, they are very shrewd, clever, intelligent people,' he said, citing Capello, Thomas Tuchel, and one particular language student who became a close personal friend, Carlo Ancelotti. 'They will use what others perceive as their lack of language in their interest. Their aim when they come to the country is to go to a club and win games and trophies. Everything else is irrelevant.'

Having seen some of his favourite Serie A managers opt against using interpreters in the long term, Patrick believes more foreign coaches would enjoy a better reputation in Britain if they were to follow Pochettino's example. 'I thought it was a very courageous choice from Pochettino. From a selfish perspective, I wish more coaches did it. I honestly think Sarri in particular would have been lauded at Chelsea if he'd had a good interpreter. In Italy he's a coaching icon. He's a brilliant mind. In England, everyone says he plays boring football, that he comes across as grumpy, that he looks scruffy. You start to judge him based on other things.'

If Sarri ever gets another chance in England, he might well be tempted to have some help by his side. It was the conclusion that his fellow Italian Giovanni Trapattoni eventually came to. When he was appointed manager of the Republic of Ireland in 2008 – Trapattoni's first English-speaking role in a career spanning three decades – he would be joined at the hip by interpreter Manuela Spinelli. They swiftly became one of the most recognisable double acts in the country, even appearing together on RTÉ's long-running *The Late Late Show*.

When Trapattoni called it a day in 2013, his time as Ireland boss amounted to the second-longest stint of his distinguished career, behind only the decade spent at Juventus. That he was able to hang around for so long was in no small part down to Spinelli, whose sense of humour and quick thinking made her popular with the press and a household name in her own right.

It is a rare and cherished moment when an interpreter is afforded the same level of attention as their subjects. 'I've never asked any footballer or manager for a selfie. Why would you when you can find a photo where you're both doing your job?' said Patrick, competing with the background horns of impatient Neapolitan drivers. 'I love that. It's a great leveller. These people are icons. But for that very brief period of time, you are their equal. They rely on you as much as you rely on them.'

In Ireland, Trapattoni came across as articulate and thoughtful, demonstrating humour that prompted people to laugh with him, not at him. Unlike his experience in Germany, it allowed him to speak freely in his native tongue, knowing every word would be faithfully relayed by a skilled interpreter that he trusted implicitly. It helped that the Italian favoured consecutive interpreting. It is not clunky, like Bielsa and his reluctant coaches. Nor distanced and impersonal, with linguists hidden in broom cupboards. It is more human, just like George Scanlan would have done it. And so too, the interpreting innovator who succeeded him. 'It's the most personal way, it's the way I prefer. When you're old school that's what you love,' said Peter, preparing to watch his fifth live game of the day. 'And when you really do a good job, it's nice to be in the limelight.'

Dedicated to Peter Clark

Several months after our conversation, Peter Clark passed away following a short illness, aged 61. He was buried in Sidmouth, Devon. I would like to thank Peter's wife Mariella for contacting me with the sad news and, in her role as co-owner and director, I wish her the best of luck continuing Clark Football Languages in Peter's good name. It remains very much open for business. Mariella wanted to express her gratitude to the loyal and tireless staff who continue to help and support her, in particular country manager Marco Pupeschi, media manager Paul Wheeler, and Peter and Mariella's devoted daughter Emma.

Peter's legacy lives on not only through the continuation of his enterprise but also via the work of the many dedicated and passionate interpreters like those featured in this chapter. Patrick, Ronan, Danny, and Marc all worked with CFL in their formative years, and some continue to do so. All speak glowingly of Peter's influence on their careers. His absence will be greatly felt in a thriving industry that owes so much to his vision.

I hope this chapter, written before his death, gives Peter and his family a lasting flicker of the limelight that he spoke of and deserved.

8

GOD SQUAD: Sports Chaplains

For many fans, following sport is an almost religious experience, akin to attending weekly mass and keeping the faith when all seems lost. But behind the scenes, the metaphor can blend into reality. When the athletes are in need of spiritual guidance in order to perform, they look to a devoted band of voluntary sages.

Shepherd of The Valley

'Lord, will You fill me afresh with Your Holy Spirit, and open my eyes to see what you are doing, so I may join in with it.' Matt Baker was reciting the prayer that he says before every visit to Charlton Athletic Football Club. It's inspired by John 5:17, when Jesus states that God is always at work. And it's served Matt for over two decades since being appointed the club's chaplain in 2000. 'If that's good enough for Jesus, that's good enough for me,' he said, having pre-warned me that he was about to get spiritual.

'When you go into a sports environment, there are all sorts of agendas flying around. But if I pray that prayer,

I don't want to come in with my agenda.' Bald-headed, bespectacled, and wearing a red polo shirt that wouldn't distinguish him from your average Addicks fan, Matt said that his task at the club is to immerse himself in other people's problems. 'That could mean I have a conversation with someone who's injured and needs to talk that day. Or a conversation with the kit man who's struggling to get all this kit cleaned in time for the next game and he's feeling the stress of it. Or the groundsman who's worried about this tractor that's broken down. Or the manager who's thinking, "When am I going to be able to sign a few more players?" I come away from there thinking I've done what God wanted me to do today.'

In 2007 Charlton were relegated from the Premier League, ending a seven-season stay in the top flight. Hopes of an instant return were dashed when just two years later they were relegated again, falling into the third tier. It was a turbulent period at the club and a precarious time for anyone associated with it. And it's in troubling times like these that the calming presence of a chaplain is sought.

Matt spoke to some of those who lost their jobs during that time. Some were angry; others were confused. Many worried about what their future would hold. In each case, Matt felt that he was able to offer a cathartic outlet for their concerns. 'In one sense, I really appreciated being involved and being able to offer that support. And in the other, I felt this is really tough. Because these are people's livelihoods. And that's the sort of thing that the fans don't see. They think, "Oh well, at least we'll win more games", or, "Don't worry, we'll bounce back up again." But when you're a chaplain, I think the highs are higher, and the lows are lower.'

Matt, who was also the pastor at the Charlton and Blackheath Christian Fellowship church at the time, was never in danger of being among those to lose their job at the club. Most chaplain roles, of all denominations, are unpaid and facilitated by Christian charity Sports Chaplaincy UK. When he got the phone call offering him the post 22 years ago he was told that, as a long-time season ticket holder at The Valley, he was perfect for the role.

But his response wasn't immediate. He consulted his wife, whose only caveat was that he wouldn't attend away games, and then took some time to think and pray. 'It was important that I examined my motives when I was offered it. That I was doing it for the right reasons.' Matt is now a national director at SCUK, and knows that potential chaplains have turned down similar offers because they have felt their fanaticism prevented them from being non-partisan. 'We're not there for freebies. That's really important.'

As for what they *are* about, SCUK's induction training outlines five values. Presence, excellence, relationship, confidentiality, and humility give a flavour of what's expected, but there's a phrase commonly shared in the community that gives a better insight into their methods. 'We talk about being pastorally proactive and spiritually reactive,' said Matt, before explaining what that means with a comparison to American football. This is not the tub-thumping, chest-beating, larynx-throttling chaplaincy of the NFL. Over the Atlantic, evangelical pastors will bless the ball, slap helmets, and kiss crucifixes at the centre of a heaving 50-man huddle. 'That's not how we do our chaplaincy here, for all sorts of reasons,' said Matt, grinning at the thought.

A British sports chaplain's place of work is not the field of play, nor even the changing room. Their toil is done quietly and sensitively over lunch in the canteen, perched by a massage table in the physio room, or chewing the fat in the ticket office. It means going in several times a week, knocking on doors, generating relationships, and creating trust. 'Then when an issue ever comes up, they will know where to come to and who to talk to. And so that's the pastoral care of everybody. Whether or not they've got a faith is irrelevant,' said Matt, stressing that sports chaplaincy is a service offered to those of all faiths or none.

In secular Britain, the majority of sportspeople fall into the latter category. And so it might be a surprise to learn that the number of sports chaplains is actually rising. 'I am a Christian. I'm a chaplain, I'm ordained. That's my identity. I'm not going to force that on anybody,' said Matt, which explained his earlier self-conscious disclaimer before sharing his prayer. 'Whether somebody is a Christian or not, I will always offer to pray for them. Most people, generally speaking, will respond positively to that. That's spiritually reactive.'

Matt is deemed so integral to Charlton's backroom that he was among the priority staff included in English football's Project Restart in June 2020. Before that, like many of us during the pandemic, he resorted to working via video calls. In a time of fear and uncertainty, he found himself the busiest he had ever been.

Chaplains across the country were similarly inundated. Unlike redundancies, which tend to disproportionately affect non-playing staff, Matt found that Covid-19 touched everyone equally. 'Covid was a leveller. That three-month period where there was no sport brought us all down to the same level. I had the privilege to have Zoom calls with some of the players at the time, just helping them in that realisation that we're all the same. It was good for everybody to have that kind of change of focus.'

Conversations are held in the strictest confidence, but one Charlton player who was happy to go on the record about Matt's calming influence during lockdown was midfielder George Lapslie. With his wife in the latter stages of pregnancy, the then 22-year-old had reservations about returning to football while this new disease continued to spread. That it was Matt who was able to reassure Lapslie sufficiently for him to resume first-team training is an indication as to why the club wanted their chaplain back from day one. It is also a sign of the esteem in which Matt is held by the players.

'I have no say on whether they play on a Saturday. We come at a different level to just about everybody else because we're independent,' said Matt. Although he is a fan, he treats the first team no differently than anyone else on the club payroll. In doing so, he finds their issues – family bereavement, illness, divorce – are also no different to those of the rest of us.

'This is where chaplaincy works because we're trusted,' he said, stressing that players will not always be comfortable bringing up personal issues with their manager, or even close team-mates. 'In a highly competitive environment, finding people that you can trust is really difficult. You can't always trust your team-mates. Because if you're a centre-half at a club and another centre-half arrives, they're after your position. You don't completely trust them. So if you find a chaplain you can talk to about anything, it's gold dust.'

Woodbine Willie

When it comes to chaplains in non-religious settings, it's the armed forces that most of us traditionally associate them with. From *M*A*S*H*'s hardy Father Mulcahy to *Catch-22*'s honourable Chaplain Tappman, they have often been portrayed in popular culture as courageous and trustworthy figures amid perilous environments.

History suggests their characteristics have not been exaggerated. Clerics who donned military fatigues and provided emotional support to weary personnel were among the many unsung heroes of the First World War. If the men can't go to church then the church must go to the men. Chaplains headed into war zones armed not with guns, but with a Bible. And, in the case of the Rev. Geoffrey Studdert Kennedy, cigarettes. Lots of them.

Nicknamed 'Woodbine Willie', Kennedy was known for his inspirational talks and bravery under fire. At the 1917 Battle of Messines, he was awarded a Military Cross for his gallantry. But his chief renown among the trenches was as a human ciggy dispenser, handing out prized smokes to eternally grateful troops more accustomed to cheap rolling tobacco. After three years on the Western Front, Kennedy would return home penniless after spending his salary on pricey pre-rolled Woodbines, sweetening the dying breath of his mortally wounded comrades. Historian Dr Linda Parker estimated that he handed out over 800,000 at his own expense in a bid to maintain morale.

By the Second World War, chaplains were even throwing themselves out of planes. Reverend Roy Ernest Price became the first to jump with the parachute regiment when he joined the 1st Battalion over Morocco in 1942. Such was a chaplain's increasing recognition at this time that the British Army introduced 'Padre's Hour', an obligatory weekly sermon followed by Q&A with the troops.

But while generals and majors were convinced of the value of having a holy presence among their squadron, it would take 20 years before sport would follow suit. This is despite football and religion going way back. Southampton (St Mary's), Everton (St Domingo's), Aston Villa (Villa Cross Wesleyan Chapel), Manchester City (St Mark's), and Celtic (another St Mary's) are some of the biggest teams in Britain who owe their formation to local churches.

Since then, the likening of football to religion has become so commonplace as to become cliché. The crowds are the faithful who worship players that entertain them on the sacred turf. The best of them are even labelled a god. But some practices, like singing the hymn 'Abide with Me' at every FA Cup Final since 1927, blur those metaphorical lines. Even zoologist Desmond Morris connected the two in *The Soccer Tribe*, his 1981 anthropological field study of the sport. He described a soccer match as a 'quasi-religious service'.

And so it makes sense that football was the birthplace of sports chaplaincy in the UK. The Rev. John Jackson was one of the first, appointed at Don Revie's Leeds United in 1962. As Revie turned the fortunes of the club around by prioritising Yorkshire's youth, Jackson's weekly visits were especially helpful to the next generation of Elland Road stars. But his spiritual guidance made the biggest impression on one of its established names.

Jack Charlton was so taken by Jackson's influence, that when he called time on his playing career to manage Middlesbrough in 1973, one of his first tasks was to source a club chaplain. Bill Hall, an Anglican clergyman from Durham, would remain at Boro for more than two decades.

Big Jack remained a staunch adherent to chaplaincy throughout his managerial career. He welcomed a resident clergyman at both Sheffield Wednesday and Newcastle, while his 1990 Republic of Ireland World Cup squad were even treated to a papal audience, arranged by the Rev. Monsignor Liam Boyle.

Graham Taylor was another important advocate in football chaplaincy's nascent days. Watford were a fourth-tier club when they appointed Taylor in 1977, with the new manager intending on forging lasting ties with the local community. Before long, Baptist minister John Boyers joined the Hornets' ranks, visiting twice a week during the club's remarkable five-year ascent to the First Division.

In *Footballing Lives*, published in 2006 by a collective of football chaplains, Boyers documented his first impressions at the aptly named Vicarage Road. 'Working where people worked was important. I met them on their ground,' he wrote. 'With the players, I was accepted in the changing room, joined in the 12-minute run, the weight room sessions, the circuit training, the cross-country, even five-a-side football at times. I was part of their world, and so with the office staff.'

So convinced was Boyers of the embedded model of chaplaincy that he began visiting other clubs to spread the word. In 1991 he founded Sports Chaplaincy UK (known at the time as SCORE), and a year later he was poached by Alex Ferguson's Manchester United. Although sad to leave Watford, the most successful club of the era was too big a pulpit to turn down. At Old Trafford, Boyers no longer needed to reach out to other clubs. They came to him.

He even outlasted Sir Alex, retiring five years after Ferguson called it a day. The Scottish managerial titan features in SCUK's promotional materials but it's not a stretch to compare Ferguson's impact on football with Boyers's own influence in sports chaplaincy.

It was his encouraging voice at the other end of the phone telling Matt he was the ideal pick for Charlton, just as he had encouraged the many other chaplains now with clubs all over the UK. Although he is now also retired from his responsibilities at SCUK, Boyers's trailblazing work means there are over 600 chaplains across British sports today. Football may have been a natural environment for sports chaplaincy to break ground, but its work has spread far and wide since.

A Welcome Outsider

Horse racing was engulfed in a damaging scandal when I spoke to Simon Bailey about his role as the sport's national chaplain. It was April 2021, and Grand National, Gold Cup, and Royal Ascot-winning trainer Gordon Elliott had just been banned from racing for 12 months, six months suspended. A picture of him sitting astride a dead horse, mobile phone in hand, had gone viral on social media.

Just weeks before he was due to send dozens of favourites to the Cheltenham Festival, the Irishman's name was manure and his reputation in the trough. Owners removed top horses from his yard, Betfair dropped him as an ambassador, and he became a target for outraged animal rights activists.

Simon, who has been based in Newmarket since taking up the post in 2014, was never going to talk specifically about whether he had personally contacted Elliott. That bond of confidence is a core tenet of a chaplain's responsibility and one that is never to be broken bar for safeguarding concerns.

Simon had even been nominated for a prestigious Godolphin Stud and Stable Staff Award but was unable to progress because the selection process required nominees to describe who they have worked with and what they have done. 'That's where the phone interview stopped. Because that's when the trust is lost, and your job becomes null and void,' said Simon, insisting that others who had been in racing all their lives were more deserving in any case.

Simon's role involves helping those facing up to the daunting spectre of a social media lynching. While Elliott's misdemeanours understandably attracted opprobrium from inside and outside the sport, many in horse racing have found themselves becoming a digital dartboard for much less. 'Horse racing is under scrutiny a lot. A horse that somebody has backed that then hasn't won, there's been a lot of attacks on jockeys.' As a man of the cloth, Simon didn't fancy reciting this abuse verbatim. Instead, he gave me a U-rating flavour of the tone. 'You didn't give that horse a great ride, you're a cheat, you've thrown the race.' He has seen a rise in the number of phoney social media accounts being used to vilify those in horse racing and felt it was too easy now to send abuse anonymously. 'That can go as far as death threats as well. Which you just shake your head at.'

As national chaplain, Simon offers support to everyone involved in racing, from jockeys and trainers to yard staff and even racegoers. He had previously been chaplain to Arbroath Football Club, but as a former cricketer (his brother is former Northamptonshire and England player Rob Bailey), Simon has since realised he works better outside of team sports. 'As somebody who's played a lot of sport I probably wouldn't be great as a team chaplain because I'd get too involved in the fan thing,' he said, sitting in front of a bookshelf crammed with religious texts and the yellow spines of *Wisden Almanacks*. 'In horse racing, there aren't any teams to cheer on. I didn't know it at the time, but I think it's probably good that I'm just there for the staff that work in the industry.'

Even without a previous racing background, it's important that Simon keeps up to speed with the form and fortunes of each yard. 'If I visit a yard I need to know how their week's gone. A horse that dies affects the staff.' He visits racing towns, yards, and farms all over the UK, and has seen first-hand what the pressures can do to people of all ages and experiences. With a lilting Potteries accent and a daytime TV warmth, Simon values face-to-face catch-ups over any digital alternative. As a qualified mental health first-aid instructor, he is a master at spotting drooped shoulders and shifting eyes even when someone is insisting they are fine. One of his tasks is to educate people on how to spot if something is off with a colleague. 'We're just trying to get the word around to those that work on yards, studs, and racecourses that it's their job as well to look out for their friends. To know what to look out for.'

He visits the British Racing School once a week, where he gets to know the next generation of jockeys. More importantly, they get to know him. For in a relentless sport where even its best proponents will lose many more races than they win, jockeys are especially vulnerable. A 2019 Racing Welfare survey found that 87 per cent of jockeys had experienced stress, anxiety, or depression in the previous 12 months. Like many young sportspeople, jockeys can struggle when the reality of professional sport doesn't align with their long-held daydreams.

It can be even worse for those no longer in the saddle. A 2020 joint Oxford University and British Horseracing

Authority study found that former jockeys are more than two and a half times more likely to suffer from anxiety or depression compared to the general population. 'The suicide rate in the sport is quite big,' said Simon, who has witnessed the trauma that follows. 'There's been those calls along the years, which is always a sad thing. The lads that take their own lives always hit home.'

With 55 per cent of jockeys admitting in the Racing Welfare survey that they felt compelled to appear 'strong' in front of their peers, opening up to colleagues can be tough. Which is when Simon comes in. 'With it being an elite sport, it's still seen as a sign that you're weak if you come out with something that you don't want to be heard. So they don't want to tell their boss. They maybe don't even tell their best mate. And so I'm here as that private and confidential first port of call that means they can get things off their chest.'

For those with drugs, alcohol, or – given its elemental role in horse racing – gambling issues, Simon can then recommend dedicated services to help them deal with their addictions. Crucially, he and his fellow chaplains aren't simply good listeners. Because their faith is the reason they do what they do, they have no ulterior motive. Nor are they there to judge. It makes them a rarity not only in sport, but in an increasingly quarrelsome society.

Somewhat unexpectedly, it was Simon who returned to the subject of Gordon Elliott. He was well aware of the damage it had inflicted on the sport's reputation but argued for calm. 'Going back to that case on social media a few weeks ago. I think sometimes when we get angry, it's best not to do anything. Not to print anything, not to write anything, not to say anything. And two or three days down the line, you can put that into perspective.'

Simon then shared a quote that he attributed to an 18th-century nun. 'She said, "There is more to a man than the worst thing he has ever done." And it always stands me in good stead. Because whatever you've told me you've done, that isn't who you are.' He mentioned that he was yet to be shocked by anything confided in him, and it occurred to me that this element of chaplaincy resembles a portable confessional. Repent your sins, unleash your worries, air your frailties, and then leave infused with belief and renewal.

'You're not going to judge them. It's about being around somebody that gives you the ability to move on. To give you the strength, to give you the hope. That this might feel as bad as it's ever going to be. But this isn't who you are. There's a chance for us all to move on and to become the best we can be.'

Olympic Sages

Mary Vickers describes her chaplaincy style as 'loitering with intent'. And she has enjoyed over three decades honing it. Humberside Police, Grimsby's fish factories, and even high-street shoppers in Worcester have all benefitted from Mary's willingness to chat about anything, anywhere. 'Chaplaincy in all its manifestations, whichever context you're in, is about being with the people where people are,' she told me. 'I just find that energising. I've got a curious mind. Some people call it nosiness, but I've got an inquisitive spirit.' A wooden cross hung on the wall above her filing cabinet. The small golden one around her neck bobbed jauntily as she spoke.

Mary's husband Peter was a military chaplain for 20 years. She didn't say if he kept packets of Woodbines handy, but they both hail from the suitably named Healing in Lincolnshire. She told me that her experience in the army community opened her eyes to the possibilities of chaplaincy. 'In the forces, you can end up telling someone your life history within the first 24 hours of meeting them. Whereas, as a vicar in a local church, it might take me six months to find things out about people in my congregation. If not two years.'

Chaplains in industry, healthcare, business, or indeed sport, possess a heroic dedication to small talk. Think hairdresser chatter, taxi driver banter, and school-gates pleasantries all rolled into one, and you're still unlikely to get to the level required.

But at the testosterone-fuelled fish factories of Grimsby, where the predominantly male workforce arrived when it was dark and left when it was darker, talking about the weather was no use. So Mary earned their trust by talking about sport.

'They don't know that it's raining or sunny outside. And they want to talk to you about Grimsby Town. You have all those conversations about that, and then all of a sudden they'll say, "Why did my granny suffer before she died?" or, "My dad's just been put on a no-resuscitation order, how do I cope with that?" or, "I'm in huge debt. What can I do?"'

One worker once confided in Mary about his addiction – to sex. It was not the sort of conversation I was expecting to have with this kindly lady in a heather-coloured cardigan. My eyes darted to the ground as she continued the tale. 'I did think it was a joke when he first started telling me. But it wasn't, and it was causing debt because he was having to buy all these videos to watch. So you never know as a chaplain what you're going to come across until it happens. And so it really keeps you on your toes. But I love that.'

As a former track runner, Mary was destined to combine her gift for chaplaincy with her love for sport. In 2005 she became SCUK's first chaplaincy coordinator for women in sport. Since then she has helped to facilitate chaplains into women's football academies, was herself in the role at Charlton Athletic's women's team, and set up a chaplaincy service at Royal Ascot racecourse.

Just as impressive is her work at pop-up sporting events. Her travels include the World Athletics Championships in Berlin, the Winter Paralympics in Vancouver, the Invictus Games in Toronto, and the Olympic Games in Athens. This intrepid itinerary is made all the more remarkable given that she wasn't paid a penny for any of it. 'I was tempted with Rio. But I looked at the fares and thought I can't do that,' she said.

Events chaplaincy requires a completely different approach to being embedded in a club or a sport. An Olympic Games lasts less than three weeks. There is no time to introduce yourself to every athlete, coach, or staff member. They come not because they know you, but because you have 'Games Chaplain' printed on your shirt. Trust must be earned in minutes rather than months. And yet for many, this is not only enough, but also preferable.

'There's a whole load of people who only want to talk about a problem to somebody who's never going to see them again. Because they'll be embarrassed if they see them again,' said Mary, comparing it to the Samaritans. 'It's not just because they're always at the end of the phone. It's because they can ask that silly question. Or they can be honest about how they feel. There are some people who like anonymity.'

In 2012, around 160 chaplains were on the ground at the various Olympics and Paralympics venues in London. Headquartered at a multi-faith centre in the athletes' village, they worked in shifts to ensure there was always someone to talk to between 7am and 10pm. Matt and Mary were among them. As too was Angy King.

Today, Angy is a regular presence with both Wales's and Reading's women's football teams and has succeeded Mary as SCUK's women's coordinator. Wearing a grey sports hoody and with her hair tied back in a ponytail, she looked every bit the PE teacher she once was. As a layperson, the London Games provided one of her very first experiences of chaplaincy. 'People would actually stop you and say, "Can I chat to you about this?" Which I was very surprised about. I'd never done anything like that before,' Angy said.

Angy remembered some athletes coming to the centre to pray before, and after, their events. 'Some of them were concerned about going back to their home countries if they hadn't done very well,' she said, alluding to the ruthless funding structures of many Olympic sports. When I asked if she had any prayers or Bible passages that she would typically offer to an Olympian down on their luck, Angy stressed that she would only do so if it was requested by the athlete. Pastorally proactive, spiritually reactive. Then she recommended that I get my hands on *Call Up*, a competitors' prayer book produced by Sports Chaplaincy South Africa.

In it, there are around two dozen prayers for specific scenarios. There are prayers to read following victory, before training, when suffering an injury, or when dealing with criticism. The prayer designated for defeat includes the lines, 'In this moment of disappointment, I choose to remember that this pain will soon fade. I choose to recall that I am not defined by defeat or mistakes but by your grace and mercy.' Sport has a habit of defining its competitors purely by the medals they win, or the matches they lose. And sports chaplains appear to be among the few within the industry to remind athletes that there is more to them than that.

It is a vital reminder that is not only offered in the aftermath of defeat. Mary remembered a story her husband shared with her when they were both in Athens in 2004: 'There was an athlete from one team who spent some time talking to my husband because he'd got a gold medal. Yeah, he'd won. But the last 15 years of his life was aiming at this. And now there was the big question of who is he now?'

These shared moments can be as profound as they are fleeting. During the first week in Athens, a Trinidad and

Tobago team member came to Mary to talk about her grandmother's recent death. 'This dear lady didn't know whether to go back or not. So I spent a lot of time with her.' Mary offered to do a memorial service to which the granddaughter and several of her team members could attend. With a six-hour time difference between Greece and Trinidad, Mary timed it to coincide with the grandmother's funeral back home. She hasn't seen this lady since, but she often thinks back to that moment.

'It has to be a different kind of person that can make relationships like that. And cope with dropping them again. Because sometimes it's really hard. I can still remember that lass from Trinidad and Tobago. Part of me says she's probably forgotten me. But there's another part of me that remembers that famous quote,' she said, referring to Maya Angelou. It seems chaplains are adept at remembering meaningful quotes and using them in their day-to-day. Me, not so much. But I was too embarrassed to admit that I didn't know the quote she meant. So after my conversation with Mary, I looked it up. 'People will forget what you said, people will forget what you did, but people will never forget how you made them feel.'

Naysayers and Unbelievers

Not everyone is convinced about the value a chaplain can bring to a sporting unit. Of the 92 professional clubs in England's top four divisions, around 20 have still to sign up for the free service. The Elite Player Performance Plan (EPPP) that outlines the roles that each club academy is obliged to employ – including sports scientists, match analysts, and teaching staff – does not feature chaplains.

'The fact that we've got 70-odd clubs that have got chaplains and some of those, like my own, have got more than one shows that they get how important the role is,' said Matt. 'But some clubs have firmly closed the door. They say they're not interested,' he added, shrugging his shoulders.

Matt admitted that it would make his job easier if he knew the reasons why some opted against the help of SCUK. But often he is stumped. 'Sometimes I've got a manager who's keen to have a chaplain because he's been a player and appreciates the role. But the chief exec or the chairman is totally against it for whatever reasons. They may be religious reasons, I'm not always a party to that.'

Certain clubs' reluctance may be down to some unhelpful misconceptions. One player-turned-manager at a League One club once told Matt that he thought chaplains only delivered chocolates at Christmas. Other views can be more damaging. The dubious work of infamous faith healer Eileen Drewery, controversially employed by England manager Glenn Hoddle in the late 1990s, is unlikely to have done much for the reputation of religion in football. 'Around 12 or 13 years ago there was a football manager who wouldn't have a chaplain because he thought it was a sign of weakness,' said Mary, echoing Simon's experience in horse racing.

Even as footballers like England trio Marcus Rashford, Raheem Sterling, and Bukayo Saka openly talk about their faith in a way that suggests it is no longer uncool to do so, chaplains insist that their role does not involve evangelising in any form. But that may not always be enough to avoid the cynical Bible-basher tag.

'The vast majority of people I work with don't have any faith at all,' said Angy, whose first few months at Reading were tough. Even chaplains who are welcomed by managers will not always find the same sentiment throughout the club. 'At the beginning, people are a little bit suspicious. I started seven years ago, and I have to say, in the first six months they really kept me at arm's length,' said Angy, who later discovered that she was originally referred to as 'the church lady'. 'I think they were just a bit wary and maybe thinking, "Gosh she's going to want a conversation about God, and I don't want to talk about God." Then they realised, actually, I'm there just for them as people.'

In a bid to ingratiate themselves, chaplains will often muck in wherever they can help. Just as Ernest Price threw himself from a plane and John Boyers joined in with the cross-country run, today's chaplains find themselves setting up obstacle courses, collecting overhit footballs, or chauffeuring players to hospital scans. It's a far cry from their usual responsibility as church or community leaders. 'A lot of ministers are very used to being the frontperson. You're the person that people look to, you're preaching on a Sunday, you're the one that's bringing direction, vision, and decisions. If that's what you're expecting in chaplaincy, it ain't for you,' warned Matt.

Instead, sports chaplains will often find themselves pushed to the perimeter, sometimes even forgotten about entirely. It's why SCUK training involves a module that covers exactly those scenarios. 'We give everybody a lemon. And we say, "Smell this, feel this, what does it feel like? Right, get used to that." It's a bit cheesy, but it works,' said Matt, smiling. 'Because you're going to feel a lemon a lot of the time. Because it's not your environment. They're not coming into your church and sitting in one of your pews. You're wandering around the dirty boot room. You're hanging around a physio room, where they're all in the kit and getting massages, and you're there feeling like a fish out of water. I'm mixing my metaphors now.' When they hear Matt say this, many chaplains are relieved to discover it wasn't just them at the end of the citric treatment.

But perhaps the most frustrating myth of all, that lingers like burning incense, is that a chaplain is only called upon during times of strife. Admittedly, it's a stigma that this chapter has done little to combat so far. Redundancies, addictions, deaths. It's not a list that screams hoot at parties. Simon recalled occasions where he's been as welcome as the grim reaper. 'I'll turn up at the hospital ward with a bag of grapes and they panic and say, "I didn't think I was that ill!" I'm just coming to see how they are. It's not the last rites!'

In Sickness and in Health

It is true that chaplains aren't always the harbingers of doom that many think they are. Sure, they'll be there when a club wants to mark the passing of a former player. Or a fan wants to scatter their old man's ashes on the pitch. When Manchester City left Maine Road for a new stadium in 2003, over 1,000 people turned up as the Rev.

Tony Porter led a memorial service for all the fans whose final resting place was soon to become a housing estate.

But in contrasting sentiments, that same year the Rev. Chris Cullwick led a half-time prayer at York City. The club had narrowly avoided going out of business, and the supporters' trust wanted to herald a new chapter with a blessing. Cullwick's prayer was afforded respectful silence before 4,000 fans responded in unison with a boisterous 'Amen'. On this occasion, the chaplain was not present to mark death but rebirth.

'Celebrating with people is as important as commiserating with people,' said Mary, who has lost count of the number of times she has been told about pregnancies before family members have been informed. Even at the Olympics, drop-ins are not always those laden with worry. Sometimes they simply want to share their serenity. In Athens, a swimmer approached Mary with news that would have been unremarkable to most. 'He said, "I was never going to win a medal. But I was good enough to be selected for my country, to be here. And I swam a personal best yesterday. I wanted to tell somebody. And God seemed like a good person to tell",' recalled Mary. 'And so it's the good news as well.'

And so it turns out they actually *are* good fun at parties too. Back when Charlton were still a Premier League side and their chaplain was still of a similar age to some of the playing squad, Matt was asked to continue the night into the early hours following the Christmas do. 'I remember sitting in a nightclub in Soho, drinking champagne with the star striker. And having a really good conversation with him. He insisted he bought the champagne, which I was quite relieved about.'

As surreal a moment it may have seemed at the time for Matt, it was a prime example of chaplaincy working. Of being there in the environments where the player felt most comfortable, rather than where the chaplain might. To explain why it works, Matt gave me a quick theology lesson. 'The Greek mindset is we compartmentalise things. We're very influenced by that in the West, and particularly in this country,' he said, hinting at his frustrations. 'The Hebrew approach is much more holistic. Life includes the spiritual, eating, and material. I'm much more comfortable in that realm. Hence, sitting drinking champagne in Soho whilst chatting to a player. It merges very easy for me.'

For chaplains like Matt, preaching to the choir holds little appeal. 'We still have to persuade the church sometimes that it's not about sitting in church waiting for people to come and knock on your door. It's about going out,' said Matt, before giving me another Good Book heads up. 'That shouldn't surprise people because that's what Jesus said in Scripture. The Great Commission was go. It wasn't sit and wait.' Mary shared similar sentiments. 'I have more conversations about what really matters in life in a chaplaincy situation than I do in church at ten o'clock.'

And so the number of chaplains in sport continues to increase apace, in both the mainstream and the niche. Along with rugby, cricket, and horse racing, there are now chaplains dedicated to Scottish shinty, UK gyms, and even the longest and most dedicated queue in sport, at Wimbledon SW19. Yet while those within sport are warming to the quiet advantages of chaplaincy, many of its observers remain none the wiser. That much was clear as each chaplain stressed the services they do not offer as much as they spoke of the functions they do.

Chaplains want you to know they are *not* psychologists. Angy, who is commonly asked about the difference between the roles, used a well-worn example to explain: 'If a player turns up at training one day and her dog was run over that morning, she doesn't need an hour session with a psychologist. That's going to cost the club money. But 15 minutes having a coffee with me talking about what the dog meant to her might make her feel a little bit better.'

And despite how often you ask, chaplains will *not* pray for wins. 'Of course, I wanted them to win,' said Mary, referring to her regular visitors from football and athletics. 'But my prayer is always that people will give their very best. And your very best might be that you come seventh. Because implicitly praying for that one to win means you're praying for that one to lose. And that I will never do.'

And then there's handing out chocolates at Christmas. Unfortunately, that's also uncommon. But when Matt had a chance encounter with the manager who once uttered those words to him, he found an enthusiastic convert. 'He said his new chaplain had been fantastic from day one and he was sorry he ever doubted it in the first place,' remembered Matt, who said he didn't need the apology. 'I told him he was the gaffer and he had to make sure it works for his team. But I thanked him for saying that and I was really pleased that it was working. And it's continued to work for the last four years.'

What chaplains *will* do, which puts them at odds with almost every other position in sport, is treat the 'talent' as equals. In their eyes, an athlete's impressive command of a ball, a horse, or a javelin, puts them no higher up in life's pecking order than, say, the ground staff, the team chef, or a visiting interpreter. And so they'll speak to sportspeople like many others don't.

'You treat them as human beings,' said Mary. 'Because if they're famous, everybody else often only wants them for an autograph, for a selfie, or a signed shirt to raise money for a cause. For a lot of famous sportspeople, the only people who beat a track to their door are those who want something. And good chaplains don't want anything.'

It's true that everybody wanting something can be a chore for sport's biggest stars. But by far a bigger worry is the day when nobody wants anything at all. Gordon Elliott knows the feeling. But in March 2022, Elliott made his return to Cheltenham Festival a year after being shamed into the shadows. He enjoyed his first winner on day two, a horse named Commander in Fleet. The 50/1 outsider pulled through against all odds.

Simon recalled one similar example among his proudest moments. 'A couple of years ago we sat in a room with a jockey who, to all intents and purposes, had blown it. It was all over. And I didn't really do anything but sit in that room when nobody else would.' Simon offered him a rare moment of non-judgemental refuge. 'He understood what he'd done wrong. He understood what he had to do to put it right. He went above that, and he's back doing what he loves. It's amazing when, against all odds, somebody pulls through.'

9

WATCHMEN: Doping Officials

*From herb-infused Roman chariot racers
to the opiate-boosted endurance walkers
of the early 19th century, the prevalence of
performance-enhancing drugs is as old as
sport itself. While the prevailing sentiment
is that the takers are always one step ahead
of the testers, high-profile busts suggest that
there is only one winner in the end. This is
how doping's shadowy combatants continue
the fight to keep sport clean.*

Hope You've Washed Your Hands

There's a story that former Ipswich Town goalkeeper Brian Murphy tells about his time under manager Roy Keane. The Irishman says that after an underwhelming second-half performance at Leicester City, Keane came into the changing room in a fit of rage. In the corner stood an anti-doping official, waiting patiently to collect samples from the players selected for testing.

As Keane began his tirade, picking off player after player, he landed upon a youngster who had struggled more than most to reach the high standards expected from this multiple Premier League winner. According to Murphy, Keane looked at this promising talent, then pointed to the official, and asked, 'Do you want to be a footballer? Or do you want to collect piss for a living like that fella?'

'That fella' would have been a doping control officer (DCO), and he would have been trained to do just what Keane described – collect urine from athletes. Along with blood collection officers and chaperones, doping control officers make up a pool of around 200 officials authorised by UK Anti-Doping (UKAD) to conduct testing at all levels of sport. That authority comes with a right to enter a changing room without prior permission from a club, or a manager. Not even a match referee can do that.

It means doping officials have been witnesses to sport's inner sanctum for many years. They have seen its murkier side, and they have been the recipient of much worse invective than Keane's flippant barb. But, unlike Keane, they are required to have a great deal of sensitivity and tact. So even as the world of anti-doping makes noises about becoming more transparent, the experiences of the testers on the front line remain largely untold. They sign confidentiality agreements, and must never reveal the names of the athletes tested, nor the sporting clubs visited. So finding an official willing to speak to me was a task as daunting as getting Keane to smile for the camera.

Nevertheless, as one of UKAD's stated aims is to recognise 'the importance of transparency and accountability in general, and specifically in providing the public with more understanding of its anti-doping regime', I felt confident that they may respond warmly to my emailed request. In the spirit of making their role more understandable to the average sports fan, I asked if they could put me in touch with a doping official who might like to share their career experiences, without infringing confidentiality. UKAD didn't get back to me.

So I tried contacting current DCOs directly, but that proved no doddle either. The role is often part-time, undertaken by people from all walks of life looking to supplement their day jobs in, say, the police, teaching, or the civil service. It means not many list anti-doping as their primary occupation on social media. The handful that I did find rejected my request outright. Or told me to speak to UKAD. So it took some time. But, finally, in a quaint little village near Melton Mowbray, I found a fella willing to speak to me.

Colin Clews is first and foremost a cyclist. That is clear before he even says a word, and his rake-thin physique isn't the only giveaway. His immaculate house is named after one of the European classics, and it is adorned with mementoes and trinkets dedicated to the sport. Even in his downstairs toilet, plastic toy cyclists have formed a nine-man breakaway around the scented sticks. Colin's name is widely known in cycling circles, having been an International Commissaire since 1991, as well as the founder of the much-loved Rutland CiCLE Classic, the

UK's only UCI-sanctioned one-day race. The event logo adorned the shoulder of the glossy blue jacket that he had zipped right up to his chin.

In his youth, Colin competed internationally for Great Britain and found some success domestically. But when kids and a mortgage came along the £4 a week pay wasn't going to suffice, so he took a job at the NHS. Unwilling to completely cut ties with his sporting passion, he moved into officiating. By the mid-1980s he had risen to the ranks of national-level cycling official.

It was at this moment that British cycling decided it was time to step up its efforts in drug testing. And it wanted its existing officials to oversee the process. 'Someone went in there protecting the rights of the rider and protecting the credibility of the system,' said Colin, reminding me that his brief wasn't just to catch the bad apples, but also to protect the clean ones from being bitten. And so, as Colin put it, he 'fell into doping control'.

For when the Sports Council of Great Britain (now UK Sport) decided to follow cycling's lead, they sought people who had testing experience. Colin was among 20 cycling officials invited to a weekend training course in Kettering, after which he had qualified as one of the country's first doping control officers. Now it wasn't simply cyclists he was testing, but any athlete from any sport that was centrally funded by the UK government. From football to cricket and even snooker.

After 35 years in the role, Colin is now retired. He called it a day when he turned 70 in 2020, which at least meant he no longer had to hear the phrase uttered to him more than any other during his testing career, 'I hope you've washed your hands.' But having been involved in British doping control since its inception, he is proud of its significant progress and his involvement in it and was keen to share his experiences.

His retirement meant that he was no longer encumbered by contractual restrictions, and he was happy to speak to me. On a bright Tuesday in May he invited me to his home to talk me through the testing process. It is a practice I would never be permitted to witness in real life. He had no intention of naming anybody, and he spoke slowly and deliberately, careful not to reveal any information that I had no intention of getting him into trouble with anyway.

But after popping the kettle on, and introducing me to his excitable dog Rosa – 'She'll be a nuisance if we're not careful' – Colin left me sat in his kitchen as he went to fetch the thing I had come to see. The bane of many an athlete's career. A Berlinger urine sample kit.

A Game of Cat and Rat

One of the first reported cases of performance-enhancing drugs (PEDs) in sport can be traced back to the 1904 Olympics. American Tom Hicks won the gold medal in the marathon event, pounding the dirt track of St Louis in punishing 32°C heat. The only source of water for the runners was a well at the halfway stage. With the British-born Hicks flagging at the 22-mile mark, his coach Charles Lucas produced a potent cocktail of brandy, egg whites, and dangerously high doses of strychnine.

During Roman times this highly toxic crystal had been used by gladiators to stave off fatigue in fights to the death. These days it is used as rat poison. Nonetheless, it worked to get Hicks through those final four miles, before he collapsed shortly after the race. Only the swift actions of four nearby doctors saved his life that day. Hicks would instead die many years later in Winnipeg, Canada, at the age of 76. He is still acknowledged by the IOC as the rightful winner and nothing he or his coach did that day contravened the rules. It would be another 24 years before the IAAF became the first sporting federation to ban PEDs.

It took the IOC until 1967 to follow suit, prompted by the death of cyclist Knud Enemark Jensen at the 1960 Olympic Games in Rome. The Dane, like many in his sport at the time, had been taking amphetamines to boost his stamina. But he lost consciousness midway through the team time trial, fell from his bike, and fractured his skull. Seven years after Jensen's demise, British cyclist Tommy Simpson collapsed and died from heart failure a kilometre from the summit of Mont Ventoux on stage 13 of the Tour de France. He was found to have empty tubes of amphetamines in the back pocket of his jersey.

The outcry from these high-profile deaths prompted the major sporting organisations to take a tougher stance on the use of PEDs. But for many athletes, the yearning for victory has proven far stronger than the fear of being caught. Or even the potential for much worse. Between 1982 and 1995, physician Robert Goldman surveyed 198 world-class athletes with a question that became known as

Goldman's Dilemma. He asked them if they would take a magic drug that would ensure they would win every competition they entered but would kill them in five years. More than half answered yes.

And so, despite the tightening of rules, there have been countless examples of athletes continuing to ingest or inject banned drugs into their bodies. Some, like the infamous East German and Russian programmes, have been state-sponsored. Others, like those involving Olympic 100m champion Ben Johnson and multiple Tour de France victor Lance Armstrong, have shocked the world. Many more have been much less documented, but no less troubling.

One case at the Rio Olympics in 2016 saw Kyrgyz weightlifter Izzat Artykov stripped of his bronze medal after he was discovered to have taken a banned substance. It was strychnine. More than a century after Tom Hicks came so close to death in St Louis, athletes are still prepared to take poison in a bid to win. And so the cat and rat game continues today, now a much more sophisticated scientific tussle than its primitive beginnings. And Colin is one cat who has seen it all.

He encountered plenty of resistance in the fledgling days of the UK anti-doping programme. 'There was a great deal of resentment amongst a lot of the competitors, towards us and the role that we undertook,' said Colin. One sport, in particular, made him feel as welcome as a mole at a flower show. 'There was a lack of willingness to be involved from people within the cricketing fraternity. Cricket was a very strange one.' He described turning up on the morning of a day's play before randomly selecting the players to be tested. Those players then had until an hour after close of play to report for the urine test. Colin found that many would wait until the final moment, even if they weren't on the field. 'You'd have the frustration where you'd be there at ten o'clock, you had a person who is 12th man, and they sat there all day,' he said. 'They were supposed to come to us and be tested as soon as they wanted to go to the toilet. It was complete disrespect.'

Colin openly admitted that he had never been a cricket fan, but the sport made little effort to convert him in his early days as an official. On another occasion he handed a cricketer the obligatory post-test paperwork, only to see the player crumple the paper and throw it on the floor. 'There were players openly smoking, lying around in the corridor drinking beer. The whole attitude and discipline of the players I found very disappointing,' he said, recalling it to be a common experience among his fellow testers. 'There were other people getting the same sort of response. The cricket authorities were hauled over the coals about it.'

If being a new face in a stubborn old sport was proving difficult, Colin would soon discover that familiarity can breed just as much contempt. In cycling, officials would often straddle dual roles. One week they would be overseeing a race as a commissaire, while the following they could be supervising a blood or urine test as part of their anti-doping purview. It led French cyclist Laurent Jalabert to describe cycling officials as a cross between Dracula and the Gestapo. 'That starts to affect the relationship,' said Colin, 'because the same group of people were involved in these two different aspects.'

To avoid conflicts of interest, the roles would eventually diverge. And when it was deemed that a governing body testing its own athletes was like a motorist writing their own parking ticket, UKAD was born.

Although funded by UK Sport, it would act as an independent agency, tasked with implementing a code outlined by the World Anti-Doping Agency (WADA). One of WADA's policies would dramatically shift the power dynamic from athlete to tester.

For Colin, it was a game-changing moment. 'The likelihood of catching somebody at a competition event started to decrease with the type of drugs that were being used. It was no longer amphetamines and steroids. It was drugs that were going to be helpful to you within training, with a lasting effect that you could then carry through into the event. So they started to develop out-of-competition testing.'

Fleeing the Scene

While Colin was out of the room getting the testing kit, my attention was drawn to a small robotic mower in his back garden. The device was barely bigger than a shoebox, and with its whirring plastic wheels it looked like something from a Pixar movie. It patrolled Colin's large lawn with an artificial mind of its own. My host returned to the kitchen and saw me admiring his garden tech. 'That's Gladys,' he said, before entertaining my stupid question about how it collects the cut grass. 'Because it's cut on a daily basis, it skims off just the top. And that goes back down into the ground. So it never really builds up.'

In a bid to stop its own field from growing out of control, UKAD took a similar daily approach to Gladys. Out-of-competition testing suddenly meant that athletes were required to provide an address where they could be found for one hour of the day, 365 days of the year. Crucially, a DCO like Colin could drop by on any day convenient for him, with no obligation to tell anyone. Not even his superiors.

'It was completely ad hoc,' he said. 'You would be asked to call upon these people within the next three months when you had time on your hands. You would just go at any time, day or night. On the basis that the more you plan them, the less likely that you were going to find anything. It was also a confidence booster for those athletes that knew they were clean.'

The random nature of his arrival to homes and places of training meant that Colin didn't always arrive at opportune moments. He once interrupted the morning of a young athlete who answered the door in his dressing gown, and was keen to return to his bedroom. Colin informed him that, as per anti-doping policy, he would need to follow him there. The young man swiftly changed his mind. 'He looked very downtrodden and unhappy about this situation.' The athlete instead offered to make Colin a cup of tea, before filling three cups from the kettle. 'After about a quarter of an hour the young lady that he'd obviously left upstairs and wanted to go back to, she came down and joined us.'

On other occasions he would arrive to test the swimmers at Loughborough University, a key performance hub for Team GB. Quite often they would be dehydrated and famished following intensive training, not ready to produce their sample. And so they would invite Colin to breakfast. He would watch the cream of Britain's swimming talent fill their faces with all-you-can-eat sausages and bacon before the orange juice finally made it through their system. 'The number of breakfasts that I've had in Tesco cafe before we've gone back and actually done the testing is nobody's business,' he said, with a smile that suggested he enjoyed the pool more than the pavilion.

If killing the romantic moment or making small talk in supermarket cafes was as awkward as it got for Colin, then some of his peers elsewhere in the world didn't always get off so lightly. In 2008, cyclist Riccardo Riccò made a run from his anti-doping chaperone following stage four of the Tour de France. The Italian, who would go on to win two stages of the Tour, was cornered by the persistent official when Riccò's ill-advised dash took him in the direction of a traffic jam. The cyclist was subsequently tested after every stage, and he was found with traces of the blood-boosting drug erythropoietin (EPO) in his system. He was kicked off the Tour and his stage wins were wiped from the record.

In 2016, a WADA report highlighted how some Russians had become especially adept at making themselves scarce when a doping official was in town. For out-of-competition testing, false addresses would be provided. Some listed their homes as being in closed cities that required military approval to enter. Doping officials reported being intimidated by armed FSB agents when they requested access. In-competition testing could be just as problematic, with many athletes withdrawing from events when they saw anti-doping officials arrive. Others simply ran off after competing. One athlete even exited the stadium midway through a race.

But fleeing the attention of doping officials rarely works out well, even when it is a successful flight. In 2019, Patrick Siele made a dash when DCOs turned up at his training camp in the Kenyan town of Kapsabet. The former steeplechaser was spotted expertly hurdling a fence and, not surprisingly for a man who could run the marathon in two hours and ten minutes, could not be caught. He was handed a ban of three and a half years.

Testing today is a lot more targeted, and any athlete behaving strangely or uncooperatively will only increase the size of the mark on their head. An athlete regularly pulling out of events at short notice due to illness, for example, would be very likely to see their name feature on Colin's list. 'In the majority of cases now when you go to an event you have a list given to you as to who they believe should be tested. And you work your way through that list.'

I had always assumed that, other than the obligatory tests for the winners, those who were being tested had been chosen completely at random. Colin had even told me the process of pulling the names out of the hat when turning up at football and cricket clubs. 'The athletes are told that it is random, yes,' confirmed Colin, after I aired my confusion. 'But I think the majority now are aware that it is intelligent testing that is being pursued, and that there are reasons why people are being tested in this way. You can get somebody who has been tested several times in a week. At a major race like the Tour de France, they can be tested four times over the course of 48 hours.'

It makes sense. But the risk in moving away from random selections in favour of information-led picks is that the insinuations that come with it risk further fracturing the relationship between athlete and tester. It also requires the intelligence behind the choices to be robust. And Colin admitted that there had been occasions when he was baffled at the names presented to him.

He was once asked to visit a prison warden, who only registered with the Weightlifting Association so that he could train some of the inmates. When Colin arrived to test him he found that the warden had only ever competed once, and had finished third. Out of three. He couldn't have weighed more than nine stone. And yet the warden's name would appear on Colin's lists on multiple occasions.

A similar case saw Colin drive 100 miles to visit the remote home of another weightlifter: 'A little guy, no more than about five foot tall, wearing just a pair of shorts, comes to the door. And, there are no two ways about it, he was an old man.' Colin asked the man if he had a son by the same name. He didn't. Colin asked him if he was a weightlifter. He was. 'And this was the guy I'd been sent to see. For some reason, the British Weightlifting Association wanted this guy tested. But he was 74 years of age. If there weren't any drugs in him, I would have wondered how the hell are you staying alive?'

This elderly man had been a competitive weightlifter for most of his adult life, but now only occasionally took part in veteran competitions. As if the scene wasn't peculiar enough, it was also the weightlifter's birthday. 'He said, "You've really made my day. I've always wanted to be tested, and you've come and tested me on my 74th birthday!"'

Both examples show that data alone can't be trusted in the battle against doping. Without additional due diligence from those on the ground, athletes who compete infrequently risk being flagged as suspect regardless of their age or standard. Colin made no effort to hide his contempt for an unnecessary 200-mile trip and duly fed back his concerns. But it wasn't a completely wasted endeavour. It was the warmest welcome he would ever receive. 'He was really enthusiastic about it. He walked straight into the bathroom, t-shirt off, shorts off, and stood there stark naked saying, "Where's my pot?"'

Gaming the System

Colin pulled up a kitchen stool and placed the Berlinger kit on the kitchen bench. He introduced it as the standard test used by doping control organisations across the world. The Swiss company behind it began life as a cotton-weaving mill in 1865, but since the FIFA World Cup in 1998, followed by their first Olympics in Sydney in 2000, they have been providing the gold-standard testing packs for sport's war on drugs. Wrapped in branded cellophane, it came in a dainty 15cm x 15cm brown cardboard box. The sort of thing you get Instagram-ready gourmet brownies in.

Inside were two square glass bottles, about two inches wide and five inches tall. One had an orange sticker labelled 'A', the other a blue sticker saying 'B'. Both had the same twisting ratchet caps that, once clicked fully into the metal teeth, could only be opened by a specialised Berlinger machine worth thousands of dollars. The same serial number could be seen three times on each bottle.

As Colin removed the wrapping with the nonchalance of a train guard checking tickets on the last train home, it seemed like he had handled this equipment thousands of times before. But in reality, Colin rarely touched the kit at all during a test. 'You start from the point whereby the athlete is responsible for whatever goes into their body, so whatever is put into there,' he said, pointing at the bottles, 'is their responsibility. And their ownership. And that's why you're going to stand back a little bit.'

To avoid any test being scratched on a technicality, Colin was never to hand the athlete any of the apparatus. Not a cup, not a box, not a bottle. 'You never get to a situation whereby you say, "There's a cup, you go off and fill it." It is to try and ensure that, from the point of view of the athlete, everything is totally correct.' Instead, there must always be a selection from which the athlete is free to make their own choice.

First, they pick a sealed plastic cup in which to pee, then they will pick a Berlinger box in which to deposit their urine. They will also be responsible for checking that the serial numbers align. After producing, the athlete will pour their samples into the respective bottles, and they too must twist the cap to seal them. It is natural to think of a doping official as someone who tests the athlete. But in fact the DCOs are there to observe. It is the athletes who essentially test themselves.

Unlike the septuagenarian weightlifter, I had no great yearning to be tested by Colin and so the next part of the process was only described by my host rather than re-enacted. Though Colin's minute-by-minute depiction left little to the imagination. 'Once they've chosen their cup, the athlete takes it into the toilet area where they're asked to remove their clothing from just below the armpits to above the knee. So as you can see exactly what's evident. You have to witness the sample, and see where it's actually coming from.'

Colin clarified that male officials will only ever monitor male athletes and vice versa, and he went on to describe the optimal method for how best to 'witness the sample' (sideways on for men, front on for women, in case you were wondering). But my mind was already wandering. As with most parts of the testing process, if anything seems unusually intricate it is likely in reaction to more shenanigans. So why, I asked Colin, do athletes need to show most of their naked torso when peeing?

'You go back to the 1970s, at the Tour de France. There's a Belgian guy by the name of Michel Pollentier. He skedaddled off up a mountainside and left everybody for dead. Took the stage. Took the yellow jersey. After the intervening period, he went to the doping control and he was discovered with a bulb under his arm with urine in it. And a tube that went down. Whether or not he was seen doing this,' Colin pumped his right arm like a chicken's wing, 'but somebody felt there was something amiss.'

In fact, when I looked into this story afterwards, it turned out Pollentier's receptacle was a condom filled with urine, and he'd managed to get away with the ruse. A team-mate, however, wasn't as adept at peeing using his armpit and aroused the suspicion of the attending official. Who subsequently asked Pollentier to lift his jersey. Thirty years later the fake penis ruse had become more sophisticated. Two members of the Hungarian team at the Olympic Games in Athens were believed to have used a urine-filled plug inserted into the rectum. From there a rubber tube led to the underside of the penis, where a valve controlled the flow of clean urine. WADA only learned of the device when it arrived, sent by a whistleblower, to its Montreal headquarters following the Games in 2004.

Another athlete at those same Games, NBA star Lamar Odom, used a prosthetic penis called 'the Whizzinator' to mask his regular weed smoking. It worked to fool US officials and he qualified for the acclaimed Dream Team, going on to win a bronze medal. His antics only became known after he admitted to it in his 2019 autobiography. In 2005, NFL running back Onterrio Smith wasn't so lucky. He was detained at Minneapolis airport when he was found with the same strikingly named device in his baggage. Produced in Las Vegas, 'the Whizzinator' comes in five colours and can still be bought online for less than £100.

The Chaperone

For every deceitful action from those athletes pushing what they can get away with, there is an equal and opposite reaction from doping officials looking to combat it. Consider it WADA's own version of Newton's Third Law. The behaviour of the few having a grave effect on the privacy of the many is a common theme in doping control. The reason athletes are supervised at all aligns with another tale that Colin told about a male cyclist in the 1960s. It is said that this cyclist couldn't produce his sample after the race, so was trusted to go home and return it when he could. 'A week later they went back to him and said, "The good news is you're clear of any drugs. But the bad news I'm afraid is that you're pregnant." It was his wife's urine.'

Colin reckoned this was a well-known story in cycling, and sure enough, I found it attributed to Belgian rider Piet Rentmeester, who for most of his unremarkable career was known as 'the pregnant cyclist'. Yet Rentmeester always denied the story and there is a good chance it may even have been an urban myth. But even if it's nothing more than a good yarn, it was one that failed to reach American basketballer DJ Cooper. He was banned for two years in 2019 for passing his wife's urine off as his own when tested as part of an offer to represent Bosnia. The giveaway was the presence of human chorionic gonadotropin (hCG) in his blood, a hormone produced by the placenta.

And so the process that Colin was talking me through has been tweaked and improved over decades in order to defeat such flagrant attempts to cheat the system. In addition to the close scrutiny supervision, chaperoning is another effective way to ensure no funny business goes on before the test can take place.

A chaperone's task is to stay with the selected athlete from the moment they have completed the event, until the time they report to doping control. For some, this can be mere minutes. For others, like the winner of an event who may be expected to attend a medal ceremony or conduct interviews, it can take longer. But at no point should that athlete escape the view of their chaperone, and under no circumstances are they permitted to go to the toilet or shower before providing their sample.

'Chaperoning was a major step forward because that was the blank period. Before you'd simply put a list up somewhere and the person then had 30 minutes after finishing their event to come to the control,' said Colin. 'Within 30 minutes, you could do an awful lot to manipulate the outcome of a future test. And everybody knows it went on. But there was nothing you could do about it.'

Even with more stringent protocols in place, there will be innovative new ways to game the system. One moment stands out for Colin: 'The person being tested, not too many years afterwards, was found to have been doing all sorts of stuff and left the sport with a black spot over them. He'd just won a major event, and while he was in the control his manager suddenly came and, whether he was feigning it or not, was giving all the symptoms of a heart attack.' Colin added that in some sports, the doping process requires a doctor to be present to oversee the sample. On this occasion, the physician was distracted by a more pressing medical need. Colin had no choice but to stop the test.

I asked if the athlete seemed at all concerned about his manager's condition. 'He didn't, no. He was giving it a glance but he didn't seem too perturbed about it. The doctor treated the manager and he was taken away. I've always thought back on that. What we know now about that particular athlete, I still wonder if that was just a cover-up, to shade what could have taken place in that control that day.' The manager made a full recovery.

The topic of cover-ups brought us to one occasion around ten years ago when Colin attended a Premier League club's training ground. In football, alcohol testing is sometimes conducted alongside the standard urine testing. Colin made air quotes with his fingers when he told me that a particular player on this day had been 'randomly' selected for testing, suggesting that the football club had all but requested that their player be chosen.

'I remember him walking into the control room, and this was a training session at 11am on a Monday morning. And you could smell the alcohol on his breath.' Colin asked the player to blow into a breathalyser. 'It just went off the scale. It was way, way up.' The player, presumably noticing the alarm on the faces of those in the room, asked if it was OK. When Colin told him it was far from OK, the footballer appeared shocked. 'He said to me, "What would you expect it to be?" And I said, "Well the expectation is that it says zero." And this guy had driven there that morning in something like £150,000 worth of Maserati outside.'

Colin believes that up until a few years ago, football clubs frequently used the anti-doping system to provide a solution to players causing them some concern. 'At that time, there was certainly a very strong suspicion that there were a lot of cases similar to that, and recreational drugs, that were never actually put into the public domain. The number of times that we would have our suspicions about a particular player, and then you would see in the press a couple of weeks later that they had a hamstring injury and would be out of the sport for three months. And then they would return.'

Stage Fright

To satisfy the DCO, athletes are expected to produce a sample of 90ml, of which 60ml goes in bottle A, and 30ml in bottle B. Thanks to the omnipresence of isotonics and dieticians it is rare that an athlete is unable to produce the required amount after a competition, though boxers who have gone 12 rounds are still prone to dehydration.

And while doping control officers develop a strong sense of when something isn't quite right, it is also understood that such an intimate situation with a complete stranger is always going to cause some unease. And so it turns out that 'stage fright' isn't a phenomenon restricted to pub urinals. 'I know of particular riders who, on a bike and generally around the place, are the most extrovert characters you could ever come across. The life and soul of the party,' said Colin. 'But put them in doping control and you know damn well you're going to be there for three hours. At the end of it, you know their life story.'

During a European tour, Colin waited 40 minutes for his randomly selected Spanish cyclist to cross the mountain stage finish line. Once at doping control, the cyclist was unable to turn the tap on. 'He was drinking these two-litre bottles of water, glugging these things down as if he was trying to fill the river. And nothing was happening at all.'

Hours later, with the crowd long gone, the finish line dismantled, and only the mobile doping control unit left, it emerged in conversation that the cyclist was staying in a hotel only 200m from Colin's. And so Colin drove the athlete the 40 miles back to his hotel in the hope that he might finally be able to provide his sample there. 'At 9pm, he finally produced a minimum sample in my hotel room,' said Colin. 'I remember thinking to myself, if this guy's number comes out again, then it's going back in.'

Two days later at the same event, Colin was once again at the finish line, this time waiting on the winner of a sprinter-friendly flat stage. And who should emerge out of the front of the bunch to cross the line first? 'It was this guy from two days ago. I couldn't believe it,' said Colin. 'But, the difference was he was obviously back on terrain that he liked. He wheeled around and before he even went to the podium, he came directly to the anti-doping control. He provided his sample, and he was out within seven minutes to take his prize on the podium.'

Once an athlete has provided their full sample, they must sign a form that, with no cameras or phones permitted, provides the sole account of what happened in that control room. You've heard the phrase 'sign your life away', but many an athlete has signed their career away on one of these sheets. It is on here that athletes can declare any medications they have recently taken. Although this is voluntary, it is in their interests to mention anything that may become relevant at this point, rather than at a more awkward moment down the line.

During a race in Portugal, a cyclist Colin had tested flagged positive for high levels of salbutamol, commonly known by its brand name Ventolin. It is used by asthma sufferers worldwide. WADA permits restricted use of the drug, with a Therapeutic Use Exemption (TUE) required for anything above the maximum stated dosage. But this athlete had no TUE. 'At that stage, he hadn't declared it,' said Colin, fidgeting with his specs. 'But suddenly, I had the team manager coming to me with a backdated prescription that he'd been given by the team doctor, for salbutamol. In my overall report of the race, I put that I believed that there was something not quite right with what was going on in this particular case and this guy should be scrutinised. I wasn't involved in any future tests. But two months later he was done for doing EPO.'

Colin picked up the bottles on the bench and screwed on the caps, which made a loud mechanical clacking sound that a barking Rosa didn't take too kindly to. Once he had twisted it until he could no more, he invited me to try to take them off. He knew I didn't stand a chance. Unless I had friends in Russia's secret service. The bottles were previously thought to be impossible to open without Berlinger's own device. But the astounding revelations about state-backed meddling at the Sochi Winter Olympics in 2014, made by Russia's former head of anti-doping, Grigory Rodchenkov, suggested that the FSB had found a way.

Bruce Draper stays alert as Honie Farrington gets the shot at the Tour Down Under in Adelaide. Credit: James Farrington

Having remembered his photographer, Luke Edwardes-Evans (on the white motorbike) chases Mikel Landa, Nairo Quintana, and Rigoberto Uran at the 2019 Tour de France.

The late Peter Clark celebrates Chelsea's 2010 title win with a language student who would go on to become a close friend, Carlo Ancelotti.

Interpreter Patrick Kendrick gets a smile from a tough crowd, sat next to Jurgen Klopp ahead of Liverpool's match in Naples.

2016 Hammer of the Year Marc Joss. And Dimitri Payet.

Chaplain Mary Vickers offers pastoral support for athletes, staff and fans at the 2009 World Championships in Berlin.

Reverend Matt Baker's congregation is not in church. It's at The Valley, Charlton.

A Berlinger urine sample kit is the bane of many an athlete's career. As demonstrated in the kitchen of retired doping control officer Colin Clews.

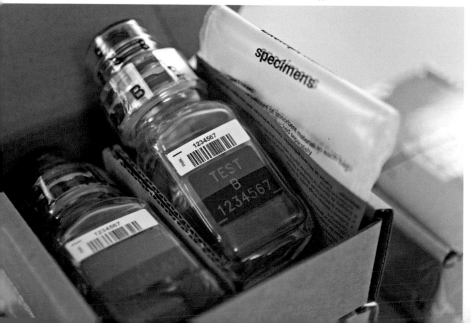

Cox Zoe de Toledo rallies her crew ahead of a silver medal at the Rio Olympics in 2016.

Following gold in Sydney, Rowley Douglas pre-empts the obligatory coxswain dip by launching himself off the winning boat.

Whether at Oakwell, Wembley, or the Stade de France, turf veteran Tony Stones insists on speaking directly to the boss. Here, Didier Deschamps tells the Yorkshireman how he wants his pitch.

After his inflatable tent helped to defeat freezing Lancashire conditions, Chorley FC groundsman Ben Kay applies the finishing touches ahead Derby County's FA Cup visit.

Leicester City's intricate pitch designs earned head of sports turf John Ledwidge the nickname 'patterns guy'. Just don't ask him to do Phil Collins's face.

Doctor James Robson punches the air after George North's hamstring held out for a memorable British and Irish Lions try in 2013.

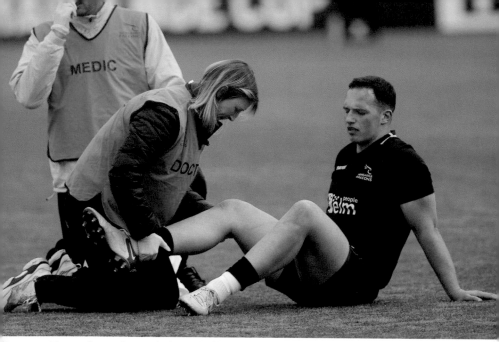

For rugby medic Rachel Scurfield, patrolling the Newcastle Falcons pitch beats working in a hospital. Credit: Chris Lishman – Newcastle Falcons

Head of medical Prav Mathema lead the Lions through a pandemic during the 2021 tour of South Africa. 'This is not a joke!' read the text he'd send to all after a player tested positive for Covid-19.

So stung by the possibility that their benchmark product had been compromised, Berlinger announced in 2018 that they were ending production of the bottles. But with the company responsible for up to 90 per cent of all tests worldwide, the departure of this family-run business could have proven catastrophic for the anti-doping movement. In January 2019, Berlinger returned to the fold, stating, 'An overwhelming majority of national anti-doping agencies worldwide asked us several times to continue our production.' Berlinger's re-designed bottles are now described as 'tamper-evident' rather than 'tamper-proof'.

The anti-doping campaign can ill afford this level of shady intrigue. It is a system that only works with the trust of the people it is meant to both protect and catch out. The whole thing falls apart if the athletes begin to question its efficacy and integrity, which is why they're involved at every step of the way. Including, and especially, when their test is shown to be positive. Or, should I say, when an 'adverse analytical finding' (AAF) has been discovered.

'The A sample is opened by the lab, and that's what the test is done on,' explained Colin. 'The B sample is the athlete's guarantee that nobody has done anything untoward with their sample. An athlete could say, "Somebody in the lab was on a downer that day, they decided that we're going to call somebody positive, and it was my sample that they picked up." So there's always that accusation that could come in.'

To counter such a claim, the athlete is invited to come into the lab with their representatives, to witness the B sample being tested. I wondered if the athletes always took up that option. 'It's debatable. Some that are wanting to prove their innocence will. But it's entirely up to them. If it was me, yes, I'd certainly want to,' replied Colin. 'You go to the laboratory and that sample has to be in exactly the condition that you saw it sealed in the doping control station. Then they see that test performed in front of their own eyes if they so wish. And then, and only then, if this finding is the same, is it declared positive.'

Yet there are countless examples when a story has broken about an athlete testing positive for a banned substance, where they are pleading their innocence while awaiting the result of the B sample. I asked Colin if waiting for the B bottle confirmation before announcing anything was a recent change in policy. 'No. That's always been the case,' he said. 'Or that *should* always have been the case. But all too often, once that A sample is declared an adverse analytical finding, the press get hold of it.' Colin suggested that in many cases it's the athletes themselves who release the news early, in the hope of controlling the narrative. 'To try and actually get the public on their side,' he reckoned. 'They can start their dialogue as to why. "Oh, I must have eaten some beef with testosterone in."'

Colin's example raised a smile. Variations on that excuse are popular among busted athletes. Tour de France champion Alberto Contador blamed a juicy steak for testing positive for clenbuterol in 2010, while veal was the offending meat in question when tennis player Petr Korda attempted to explain the nandrolone in his system in 1998. In 2015, heavyweight boxing champion Tyson

Fury attributed traces of the same drug in his body to tucking into uncastrated wild boar. And back in 1983, cyclist Adri van der Poel blamed his dad's pigeon pie for the strychnine found in his system. Given what we know about that particular ingredient, it's hoped that van der Poel's old man didn't cook too often.

The Battle Continues

Before I asked Colin for directions to the best place in Melton Mowbray to get their famous pies (pork, not pigeon), I was keen to know his thoughts on the current status of sports doping. From his perspective, doping control officers are now an accepted, and indeed an integral, part of sport. They may still deal with the occasional Roy Keane-esque quip, but he was pleased that sharing a coffee with athletes is now more commonplace than picking up their crumpled, discarded forms.

And as for their effect on the integrity of sport? WADA's reports are published on a two-year delay and its data for 2019 shows that there were 278,047 blood and urine samples analysed in WADA-accredited labs. Of the 2,702 positives, 1,537 led to sanctions. That's just 0.5 per cent of all athletes tested that were deemed to be cheating.

WADA only began publishing their violation report in 2013, when the figure stood at 0.8 per cent, from 207,513 tests. On the face of it, not only has testing increased but the number of those caught doping has dropped. Of course, the word 'caught' is doing some heavy lifting in that take on the data.

'Certainly, from where we were, the whole of sport has made absolute massive strides in the last 20 years,' said Colin, packing up the Berlinger bottles as one of the most unusual souvenirs I have ever been given. 'Across the whole of doping control so many of the little gaps that existed before – of people not having to come to the control quickly and doing their own thing for periods of time – those doors have now been shut. It's a much tighter system that we're operating right the way across the board.'

When WADA's 2020 violation results see the light of day, they should make fascinating reading. Some of those doors that Colin references were, at least temporarily, taken off their hinges by an unlikely ally for dopers. Covid-19 meant lockdowns and travel bans made it difficult for DCOs to conduct the out-of-competition tests that keep potential cheats on their toes, and social distancing rendered the concept of chaperoning completely unworkable. It is very likely that some took it as an opportunity.

'You're always still surprised by what lengths and what methods that sportspeople are prepared to do,' said Colin. 'I think everybody involved in doping control would love it to be a proactive purpose. But unfortunately, time and time again, it's been proved that the athletes and the people that manage the athletes are finding new ways of producing performance-enhancing activities. They're one step ahead.'

He mentioned PEDs that may not yet be detectable by the authorities. Like in 2003, when high-profile sprinters including USA's Marion Jones and Tim Montgomery, and Britain's Dwain Chambers, were among 20 athletes implicated in the BALCO scandal. Had a whistleblower, now known to be Jones's coach Trevor Graham, not sent a syringe filled with a new designer steroid to the US Anti-Doping Agency, their misdemeanours may never have been uncovered. Colin worried that athletes might be doing the same today, taking new drugs that are not only undetectable by authorities, but whose long-term side effects may be unclear.

It brings us back to Goldman's Dilemma, and the fact that more than half of all athletes three decades ago said they would take death in five years if it meant guaranteed victory until then. 'That is the psyche of a sportsperson at that time, in those institutions,' said Colin. 'I think it's so telling. And that's what anti-doping is all about. To try and prevent that. I would hope to think that percentage has dropped significantly now.'

In 2013, a study conducted at Canberra's University of New South Wales revisited Goldman's Dilemma, with the aim of 'replicating the results in the post-World Anti-Doping Agency context'. They surveyed 212 athletes at an elite-level track and field event in North America, offering them the same Faustian pact devised by Goldman in 1983. Only two said yes.

10

HUMAN DRUM: Rowing Coxswains

The job of a rowing coxswain is as complex as it is misunderstood. These diminutive figures may be dwarfed by their hulking team-mates but there is nothing small about their role. Find out how Britain's top coxes exert physical and psychological control of their shells to inspire their teams to victory.

The Pipes Are Calling

At the 1868 Henley Royal Regatta, a stubborn rower decided to make a splash that would leave a lasting ripple. Walter Bradford Woodgate, representing Oxford's Brasenose College, ordered one of his crew to walk the plank. Despite his slight build, Woodgate had become one of the finest oarsmen of his generation, a regular winner at the event in the seven years since his first victory in the coxless pairs. But two memories had left an impression that led him to hatch his daring plan.

The first came in 1861 when he suffered an injury that put a temporary halt to his fledgling rowing career.

According to Brasenose historian William O'Chee, Woodgate became embroiled in 'animated shenanigans' with coxswain Charles Parkin. It resulted in the rower receiving a serious knife wound to his right hand. Six years later, Woodgate watched in awe at the International Rowing Regatta in Paris. An unfancied Canadian four, composed of three fishermen and a lighthouse keeper, defeated champion crews from all over Europe. They did so without a cox on board.

Woodgate was determined to replicate their success and chose Henley's Stewards' Challenge Cup as the event in which to do so. Although traditionally contested between coxed crews of four, the future barrister had noted that there was no rule obligating the use of a coxswain so he opted for a shell designed with only four seats. Rival teams lodged complaints when they realised what Woodgate was planning, prompting the Henley committee to enforce a new law requiring a coxswain to appear in all races of fours and eights.

Unable to change his boat, Woodgate asked cox Frederic Weatherly to perch on the stern for the start of the race. Weatherly, who would later pen the ballad 'Danny Boy', was instructed to abandon ship as soon as the start was given. The future songwriter did as asked. But as the swiftly discarded cox became entangled in reeds and lilies, the popular funeral number was almost nixed from existence due to the premature demise of its writer. Fortunately Weatherly managed to free himself in time to see his fleeting Brasenose crew-mates cross the line first.

They were immediately disqualified but Woodgate had made the waves he had intended. The following year, the regatta introduced a new race. The disruptor who saw coxes as nothing more than barking ballast had become the founding father of the British coxless four. By 1873, the Stewards' Challenge Cup had followed suit.

Yet, like the lyrical Weatherly, the role of the cox did not perish that day. While coxed pairs and fours are no longer seen at Olympic and World Championship level, no eight will depart without a ninth member crouched in the hull. But a wider appreciation of what the cox brings to a crew was less enduring.

Just two months after coxing Britain's men's eights to Olympic bronze in Tokyo in 2021, Henry Fieldman told me about his typical interactions with Joe Public. 'Normally, when we're travelling together in the airport, there are eight massive guys, and then me. People generally get that it's probably rowing. But then they say, "So you're the guy with the drum?" I used to say no and explain it. But I've had it for eight years. Now I'm like "yep".'

Zoe de Toledo, who won silver with the women's eights four years earlier in Rio, remembered similar exchanges: 'Whenever I say this is what I do, people are like, "Oh, so you just sit there and shout 'stroke, stroke'".' These views are not confined to those whose interaction with the sport occurs only when the Olympic rings appear on the screen. It seems that Woodgate's disdain lives on in some within rowing itself. 'Even a lot of rowers don't understand what a good cox can add until they've had a really good one. They won't go out of their way to find someone. That's a shame,' said Zoe, speaking to me shortly after passing her medicine school finals. 'The role of the cox is definitely underappreciated, 100 per cent,' said Zoe. 'But at the same time, I've won an Olympic medal, and I literally sat on my arse and shouted at people.'

It is true that the role of the coxswain differs from others featured in this book. They are not hidden in the bowels of a stadium or under helmets in a pit garage. Rather, they are a visible part of the crew. They are categorised as athletes. They wear the same kit (albeit five sizes smaller). Like the rowers, they are even awarded medals. But while the coxes themselves may not be concealed, their talents often are.

And so, just like a Formula One mechanic or a football grounds manager, coxes are usually only noticed at times when they would really rather not be. So with Walter Bradford Woodgate's leading question still lingering for many outside the sport – and some inside – over 150 years on, it is time to answer it. Just what is the point of a rowing coxswain?

Bum Steer

When Rowley Douglas dialled in from his home in New York, the first thing I noticed was the potent ticking of his living-room clock. It provided a metronomic soundtrack to our conversation and meant that I was conscious of the ebbing time before Rowley had to dash off to his job at a Big Apple start-up. Perched on the mantlepiece above a brick fireplace, the clock's presence meant I avoided digressions. It sharpened my focus. For this 90-minute interview with a gold-medal winner, the timepiece essentially acted as my very own cox.

Although he is now back in the nation of his birth, Rowley was nine when he and his British parents moved to the UK. He represented Team GB at the Sydney Olympics in 2000. And it's the country of his ancestry and upbringing that is reflected in his accent and his bawdy humour, though there is the occasional transatlantic nugget thrown in. 'A lot of racing car drivers have said that they need a really good ass to get the feedback of what the vehicle's doing underneath them,' he said. 'A lot of what I did was based on feeling what the boat was transmitting through my ass because it's telling me a lot about how's it moving. And then you have to figure out how to interpret that.'

Probably due to that unnerving clock, I opted against becoming the umpteenth person to remark upon the aptness of Rowley's name given the sport he took up at 14. Back then, he had been keen to pick up an oar but he was urged to try coxing. Although he was daunted at the prospect of shouting at kids two and three years older than him he soon settled into the task. 'What's not to like about telling other people what to do, you know?' he said with a grin. 'Everyone's an equal in the boat, with the exception that one person has the voice. And you listen to that voice. Because those kids had all been rowing for five years, they'd already been taught that. So they weren't questioning me. They wanted to know that I was good enough. They didn't care that I was their junior.'

As a cox, the proof that you're good enough comes long before you've uttered a word. It may be the most visible aspect of the job but knowing what to say during a race is the least important concern. 'The way coxing is seen is that your main job is to shout the rowers on. To tell them to go faster or harder. I always say that is the icing on the cake, the last thing you should be focused on,' said Zoe, who also tutors young coxes alongside her new career as a doctor.

'You need to know how to manoeuvre the boat, you need to have watermanship skills, you need to know how to manage your boat when there's a stream and there are bridges. There's stuff that can throw you around in all different directions.' Like Rowley, Zoe said that a good cox can sense when a boat has a problem: 'Because you're sitting there in the hull, you can actually feel a lot of technical problems. Or when the boat's running well. You need to develop all those things first. Then worry about the motivation side.'

The length of an eight is around 19m, longer than a double-decker bus and equivalent to a ten-pin bowling lane. As the quickest rowing boat on the water, the carbon-fibre-reinforced plastic shell of an eight can reach speeds of 18mph. When all are on board a women's eight can weigh more than 700kg (110st) in total, a men's eight over 800kg (125st). And this water dart is navigated with a steel rudder often no bigger than a credit card. This is connected to two handles which are in the steady clutches of the trusty coxswain.

Moving the right hand up will see the boat veer starboard, push with the left and the eight will head off towards port. But the boat will not respond immediately. Even the captain of the *Titanic* saw the iceberg. And so, it can take one or two strokes before a shell reacts to the movements of this rudimentary metal fin. On a straight-line rowing leg like the courses at the Olympics, a cox will be tasked with steering bullet-straight. A crew who find they were forced to row more than the required two kilometres will be less than understanding. On a winding course such as the annual University Boat Race on the Thames Tideway, the idea is not only to identify the fastest racing lines but also to prevent crashing into your opponent.

Given the speed of travel and the small matter of eight grunting rowers in your eyeline, identifying and avoiding pesky flotsam isn't always a doddle. 'Training on a river is like a road. There's two-way traffic. There are corners. There's shit floating down the river. I've come across bodies on the Thames,' said Rowley, who once helped a police officer dredge up a dead body from a lake in Switzerland. 'You've got to pay attention to what you're doing, not least of all because of safety. You pile into Hammersmith Bridge, and that's not going to be a good thing.'

Although many coaches will advise a cox to avoid oversteering, what they mean is the type of overcorrecting that slows the boat down and churns up vital metres. The best coxes will be constantly steering with intricate adjustments that eventually become second nature. 'If the stream's coming downriver, you want to be tucked into the sides. If you're going with the stream you want to be in some deep part of the water,' said Rowley, adding that a straight-line course was often harder than a twisting one. 'Because you can see when you're not going straight. And not steering straight is costing people time.'

At Henley in 1868, Walter Bradford Woodgate was able to throw his cox overboard because he had designed his shell with a footplate linked to the rudder. The technology that allows rowers to steer the boat themselves hasn't changed all that much since. But while pairs and fours are lighter, smaller, and therefore easier to steer, every so often there comes a reminder that managing without a cox is not as simple as Woodgate made out.

At Tokyo in 2021, Great Britain's men's four were bidding to make it six consecutive gold medals in the event, stretching all the way back to Sydney in 2000. They looked in great shape to do that when they comfortably won their heat. And in the final, Team GB were well placed just a second behind leaders Australia with 500m to go before it all went wrong. On the last push the Brits in lane four veered wildly into the direction of the Italians in lane five. On the TV coverage, co-commentator Katherine Grainger could be heard gasping 'no, no, no!' in anticipation of a grisly collision. It was only averted because Italy steered themselves out of the danger, and out of contention for silver. A shellshocked British team finished fourth and a two-decade-long dynasty ended because of a steering error.

Oliver Cook, the man whose foot was on the plate, burst into tears during an emotional post-race interview. 'I feel I screwed up a bit. As I was closing in at the end and taking big strokes at the end, going for the line, I forgot the steering. And that's what cost us to be honest, cost us a medal,' he said. Tweeting after the race, Matthew Pinsent weighed in on the criticism directed at Cook: 'Ollie Cook in absolute tatters in that interview. He realises it went wrong. Steering a fast four under Olympic pressure is not easy in a crosswind. I never had to do it and I wouldn't have fancied it today.'

Henry recalled the conditions in Tokyo made for difficult navigation in the eight. 'It was crazy. We started off in a tailwind. And then it became direct-cross. And then it became cross-tail, and then it became tail. All in the space of five minutes and 20 seconds.' As a race progresses, it's not only the weather that a rudder must tussle with for dominion over the boat's direction. With four oars on one side of the boat and four on the other, each operated by a single rower with depleting energy reserves, it is up to the cox to compensate for any telling contrasts in power output.

'If one side is stronger than the other, then you're not going to go in a straight line either,' said Zoe, as I fought the urge to compare it to one-legged ducks swimming in circles. 'So that's the primary role really. It's keeping the boat safe. You are essentially the captain of the ship.' It was a sentiment echoed by Henry: 'It's your responsibility to keep the crew and the equipment safe. Being on the water, things can get out of hand pretty quickly.'

Fighting the Tide

In 1984, Cambridge cox Peter Hobson discovered that things could get out of hand before a race has even begun.

As he led the Light Blues through a warm-up on the Tideway, Hobson managed to steer into a moored barge in front of hundreds of spectators at the Putney Bridge start line. With a mangled bow pointing to the heavens and his sopping crew scrambling to the river's edge, Hobson had etched his name into Oxbridge infamy. 'It was in my blind spot,' the sheepish cox told a giggling press corps after making it to dry land.

As Cambridge went off to find a new boat, the race was re-arranged for the following day. Oxford proceeded to rub Thames saltwater into their rivals' wounds by winning by three and three-quarter lengths. Hobson went on to cox internationally, but nothing he did after managed to rehabilitate a reputation as the man responsible for the first Sunday Boat Race. To Hobson's credit, he is now at least able to laugh about it in public. At a 2014 talk at Christ's College, his icebreaker line was, 'They said I had ten minutes [to speak]. That's not long enough to cover all the crashes.'

If it took 30 years for Hobson to see the funny side of a steering error, then it might take longer for Zoe to get over her own Boat Race trauma in 2012. Her tone noticeably shifted when I brought up the subject and it's no surprise that her experience as Oxford cox in one of the most dramatic men's Boat Races in history is not a favoured topic. 'It was nearly the end of my career. Because I didn't want to get in a boat again afterwards.'

With both boats level at the halfway mark, assistant umpire Matthew Pinsent spotted someone in the water on the approach to Chiswick Pier. The race was halted as a protestor with a death wish came only inches away from being struck by an Oxford oar. After the troublemaker's cuffed removal, the race recommenced half an hour later. But with the motorboat salvage operation resulting in choppier conditions the two rowing eights found themselves coming closer together.

Zoe was on the receiving end of a warning from umpire John Garrett, but it didn't prevent a clash between the two crews. When Oxford's Hanno Wienhausen removed his oar he found it no longer had a blade attached. The race was effectively over for Zoe and Oxford but the drama would continue. After crossing the finish line four and a quarter lengths behind Cambridge, Oxford's crew watched on in horror as exhausted bowman Alex Woods collapsed and lost consciousness. Cambridge cancelled their celebrations while Woods was rushed to hospital, where an overnight stay saw a full recovery.

The disappointment of the day has stayed with the cox, who found herself the target of blame in some quarters of the sport. 'At the time, I was being warned. So that's my fault. And we lost the race. That was easily the worst I've had, not least because it's watched by millions of people. And so I think that was definitely my lowest point.'

The day wasn't a complete write-off for Zoe, and the story comes with an unlikely happy footnote. Earlier on in our conversation she joked that 'rowing's a small world, and we all marry each other' and I soon found out just how true that was. 'If I hadn't been in that race with those people and had the experience I had, I probably wouldn't be married to my husband now, who was in that boat,' said Zoe, referring to Alex, her stricken team-mate that day.

The pair were married in 2018, and Zoe credits his support and encouragement as one of the reasons she returned to rowing. 'I'd rather it have not gone the way it went. But if I am where I am now because of it, then it was worth it,' she added sweetly, before glancing behind her to see if Woods, also a doctor, had overheard from the next room. As she did, I noticed the picture on the wall behind her. At first glance, it appeared to be Hokusai's *The Great Wave off Kanagawa*. I wondered if it had a deeper meaning for Zoe, until I noticed it was a spoof version of the famous print. It wasn't a wave. It was the Cookie Monster. Zoe doesn't take herself too seriously.

Given the typical life of a cox, Zoe's love story is a rare drop of harmony amid a tide of friction. Being the person charged with eking every exertion from rowers who have no more left to give is not usually conducive to an affectionate relationship.

Henry, who speaks so delicately it is hard to imagine him roaring at giants who tower above his 5ft 4in frame, admitted that coxing can be a lonely place. 'The training programme is designed to make the rowers tired the whole time. They're always in some level of fatigue. And you're there saying, "I need it to be better." They're all fucked. But it's still your job to push it forward. That's sometimes an uncomfortable role to fulfil. It's not your job to be their friend,' he said, his voice deepening. 'You've got to be that guy that sometimes people don't want to hear from.'

Talking Tactics

If the skill and awareness required for steering the boat showcase the cox as an athlete, then their next responsibility places them firmly in the guise of a skipper. A coach has no further influence on a crew once they are on the water, and so will rely on their cox to help execute a pre-determined race plan. Coxes will also be trusted to instinctively change plans mid-race should circumstances require it.

And while the over-arching themes of starting quickly and getting into a rhythm will be true of every boat, staggered intensity levels will differ for each crew. 'I could go and give someone our race plan but it doesn't mean they're going to be able to execute it. From a physical, mental, and technical point of view,' said Rowley, adding that the same would be true if he was given a rival's instructions.

While some teams will aim to establish a lead and cling on, others will be happier in the chase knowing they possess a strong finish. In Sydney in 2000, Great Britain encountered an Australian crew intent on the former. It had worked for them in the opening heat, as the host nation led from the front and refused to wilt to the advancing British crew. They finished two seconds in front and qualified directly for the final.

Rowley and his eight crew-mates, bidding to end an 88-year British drought in the event, were forced to contest the repechage heat. This time it would be Team GB front-loading the race, exploding out of the blocks at 51 strokes per minute to build a commanding lead. After just 500m they were already a length clear and a place in the final was secured with a three-second cushion. By the time it came to contest for the gold medal, Rowley decided not to dwell on the tactics of his rivals.

'I don't think you make your race plan specifically around another boat. That would be a mistake. But you probably should be conscious of other boats' strengths,' he said. Rowley knew that an inexperienced Croatian team could get out of the blocks fast on their day, but struggled to keep the pace if they found themselves behind. Likewise, the Americans were not to be left to dictate the pace. 'If they got out in front chances are you're not seeing them again. So you have to be conscious of these things but not centre everything you do around them. In our race, the Americans were triple world champions. They came [second] last. So if we'd have been racing them we'd have been fourth.'

Instead Great Britain led from the off. Holding his microphone in place, Rowley's blue headband could be seen bobbing side to side as he kept his crew informed throughout. Just how truthful one should be in this situation is another judgement call for the crafty cox. Some may be tempted to underplay slow starts so as not to demoralise their crew while fibbing about how long is left in a race is a known rowing hack. Tell a crew to push for the last 50m when there is really 80m to go might just squeeze out that extra kick. But it's also a big risk. For what might work once may never do so again if the crew interprets your white lies as broken trust.

Rowley had no such concerns in the final. After 500m the crew could see every boat behind them. At a kilometre the Brits had extended their lead over the entire field. Every glimpse of Rowley showed him hunched and screaming, veins bulging from his neck, his fair-skinned face reddening under the Sydney sun. With 500m to go his crew were two seconds up on Croatia in second, nearly three on Italy in third, with the Aussies even further back. But the home boat had the backing of a roaring grandstand, and it was an inspired Australian outfit that finished the fastest.

They claimed silver, coming in just 0.8 seconds behind a British rowing unit that was too exhausted to celebrate. The eight tumbled backwards and slumped forwards after crossing the line. In contrast, an adrenaline-fired Rowley leapt to his feet and waved his clenched fists towards the Union flags in the grandstand. While the Aussies rued running out of track the Brits had nothing left to give. For Rowley, it represented a perfectly executed race plan. 'I have a reasonable memory of it, albeit it's a little while ago now. We win by more every time I talk about it.'

Straddling the dual role of instructor and competitor can be a complex proposition for coxes. For they are not only tasked with realising the coach's vision on race day; they are also running gruelling daily drills on the water, before reporting back to the coach with their thoughts on technical areas in which the crew can improve. It is not unfeasible that a struggling rower fearing for their place may perceive the cox as an unwanted whistleblower. And so being caught between the devil and the deep blue is a common problem.

'I definitely feel like I'm more in the boat than out of the boat,' said Henry, noting that he is on the podium if all goes well. 'But you are definitely a conduit between the coach and the crew. Me and the coach will talk separately about things. He'll say, "This is my vision for the next race and I think you can help bring that out by doing this." Different coxes might see it differently, but I see myself more as one of the athletes than one of the coaches. But you have a foot in each camp.'

Saying Boo to the Geese

Rowers are notoriously driven characters, and Henry's eight in 2021 was no different. It included Moe Sbihi, the imposing 6ft 6in Team GB flagbearer who had followed an Olympic bronze in 2012 with gold in 2016. As such, a bronze medal in 2021 was not initially seen as anything to celebrate, and Henry mentioned a 'media shitstorm' in the aftermath. He was referring to bowman Josh Bugajski's comments criticising former coach Jürgen Gröbler, though Henry was careful not to name him. 'One of the guys said some stuff in the media that probably none of the rest of us agreed with. He's a good guy. He's a challenging guy. We've had guys in the past that have been challenging.'

When he was younger, Henry had posters of Michael Jordan on his bedroom wall and after watching Netflix's *The Last Dance* he recognised many similarities between Jordan and the rowers. Especially Sbihi. 'There were bits in it where I thought to myself, that really reminds me of the way Moe is day to day,' said Henry, before throwing in an immediate caveat. 'Not the negative stuff. I'm not saying he's punching people in the face. But that drive. The intensity. He probably feels how Michael Jordan felt, that it's not just his job to score baskets or row good strokes, he's also got to lift the team forward and hold them to a standard that he thinks is acceptable. Which might be higher than maybe other people think. In that way, they're really good people to have around.'

I wondered if it could be daunting for a cox to not only work alongside such intense characters but also be expected to push them to new levels. Henry said he had never encountered any animosity that had overwhelmed him. But at a lower level, he had heard stories of coxes being intimidated and bullied. 'You've got to be thick-skinned about it. Sometimes if I see it, which is rare, I'll call it out. Nothing grinds my gears more than seeing a kid getting ripped into when everyone's trying their hardest.'

At an Olympic level, Henry said he had only ever come across athletes who were eager to accept feedback on their techniques. This desire to be constantly improving was an attitude that Rowley also encountered in the lead-up to Sydney, even among the heated exchanges. 'We definitely had some pretty explosive run-ins, shall we say,' he said smiling. 'I was probably at the centre of a few of them. But when you're pushing things hard, shit breaks.'

Other than Ben Hunt-Davis, who had appeared in Barcelona in 1992 and Atlanta in 1996, Rowley's team were Olympic virgins. 'We were 20-something-year-old, stupid, egomaniac, moron blokes. Of course, we were going to make mistakes, it was just inevitable. What we were good at doing was limiting that and channelling that.

But sometimes it went over the edge. There are at least two occasions where someone nearly knocked my block off.'

It is during these testing occasions that a good cox will earn their keep – and their medal – by refusing to cower to crew-mates who are all much taller and stronger than they are. 'You've got to call it as you see it, even when it's tough to do so,' said Rowley. 'Going through life, it's easier to just politely agree and move on. But you can't do that if you want to push everyone and everything to get where you want it to go.'

When their technique is being questioned, when their will is being challenged, and when their chance of a medal is being doubted, gratitude is rarely the sentiment that rowers feel. But eventually, Rowley insisted, the best of them will appreciate the most obdurate of coxes: 'Any rower that's actually good, they'll fucking thank a cox for that, right? Because they know that they're only being pushed, and having strips ripped off them because that person is trying to get them a gold medal too. You need to improve, and I'm here to improve you.'

If improving a team includes steering, coaching, liaising, and keeping the crew safe, one thing it doesn't involve is being the dogsbody. Sure, coxes can help tune the boat and mend equipment. But any self-respecting coxswain will only go so far. 'One thing I was never going to do was just be subservient to the crew,' said Rowley, becoming so animated on the subject that his clock seemed to tick faster. 'Carry this shit around for them, make tea for them, and fucking toast. I say that complete with curse words because it just pisses me off. And some people get selected for that. Basically, you're getting selected for being a butt-kissing slave. What value are you really adding just being someone's skivvy?'

Rowley sneered at a memory from the World Championships in Cologne. There, he watched on in amazement and disdain as the Romanian coxed pair pulled up on the dock before the cox rushed off to collect their shoes. 'Then he kneeled on all fours and they used him as a bench. They sat on him to tie their shoes.' Rowley's laugh was raucous but there was a serious point hidden within the description of a Marx Brothers moment. Without respect, the cox's most well-known function is a complete non-starter. Just like trust, if there is no respect then there is no inspiration. Rowley made that abundantly clear to his crew from day one.

'I said if people want me around to make tea and shit like that, I'm not your guy. I don't think people respected me for the statement. They respected me for the work I put into being the other guy. You want people to look at you as the guy we need on board. "That person will help us get a gold medal." Because that's how I'm thinking about the other eight people. You don't want, "That's the person we want on board because they tie our shoelaces."'

It was clear the topic of respect and motivation brought out a different side to Rowley. The ribald locker room humour – lines like 'you don't shout "stroke, stroke, stroke" unless you're at a brothel' and describing rowing techniques as 'like an erection, the more you think about it, the harder it gets' – was put to one side. After all, a laughing oarsman is a rower wasting energy. And as he furrowed his brow, I got a glimpse of the Rowley that the rowers faced in the boat.

Magic Words

Every word that a cox utters during a race will boom out of speakers all the way down the boat. The effect of those words may be marginal at best. But when you consider the margin of victory enjoyed by Rowley and his crew over the Aussies in Sydney, those words can be the difference between gold and silver. Yet what may work for one crew member may not work for another, and the best coxes know exactly what to say, to who, and when.

'If I swore and cursed at one of the guys, man, he'd go crazy. He would pull so frigging hard but he'd probably blow up in 20 strokes and then be baggage,' remembered Rowley. 'You've got to manage that in the right way. There was another guy, if I swore and cursed at him, he'd just think, "Why are you swearing at me?" He needed a totally different type of motivation. He responded well to essentially what amounted to responsibility.' During the Olympic final, Rowley remembered exactly how he dealt with the latter rower. 'I said, "If ever we've needed you, and the power you can deliver, it's right fucking now." And all of a sudden he's turning on the gas like nobody would believe.'

Although coxes aren't always expected to join their crew in the gym, Rowley found it useful to attend the weights sessions. For it was there that he could pick up pointers on what would drive each individual to reach their physical peak. 'The guys would often be pushing each other on the weights to get one more rep out. It was always interesting to see who responded to what. Then you do a bit of trial and error in the boat. You try things out with pitch, tone, words, singling people out, and picking subgroups within the group. It was all about test and fail, test and fail, test and succeed.'

Henry said this vocal stimulation was 'where the magic happens', recalling Michael Jordan once again by describing it as where he can find an edge. When I asked him to give examples, it was revealing just how much emphasis was placed on *how* he said the words. There was almost a musicality to it. 'I'm using my voice to maybe change the rhythm a little bit, to try and convey that as well as just the word. So I might say, "Just roll out a tiny bit more therrrre,"' he said, deepening his voice and extending the word 'there' for several seconds so that it became like white noise.

He gave me another example, saying, 'Let's just *sting* it through a little bit more,' emphasising the sharpness and brevity of the word 'sting' to give a sense of pace. I suggested that, with intonation seemingly as important as vocabulary, maybe those questions at the airport weren't so silly after all. Only he is not the drummer. He is the drum. Henry accepted that there was some truth to it. 'I suppose your audience when you're a cox is someone who's just in terrible pain. The intonation is something that can really get through. But also you're trying to keep what you're saying quite concise because they're not able to focus so much.'

Zoe, who also has a degree in psychology, advises her students that coxing is about more than pithy one-liners.

She believes that overthinking the lingo risks undermining a race rather than strengthening it. 'I think it's important for them to understand that a lot of it is about when you say things and how you say things. If you've sat at home and thought, "This is a great call, I'm going to make this at 500m to go", you're then trying to shoehorn it in and it doesn't make sense in the race that's playing out in front of you.'

While she cautioned me that all coxes do it differently, Zoe nonetheless wanted to share an example of just how effective a cox's voice can be. She sent me a link to a 2010 recording of US cox Katelin Guregian's audio during an eights race in Lucerne, Switzerland. It's a revealing listen. For six minutes Guregian barely takes a breath, talking her crew through every stroke while offering collective pleas – 'we're gonna send a fucking message to Canada!' – in addition to individual prompts like, 'That is your fucking rhythm, Amanda. Solid!' There are monosyllabic cues, lyrical descriptions ('I'm sitting right on their bow ball'), and onomatopoeic grunts that would have loved ones calling the doctor if uttered in public. Guregian's voice begins calm and composed, then builds to a crescendo just as the eight cross the finish line first.

Although some vocabulary will overlap, most crews will work to a completely different set of commands to their rivals. 'You create a language for your own tribe,' said Rowley, explaining that the words he used were based on shared experiences over four years together. 'They're micro-terms that are only maybe two words long. But two words to that group of guys was the equivalent of 2,000 miles of training.'

At the 2006 Head of the Charles Regatta in Boston, American cox Marcus McElhenney shouted 'shake and bake' to signify a power move, a catchphrase from Will Ferrell movie *Talladega Nights*. It worked to inspire his crew to victory. When I asked Henry if he had anything similar, he sheepishly admitted that during training for Tokyo his eight enjoyed their own unusual source of linguistic inspiration. 'It's funny the way languages work, even off the water. Because you spend so much time together we have all these catchphrases. For some reason, there was this endless fascination with *Les Mis* [*Les Misérables*] in the team. People would just be in the corridor and they'll say a phrase, and the guy passing would complete the line. It's weird.'

The most famous phrase to emerge from the mouth of a British cox occurred at the Barcelona Olympics in 1992. Brothers Greg and Jonny Searle were competing in the coxed pairs against the heavily fancied Italian brothers Carmine and Giuseppe Abbagnale. The Italians were seven-time world champions and led the race by nearly five seconds at the halfway stage, with the Searles lagging in third.

With 200m to go they remained a length behind, prompting cox Garry Herbert to utter his immortal words from the bow, 'If not now, when? If not you, who? How much do you want this?' An extraordinary climax saw the Searles overtake the faltering Italians with just metres remaining to take the gold medal. Afterwards,

Greg credited Herbert's words as a significant factor. 'We knew then that we wanted it more than them,' he said. Herbert's tears on the podium became a defining image of the Games.

Soul of the Boat

At international level, both male and female coxes must weigh a minimum of 55kg. Anything under that and they are required to carry dead weight in the boat to make up the deficit. Given that any cox tipping the scales above that will soon find their diet scrutinised by coach and crew, weight management is an under-appreciated element of coxing. 'It's a bit of a challenge sometimes, especially when you get older,' said Henry, adding that while the rowers enjoy five meals a day totalling over 6,000 calories, he will stick to two meals amassing no more than 1,500.

Although they are not expected to be warrior specimens like those wielding the oars, coxes do need to be in good physical nick. With the boat constantly accelerating and decelerating, having a strong core is vital for steady steering. 'You're basically tensing the whole time. So you build up this weird body shape. I'm pretty heavy on the leg and butt region. One-legged squats are my jam,' said Henry, who was born in Hammersmith and grew up near the river. His school-age memory of being lined up in height order during PE is a common one among coxswains. There may not be a height restriction, but given the weight target and how little space there is in the stern, tall and leggy coxes are rare. Very much like horse racing jockeys, the smaller the better.

And while Henry shared a biological trick that lets him marginally game the system ('I'll try and get down to 54 kilos, drink up [for weigh-in] and then piss it out. So that I race a bit under and just sneak a tiny advantage'), Zoe warned against focusing too much on what the scales are saying. 'I've seen it so many times, coxes turning up who've been crash dieting. They get into the boat dehydrated and dizzy and they cox and steer terribly because they can't concentrate. And they've done that for a kilo,' said Zoe, referencing a University of Oxford study that showed an extra ten kilograms of weight accounts for less than a second over two kilometres.

'There's coxes going out when it's really cold in hardly any kit because they don't want to carry extra weight in the boat. Then being so cold that they can't perform properly. You don't want a cox who's 80kg. But a 53kg or a 55kg cox is probably not going to make a difference, especially if they're the best person for the job in terms of everything else they can offer.'

We now know what everything else entails. Coxes may be commonly known as the voice of the boat but they are also its eyes and its brain. And when it comes to the best of them, they are often its soul, too. In BBC submarine drama *Vigil*, the onboard coxswain describes himself as a walking HR department. It is an accurate description of the namesake role in rowing too. Coxes are there to resolve everybody else's problem while being expected to leave their own issues on dry land.

'A coach of mine once said to me "rot spreads",' said Rowley, discussing the importance of setting the tone. 'If

I'm down everything I say has a tone of, "I'm down." That is today's rhythm. So I have single-handedly ruined the day. Whatever it is that you come down to the river with you've got to dump it off real fast. That can become quite wearing. It's like working in a Christmas store all year round. Everyone thinks it must be great, but it's awful.'

Zoe used the same word when describing the harsher elements of the job. 'Honestly, coxing is sometimes awful. You're sitting there in the freezing cold, you're soaking wet, you aren't moving. Unlike the rowers who are exercising and getting warm, you're sitting there getting colder and colder, your back's hurting because you're sitting in this hunched-over position. And it can be really miserable.' Even when they have led their crew to victory, a cox's traditional reward is to be picked up and thrown into the water.

But every backache, every death stare, and every exasperated remark of 'easy for you to say' is worth it for those rewarding occasions when every element – steering, coaching, and inspiring – comes together over a perfect two kilometres. Those days when a cox is certain that they made a difference. For Zoe, that happened at the 2016 European Championships.

The first outing for the eight who would go to Rio three months later had seen a win in the opening heat. Heat winners get one of the plum central lanes in three and four, which not only gives the best view of the field but tends to be sheltered from any swells in the water. However, on this occasion in Brandenburg, commentators remarked how Great Britain and fellow heat winners the

Netherlands were unlikely to be able to win the race from where they were, with brutal conditions favouring those in lanes one and two.

'It was probably the worst conditions I'd ever ridden a two-kilometre race in. It was horrendous,' remembered Zoe. The wind was so rough that British blades were constantly paddling at the start line just to keep the boat facing straight. As the race went off, the Russians in lane two built a commanding lead. Zoe would normally expect her eight to set off rowing anywhere between 40 and 45 strokes per minute before settling into a race pace of around 35 strokes; the reading on her cox box device showed her crew doing just 31. But she didn't panic in the choppy waters. 'We were relatively relaxed in these awful conditions where stuff's just blowing around everywhere. And we just got dropped like a stone. The crews out in lanes one and two were way ahead at the start. And the Netherlands in three were ahead of us as well.'

By 600m the commentators had already dismissed Team GB's chances, deeming them already too far behind in the squall. After a kilometre Russia's lead had been reduced by the Dutch, who Zoe had been keeping a close eye on under her white peaked cap. 'The Netherlands moved through and we kind of went with them. But even with 500m to go, they were still a full boat length ahead of us.' Having paced themselves superbly, and with the conditions now improving, Zoe sensed the moment. 'Suddenly, we were feeling quite fresh compared to the other crews that had been battling through the rough conditions in the early part. And we just started coming back to them. And we were catching them so fast.'

As the buoys went from yellow to red, signifying 250m to go, Zoe chose this moment to unleash her battle cry. 'We were running out of racetrack, but we were moving really quickly through them. And I just said to the crew, "I wish you could see what I could see! I wish you could see how fast we're catching them!" Which is obviously not something you'd ever sit down at home and think, "Great call, I'm going to write that down and use that." But it was just what I felt in the moment. And it was just what was happening.'

After the race, the crew told Zoe that it was not only her words that spurred them to overtake the Dutch and become European champions with barely a stroke to spare. They remarked upon how excited she sounded when saying it. They felt energised by the confidence and belief in her voice. 'It was one of the races where I really think that what I added made a difference to the outcome in the actual race itself,' said Zoe.

When I asked Zoe about the traits required to be a top cox, she told me that being calm and having the ability to bullshit were important. She then shouted towards the next room to ask her husband's opinion. 'Gobbiness!' came Alex's response. 'There you go,' said Zoe, rolling her eyes. 'So that's the rower's perspective.'

In Rio, Zoe needed to combine all of those characteristics for the silver medal. Like in Brandenburg, Great Britain started behind. Zoe figured that their rivals had gone off too quickly and would be unlikely to maintain their pace. Even with her crew in last place at halfway, she advised them to maintain their steady pace. They ended up pipping Romania to silver in a photo finish. 'I think that decision helped us win the medal that we did, because I think if I'd panicked, they would have panicked, and it could have all gone to shit,' said Zoe. 'Sometimes the decision to do nothing is harder than the decision to do something.'

While Zoe and Rowley are now retired from international rowing and using their coxing skills in their impressive post-Olympic careers, Henry has Paris in his sights. Which means fielding more strange questions in airports, not that he'll get a complex. Henry, like Zoe and Rowley, has an unyielding belief in what he brings to the team.

Distilled to its fundamentals, it is not all that different to those in the boat with him. 'The primary role is to be a part of what makes the boat fast,' said Henry. 'In that way, you're very similar to the rowers. Your purpose is completely aligned, but the way you do it is very different. And probably quite unique in the world of sport.' He told me that nothing would please him more than to be hurled into the Seine in 2024. Not – as Woodgate would have it – before the race, with reeds around his feet. But after it, with gold around his neck.

11

COUP DE GRASS:
Football Ground Staff

For most viewers of a football match, the pitch
is merely a blank canvas awaiting its art.
But before the artistry must come the science.
These days it takes more than a pitchfork
and a mower to get the game's top turfs up to
standard. Discover how today's ground staff
have transformed from crabby greenfingers
into techie agronomists.

Cold Sweats

It was the early hours of Saturday, 9 January 2021, and
Ben Kay was engaged in a thermodynamic battle. As head
groundsman of Chorley FC, a semi-professional football
club in the sixth tier of English football, it was down to
him to ensure that the biggest game in the club's 138-year
history could go ahead.

In a matter of hours Derby County, the Championship
team from four divisions above, would be arriving at
Victory Park to play in the third round of the FA Cup.

BT Sport's cameras would be there, along with Premier League referee Kevin Friend. Friend's first job would be to inspect the pitch which, due to temperatures that had dipped to as low as -5°C, was as frozen as Mr Whippy's last ice pop.

With Covid restrictions preventing fans from attending, the club had welcomed the injection of television cash. Ben was less enthused. The earlier 12.15pm kick-off had robbed him of three hours of sun, still his most reliable ally. The second most potent weapon in his armoury was a heated inflatable tent. Looking like something from the decontamination scene in *E.T.*, it was provided by the FA at a significant discount to ensure the game could be televised.

'It's like a big blimp,' Ben told me when we spoke that summer. 'It's 100m long, and you blow hot air into little vents. Once in the ground it thaws it out. But we had some areas in the corners that weren't doing that. On the Friday night, we still had a frozen pitch.'

The pitch had been a block of ice since 27 December, meaning that Ben hadn't been able to do any work on it since Chorley's Boxing Day win over AFC Fylde. On the night before the FA Cup tie Ben and his staff had a sleepover to keep a close eye on heaters that they had pushed closer to the tent. They used free-kick mannequins to keep the flapping canvas a safe distance away. 'If it had been three o'clock [kick-off] we could have got the tent off earlier and let the natural sunlight thaw it out. But we had freezing conditions. So that's why we made the decision to sleep there.'

As a 19-year-old, Ben had been on the books at his hometown club Wigan Athletic. He spent a year on professional terms before being cut adrift and forced to join the dole queue. 'I went in and they asked what my previous job was.' He was embarrassed to say professional footballer. 'They looked at me a bit funny. I knew I needed to get a career.'

He spent 14 years looking after local pitches for Wigan Council, but as a former pro he became frustrated at the lack of care shown towards grassroots grounds. When he got the job as head groundsman at a Preston high school, it seemed only a matter of time before he would be back in football. A consistent non-league performer for the likes of Marine, Warrington Town, and Leigh RMI, his contacts in the game eventually led him to Chorley.

The Magpies' budget meant that Ben had to work with second-hand mowers and decades-old frost covers, with no irrigation system in place. Undersoil heating was, quite literally, a pipe dream. It meant the money generated from an FA Cup run would be vital for the club's future. As Ben considered methods old and new ahead of the referee's inspection, including manning 20 volunteers with buckets of hot water, he knew getting the game on could be worth up to £200,000.

Chorley had already beaten Ben's former club Wigan in the first round and Peterborough United in the second. A historic spot in the fourth round was well within the team's grasp. Derby's first-team squad and manager Wayne Rooney had all been forced to isolate due to positive Covid tests.

'Derby's ten-day Covid isolation finished on the Monday,' remembered Ben. 'That was added pressure, knowing that if this game doesn't go ahead on the Saturday it's going to be on Tuesday playing Derby's first team. The game had to go on no matter what. We were playing Derby's under-18s.'

The groundsman's dedication would soon be apparent for the world to see after he took his turn for an hour's shuteye under the tent. It was 4am and, with his pitch now acting as a makeshift mattress, he dozed off wearing only his coat. A kindly colleague placed an M&M's-branded blanket over him. Then took a cheeky snap. When the game was given the green light a few hours later, the club tweeted a thank you to their ground staff alongside the candid photo.

The picture went viral and before long Ben was being interviewed on BBC radio and featured during BT Sport's coverage. His efforts were given superhero status in Chorley. Not so much Thor, more like Thaw. It was a rare moment of credit for the hardworking souls whose graft ensures games like this one can be played all over the country.

To top off Ben's successful salvage job, Chorley won 2-0. Their reward was a lucrative tie at home to Premier League Wolves. 'Any groundsman would have done the same just to get the game on. Because that's our job,' said Ben, stressing that it was a team effort. 'I wouldn't like to do it again. It was probably the worst, and the best, week of my life. Though I was hoping I'd get a year's supply of M&M's, but they never got in touch!'

Ben's newfound attention didn't just increase his Twitter followers. His 12th-round knockout of Jack Frost caught the attention of clubs higher up the pyramid. Three months after Chorley's memorable win, Ben was announced as the new head groundsman at League One's Accrington Stanley. He was back in the professional game that had once deserted him.

He was also invited by Wembley grounds manager Karl Standley to work on the most famous pitch in the country on the weekend of the FA Cup Final. It proved more than the watching brief of a competition winner. On the eve of the game, Ben was trusted to mow the turf. 'As I was on the Honda I was just looking around thinking, "Fucking hell, I'm in the middle of Wembley, I hope nothing goes wrong here." I was shaking.'

By Saturday Ben felt like a fully fledged member of the team, and he thrived on the chance to work with some of the best facilities in the world. 'As a footballer, you want to play on Wembley so this is kind of the next best thing. How many people do you know that have said, "I've walked on to Wembley's pitch"? Not many get to do it, and I spent three days helping to prepare for the FA Cup Final.'

Didier and the Yorkshireman

One man who is as familiar with the Wembley turf as he is with his back garden is Tony Stones. I met the experienced groundsman at a south-east London coffee shop just over the road from The Valley. Charlton Athletic's pitch is one of several that he consults on after three decades of tending to some of the world's most famous turfs. His thick Yorkshire accent barrelled around the cafe as he told me stories from his career, punctuated with the occasional swear word and gravelly laugh.

Thickset, shaven-headed, and tracksuited, Tony seemed to be the archetypal groundsman. The say-it-as-I-see-it, get-off-my-pitch type. Cut him and he bleeds grass. He too began minding pitches for the local authority, including cricket squares, bowling greens, and golf courses. He progressed to the groundsman's job at Barnsley before, in 2009, he was handed the dream opportunity to become head groundsman at Wembley – the most sacred surface in soccer.

In 2016 his career took a path that suggested there is more to Tony than meets the eye. He took a job at the Stade de France in the year that it was hosting the Euros. The commute from his Hitchin home was four hours. I asked him if he spoke any French. His giddy eyes had anticipated my question. 'Zero!' he barked before his laugh made the crockery clink.

On his first day, the man nicknamed 'Thunder Shorts' was given a polite warning from the managing director. 'We French like a revolt,' she told him. Tony took the advice, but wouldn't be cowed. When the national team arrived to train on the pitch, Tony asked to speak to manager Didier Deschamps. His suggestion was greeted with horror. 'They said it was forbidden. But I needed to see what pitch he wants.' Tony had enjoyed a close working relationship with England manager Roy Hodgson and his assistant Gary Neville, though Fabio Capello would only communicate via a liaison officer. The Yorkshireman much preferred the former approach, and he told his new French colleagues as much.

Amid the disagreement, Deschamps made a beeline for the new guy. 'You must be the English guy I've been hearing about. Call me "Boss",' said the World Cup winner, before shaking hands with Tony. He wanted the pitch firmer, wetter, and cut to 24mm. Tony's new communication route was now the norm in Paris. 'I said, "No problem, Boss, that's how we'll run." And that's how it always was after that.'

The language barrier led to the occasional mishap at the beginning of Tony's tenure. One of his first jobs was to transition the pitch from rugby to football, adjusting the line-markings accordingly. He would use a knapsack sprayer, which he had been assured, in broken Franglais, had no weedkiller in. Three days later the translation failure was all too apparent. Rugby's ten- and 22-metre lines were gone. But so too was the grass underneath it. 'All dead,' said Tony.

Although they were able to re-seed, the newer grass would grow back a lighter shade than the established turf. Tony was panicked. 'We've got the Euros coming and it's going to look an absolute shitter. So, what do we do? Well, this is another trick up the sleeve.' This time it was my turn to second guess Tony, and I asked if he'd simply painted it. 'I did!' came the happy response. Now it was me laughing.

Using 250ml of green dye and 20l of water, Tony found the formula to create the exact shade required. To those watching at home the pitch appeared immaculate. Throughout the entirety of the Euros, Tony gave the turf its Just for Men treatment at midnight every night. 'I was walking on with green spray when there was nobody in the building.' He said only six people knew of this covert operation, but I risked his wrath by asking him about another misadventure that many more had witnessed.

During the final between France and Portugal, a plague of moths disrupted the players throughout the 90 minutes. One landed on Cristiano Ronaldo's head. The story at the time, as repeated by the BBC's Gary Lineker, was that the beasts had arrived overnight when a member of the ground staff left the floodlights on. When I put this to him, Tony responded just as I had expected. 'Fuck off, we hadn't been in all night! The lights weren't left on. We arrived on the morning of the final at 4.30am.' The first mow disturbed the moths, and it was then Tony knew they had a problem. 'Some were as big as my hand. They were everywhere in Paris, it wasn't just the stadium.'

The June rain had been so persistent that it had caused the River Seine to flood. Only two matches at the Stade de France had seen dry conditions, the opening game and the final. The unusual climate led to the unseasonal infestation. 'Because it had rained so much, they hadn't hatched. As soon as it stopped raining and the temperature went up, all these fucking moths hatched out.' The problem didn't end at the full-time whistle. The moths had left their babies behind. 'During concert season caterpillars were coming out of the boards covering the pitch. There were people going to gigs knocking caterpillars off their legs. It was just a freak of nature.'

Despite those bumpy first weeks, Tony enjoyed a successful four years in Paris. Had it not been for the pandemic it is very likely he would still be there today, enjoying a more relaxed working environment than he was used to in the UK. The first time he completed an 18-hour shift, the MD wanted another friendly word. 'She pointed to my chest and said, "I don't do workaholics. Go and see your family." I've never been in trouble for working too much.'

His time in France made Tony rethink his work ethos. 'Working out there made me a more rounded person. Because everything doesn't happen at 100mph over in France. So I'm not as pushy to get stuff done.' A more relaxed approach was a far cry from his time in charge at Wembley. When we met, Tony had just come from The Valley, where Charlton were expecting 99 playing hours on the 2021/22 pitch. When he was at Wembley they would typically see over 230 hours of playing time. 'I always call it the biggest goldfish bowl in the world,' he said. 'Because the eyes of the world are always watching that pitch. My first year there was horrendous.'

Wembley Woe

When Tony arrived at Wembley in 2009, a pitch that was for decades renowned for being the plushest lawn in the land was close to becoming a national disgrace. Despite the new £750m stadium being on the same site as the original, what was once a hallowed turf had become a hollow one. Intended as the permanent home of football, its sand-and-soil pitch struggled with its multi-purpose role as an ad-hoc base to everyone from Lady Gaga to Tom Brady.

Big-name managers including Alex Ferguson, Arsène Wenger, and England's Fabio Capello lamented a surface as stable as a toddler's ball pool. After a slip from Tottenham defender Michael Dawson resulted in an extra-time goal for Portsmouth in the 2010 FA Cup semi-final, Spurs boss Harry Redknapp made his feelings clear: 'It's a disgrace. How can you play on a pitch you can't stand up on?'

Tony recalled the flak. 'We're always the first person people point the finger at. No one ever considers if a team has trained on it the day before. Or the morning of.' He remembered that the very same Portsmouth team had every intention of using the choppy pitch to their advantage. On the eve of the FA Cup Final against Premier League champions Chelsea, Avram Grant's side trained for 90 minutes on the turf. They finished the session with penalty practice. Tony was incensed. 'They destroyed the penalty spot. It were fucked.' When it came to their turn to train, Chelsea were less than impressed. 'Petr Čech walked on and said, "Why am I playing on a potato field?"'

After replacing the butchered turf, Tony endured a sleepless night praying that no spot-kicks would be awarded. The last thing he and Wembley needed was the FA Cup being decided by shifting sands. Unfortunately for him his appeals went unheard and the next day, referee Chris Foy pointed to the spot. Twice.

The first penalty went to Portsmouth, at the opposite end to where the turf had been cut up. But, in an act of karmic comeuppance, Kevin Prince Boateng scuffed his shot and allowed Čech to save with his legs. The second penalty went to Chelsea, and Tony could barely watch as the ever-dependable Frank Lampard placed his ball on the replacement grass. 'I was in the office with my head in my hands, thinking, "Please do not fucking slip."' Lampard didn't slip but he also failed to make a clean connection, shanking the ball wide of the post. Only a match-winning free kick from Didier Drogba allowed Tony to emerge from his office without worrying about more headlines.

Underdogs seeking any advantage that they can get from the playing surface is nothing new in football. When there is a gulf in class between teams, one way to ensure an even playing field is to face each other on an uneven one. And while no self-respecting grounds manager would agree to sabotage their own pitch, there have been plenty of other ways to create conditions best suited to the home team.

When Stoke City were promoted to the top flight in 2008, manager Tony Pulis requested the Britannia Stadium pitch be squeezed to its minimum permitted dimensions. At 100m long by 64m wide, it was five metres shorter and four metres thinner than the pitches at Manchester United and Arsenal. Pulis knew a smaller pitch would maximise a secret weapon that would rattle the country's top sides, and ensure survival for a club the bookmakers had tipped for an instant return to the second tier.

The manager's ace card was a dependable but hitherto unremarkable midfielder called Rory Delap. More specifically, it was the Irish international's long-distance, high-speed, and low-trajectory throws. With the slimmest pitch in the league, Pulis's human trebuchet contributed to eight goals at the Britannia Stadium that season, including two in one afternoon against a shell-shocked Arsenal. By contrast, Delap's killer throw-ins contributed to only a single goal away from home.

Arsène Wenger was among those crying foul about the pitch, even going so far as to write to the FA to complain that another of Stoke's stifling tactics was to grow the grass long. It would prove to be a regular bugbear of Wenger's throughout his time in England. As late as 2014 he said, 'I know perfectly well that some managers give orders to their groundsman sometimes to not cut the grass because they play against a team who passes the ball well.'

Tony remembered similar tactics being employed during his time at Barnsley. 'We'd leave the grass longer in the corners to slow it down for the wingers.' Once at Oakwell he was even cited for watering only half of the pitch. 'One of the away fans timed that I watered one half more than the other. They said I was fixing the games.' The accusation prompted a Football League enquiry. Tony had an explanation ready. 'It was because of the stadium, the south side is open so the wind blows through and it dries out quicker. The north side holds more water.'

Today the guidelines are stricter. The entire pitch must be watered equally and visiting managers must be informed when the sprinklers will be on. Pitch dimensions have also been standardised. Unless a stadium layout prevents it, all Premier League pitches must now align with UEFA's guidelines, 105m by 68m, the dimensions that Old Trafford and the Emirates already favoured. And as for keeping the grass long? 'You can't do any of that nowadays,' said Tony, adding that the maximum grass length is now 30mm and the entire pitch must be cut to the same height.

While the homogenisation of England's professional pitches might sap some of the individuality out of the game, Tony is not too upset if it keeps him out of trouble. 'If you're doing what the manager wants and then there's a comeback, it's on my shoulders. At least this way it's easier.' Not that Tony has ever shirked from confrontation when it comes to defending his pitch. There is a reason he earned his nickname. At over six feet tall and with a pitchfork in hand, it would take a brave person to get on the wrong side of him. But several have.

There was a crash course in Nordic expletives from Iceland's goalkeeping coach during Euro 2016. Tony had prevented the goalkeepers from training in the goalmouth on the eve of their quarter-final clash with France. Given the amount of rainfall that month, he was in no mood to repeat his Portsmouth Wembley nightmare.

He also recalled a feisty exchange with a Plymouth Argyle fitness coach ('I called him Blue Gloves') whose sprint drills weren't welcomed by the grounds team, nor the notoriously uncompromising Barnsley captain Chris Morgan. Fisticuffs were only just avoided.

But Tony saved his biggest laugh for the time he asked a visiting substitute goalkeeper to use the portable goal at the side of the pitch rather than damage the goalmouth. His request was met with a curt response. 'He told me to "fuck off you fat bastard".' Tony admitted that 'a few proverbials' followed before the goalkeeper continued his warm-up. As he went to collect a cross, he turned and fell on to the goalpost. 'He got a gash above his eye,' said Tony, smiling. 'As he walked past me, bleeding with a towel on his head, I said, "That's what you get you fucking wanker. Use the portable next time."' The crockery rattled again.

Green and Pleasant Lands

If the long-established trope about grumpy groundsmen appears to have some foundation, it is hard to begrudge it in an industry that has proven itself to be ruthless. Steve Welch, Tony's predecessor at Wembley, was sacked following the well-publicised issues despite being a former groundsman of the year. And it's not just at the elite level where sentiment is in short supply. In 2017, Southend United groundsman Ken Hare was dismissed after a frozen pitch forced off a game against Bolton Wanderers. He had been at Roots Hall for 27 years.

Now that he was dealing with the increased pressures and demands at a higher level of football, Ben admitted that the criticism was difficult. 'You're on a global stage all the time. Our game will finish and Sky Sports News will be showing the goals for the rest of the week. And with social media, there's no getting away from it now. Because somebody will post something like, "Look at the state of this pitch at Accrington, have they been on the piss all night?" At the end of the day, you take that to heart.'

Following every game, the referee and visiting manager score the pitch out of five. At the end of the season the marks are tallied up to crown the division's top grounds team. In 2021 Manchester United, Watford, Doncaster Rovers, and Forest Green Rovers took the awards for their respective divisions. But with referees unlikely to consider external factors, and with away managers often swayed by the emotion of the result, it's not a flawless review process.

Only weeks into his new job, Ben remembered Portsmouth manager Danny Cowley being less than complimentary after Accrington snatched a late draw. 'What he [Cowley] doesn't see is what's gone on through the week,' he said, adding that the team had been training on the pitch because of a lack of facilities. 'We've had to work our bollocks off just to get the game on. But people don't see that. Because for ten seconds they see the Portsmouth manager saying "that was bobbly, that's shit, there's no grass on it". Well, spend a week in our life and you'll understand why.'

A week in Ben's life is usually a wet one. The east Lancashire town of Accrington saw over 150 days of rain in 2021. 'We're surrounded by mountains, and most days you can't see them because of the mist and rain,' said Ben, wearing Accy's blue Adidas training kit. 'We have proper winters with snow on the hills. No one's ever winning pitch of the year over here.'

But if besieged UK ground staff feel a little unappreciated by the watching public, the same cannot be said about their reputation within the industry. Tony is one of several British turf pros who have been headhunted by the biggest stadia in Europe. The pitches at Real Madrid, Atlético Madrid, and Paris Saint-Germain may be foreign fields, but, to butcher Rupert Brooke's poem, those growing them are forever England. Tony attributes this popularity to a very simple reason. They get a lot of practice.

'We start from scratch every summer. Whereas in Europe, they think, "The pitch is good, it'll go another year." Then it starts falling apart because you get weed grasses.' Most professional football clubs in the UK renovate the pitch every season, regardless of its condition. Tony reckoned the alternative was too risky. 'When we went into administration at Barnsley, we didn't have the money to renovate. So we scarified it, and that's the worst December I've ever had. Kevin Betsy went in for a sliding tackle and his foot just slid. I went to [the divot] at half-time and it were five foot long,' said Tony, holding his arm in the air as if the offending strip of grass were in his hand. 'If you look on European pitches you'll see big blobs of different-coloured grass. It's a lighter green, which is annual meadow grass. Its root is shallow but it spreads massive leaves, and it's shit. So take it up, and start again.'

It is an annual process that has become even more effective following the advent of hybrid pitches. These are not to be mistaken for the controversial plastic surfaces seen in the late 1980s. Trampoline turfs like those at QPR, Luton, Preston, and Oldham were banned in 1995. Today's synthetic pitches are more sophisticated, strengthening the natural grass rather than replacing it. Tony credits

Wembley's resurgence to the installation of a Desso Grassmaster pitch in the summer of 2010. That came following the FA Cup Final and its two missed penalties on what was the ground's 11th relaid pitch. With the home of English football set to host the Champions League Final the following year, Tony said pressure from UEFA was the factor that eventually told: 'They said, "We want a pitch that we can guarantee will be safe for play and will not get bad publicity." So that's when upstairs made the decision.'

A reported £250,000 was spent to install the system first used by Huddersfield in 1997. It works by injecting 20 million polypropylene fibres into the base, 18cm deep. Just two centimetres of each fibre protrudes from the surface into which the natural grass is seeded. As it grows, the roots entwine with the artificial strands, anchoring the grass and creating a firmer and more stable playing surface. Only three per cent is synthetic.

Most Premier League and Championship clubs now have hybrid turfs like Grassmaster, though with installation costs now upwards of £500,000 the likes of Accrington do not. 'We're very basic. We just have a sand-and-soil pitch,' said Ben, whose weekend at Wembley must have been akin to a kid trading in his Connect 4 for an Xbox.

Tony, whose experience with Wembley's hybrid turf was the reason for his appointment at the Stade de France, said it has revolutionised the job. 'When we went with Grassmaster, that Wembley pitch was amazing after six months. It were never talked about again.' He compared the structure of the hybrid turf to a concrete pillar: 'If you have no steelwork in it, you can hit it and it'll fall over. But put steel rods in it, and it's not possible to knock it down. That is what Grassmaster does to the sand. It can take a divot because obviously it's got to be movable for players not to get injured. But the players don't interact with the plastic fibres, they only interact with the grass.'

It also reduces the headaches that used to come with pitch-destroying gigs. Rather than having to re-turf, grounds staff simply take off the top two centimetres of grass to remove all weeds and thatch in a process called fraise mowing. Tony showed me a video of one of his favourite toys in action at the Stade de France. The Koro Field Topmaker is an industrial mower that strips the surface down to its synthetic tufts in just a few hours. Once re-seeded, a pitch can be back to its cup-final best within weeks. The once-dreaded concert season no longer holds any fear. 'It's brilliant,' said Tony. 'They get to make money, and I get a new pitch.'

The One Per Cent Club

With the era of the new-age pitch, comes the dawn of the new-age grounds manager. In October 2021 I visited Leicester City's state-of-the-art training ground in rural Seagrave. Less than a year old, the 180-acre project cost £100m to build and cemented Leicester's place among the most forward-thinking clubs in the country. Taking me on a tour was the club's head of sports turf and grounds, John Ledwidge. And his bouncy six-year-old cockapoo, Harley.

John placed his thumb on to the biometric entry system before talking me through the headline innovations at a facility that manager Brendan Rodgers described as the most significant investment in the club's history. There are 21 pitches, including a floodlit 499-seater show pitch. Mounted spider cameras film training sessions at every age level. Off the pitch there are 30 acres of lawns, a fishing lake, a gym, a nine-hole golf course, hotel rooms, a vegetable garden, and cryotherapy facilities. Housed under the turf-walled dome is one of only three full-size covered pitches in the UK. Refreshingly for a Premier League operation, the complex isn't slopped in garish club colours. Instead the copper-toned buildings blend into the countryside.

John told me the architects designed the entire site around aspiration, with the first-team areas boasting nicer furnishings and better facilities. When I asked him for some examples, his first thought was the thicker carpets. Even indoors, he can't help but analyse what's underfoot. Leicester's first-teamers get exclusive use of the golf course and an individually allocated hotel room. They also play on better turf. 'Aesthetically, they look the same,' said John, 'but the pitches upgrade as you go around.' Just like the economy class enviously watching business flyers supping complimentary fizz, it all begins at the front door. 'As you come down the driveway, you turn left if you're in the academy, but if you turn right you've made it. You're with the first team,' said John, whose fluency in corporate speak hinted at the reason I was visiting.

As part of the development, he persuaded the Leicester board to launch the UK's first Sports Turf Academy. He had the idea many years ago, back when he was the Football League's youngest head groundsman at Coventry.

'I wanted a place where people can follow a journey like I've had, but in a much more professional setting. But it fell on its arse a bit because I needed about £13m to get it off the ground.'

When John joined then-Championship side Leicester as a 27-year-old, his ambition was to become a Premier League groundsman by the time he turned 30. The following season, Leicester's promotion saw him achieve that goal two years ahead of schedule. Improbably, by the time his 30th birthday came around, the club were Premier League champions. John admitted that it was a fortunate case of right place and right time. 'The signs were there when I joined back in 2014. It was like a marriage made in heaven. I feel like we both had the ambition to do the same thing.'

Knowing of the club's desire to invest in world-class facilities, John dug out his old notepad and presented his business case. 'They supported me with it. Fast forward four years on from when I first pitched it, we're sat in this multimillion-pound building for us to develop the next generation of people like me.'

The turf academy contains classrooms, a canteen, a mechanics' workshop, and a laboratory. The first-floor dining hall leads out on to a balcony overlooking the entire training ground. 'If you went anywhere else in the country, there's nowhere that you'd find a facility for ground staff like here. We're so lucky in that sense.' John pointed to a storage barn in the distance. 'Typically what you'd find in any setup is all of us would have been in that big green shed.'

John intends for the academy to become a gold standard in the training and education of ground staff. Referencing the success of Sir Dave Brailsford and British Cycling, his ethos positions a football pitch as a club's most important resource. One that should aid, protect, and maximise its prized talents. 'The largest asset at a football club are the players,' he said. 'And what they do on a daily basis is train and operate on something that you're producing. I call us the one per cent club. Because in terms of an operation, we are about one per cent of the club's turnover. But we are those marginal gains that can make a difference.'

When John joined Leicester he was in charge of a team of six people. Today that number is 52. That includes 18 ground staff, ten gardeners, four greenkeepers, four mechanics, a head of sports science, and an in-house doctor of sports turf. 'That exists, believe it or not,' said John, before introducing me to the man himself. Doctor Jonathan Knowles was sat by his laptop in the lab, surrounded by microscopes and gas taps. 'We had an issue on one of the pitches where we thought we had a certain disease,' said John. 'Whereas before we would have had to send [a sample] off to be analysed, Jonathan brought it in here and analysed it in five minutes.'

'We're like French chefs, we're so passionate about what we do,' added Jonathan, before going into detail about some of the 15 trials he is currently overseeing. One focused on the tines that punch holes in the pitches to get water and air to the roots. Traditionally, this small circular puncture tends to soften the turf. So they'd been experimenting with alternatively shaped tines in a bid to maintain firmness.

John compared it to jogging on the beach. It's much easier to run on sand that is wet and firm rather than dry and soft. 'A soft pitch can be really sapping. If we punch a load of holes through it, it zaps all the energy out of their legs. Whereas a player might normally be getting 60–70 minutes of high performance, all of a sudden that goes down to half an hour. We work with sports science to try and make sure that we're hitting an optimum all the time.'

What is optimum for one player isn't always the case for another. A forward whose game centres around speed will thrive on a vastly different turf to that which would benefit a centre-half reliant on an ability to read the game. In a sport increasingly obsessed with analytics, the pitch is another piece of data to consider.

'Pitches are the same as whether they've eaten, they've slept, they've shit, or they've shagged their missus the night before,' said John. 'It all has an effect on players, and all players are different.' Leicester know the exact pitch firmness required for striker Jamie Vardy to hit his top speed. 'But that will not benefit a Wes Morgan or a Jonny Evans. We've been doing that work for about four years now, trying to work out what suits what player.'

As requested by Brendan Rodgers, all of Leicester's training pitches are cut to the King Power Stadium grass length of 22mm. Like Tony, John is a firm believer in establishing a relationship with the manager. For him, dialogue should never be one-way. A manager shouldn't simply be issuing edicts to his ground staff, he should also be aware of their challenges. When Covid prevented Leicester from reconstructing their pitch as planned, the surface began showing signs of wear. 'The players were slipping, we were picking up injuries, and I couldn't control it because it had become so inconsistent. I went to Brendan with my head in my hands and said, "I'm so sorry."'

John had used three years of data to strengthen his case for reconstruction and had kept Rodgers in the loop throughout. 'I'm not one to hide and say it's not my fault. I'll front it out and say this isn't good enough.' It meant that when the media started asking questions, an informed manager was ready to defend his grounds team. 'Because we built that relationship, and because he knows how detailed we are, he was able to deflect those questions away. He understood what was happening.'

Outside, as Harley lolloped around in the black crumb rubber of the artificial pitch, John described the fear that drives him. 'If a player goes down injured I'll look at what's on the bottom of his boots. If there is a load of grass and crap, that means I haven't done my job properly. That will cause me sleepless nights.' John's recurring nightmare imagines Vardy lining up to take a penalty in the 89th minute of the final game of the season. 'And he goes arse over tit and slips because the pitch isn't right,' explained John, his sky blue eyes widening at the thought. 'It could cost us £40m if we've just missed out on the Champions League. Who are they going to come to? Me. And rightly so, because that's what we're here to do. We're here to produce a platform that they can perform on.'

Patterns Guy

As he handed me a cup of tea in a Sports Turf Academy-branded mug, John admitted that he wasn't always the science-led groundsman that he is today. 'When I started at Coventry, we were almost conditioned to stand in the goalmouth and wait for a fight.' Describing himself as a 'cocky little shit' when he pestered his boyhood club for a job at just 16, his attitude gradually shifted thanks to 14 months as assistant to Jonathan Calderwood at Aston Villa. Calderwood is now the grounds manager at Paris Saint-Germain.

When he was offered the top job at the Ricoh Arena, John returned with a progressive mindset and a new appreciation of the football business. In 2012, with Coventry chosen as one of six venues to host Olympic Games matches, John was told that the pitch was to be made a priority and assured that there would be no summer concerts. 'That was music to my ears. Until Coldplay turned up with a big fat cheque and said, "Can we play?"'

With the cash-strapped club in no position to turn Chris Martin away, John had five weeks to get the pitch ready for 12 games over eight days. 'The main lesson is that it's a business, it's got to make money. Non-matchday revenues are becoming so much more important to football clubs. It taught me to be open-minded, versatile, and flexible.'

John's commercial savvy will be vital for his academy to succeed. To ensure it runs a profit that will prevent Leicester's owners from turning the lights off, the plan is to hire it out for industry events. A 60-strong delegation from John Deere had been the latest to visit.

Generating more interest shouldn't be a problem for John. At around the same time as Leicester's Premier League win, their staggeringly intricate pitch patterns were making him the most famous groundsman in the world. 'It was a great opportunity for us to get more people talking about the industry. All the platforms were picking it up, and our lads were chuffed because [social content website] LadBible were showing their pitches. It was the opportunity for us to showcase what groundsmanship can do.'

From circles, stars, and zigzags to eye-catching 3D effects, Leicester's pitches mystified fans. And even some fellow grounds managers. Traditionally, the contrasting light and dark green lines on a pitch are created by simply mowing the grass one way and returning the other, using string to mark out the route. Astonishingly, given the detail involved, John insists that this manual method was used for every pattern except one.

The club crest, displayed in the centre circle, was achieved thanks to a state-of-the-art GPS mower from the USA. 'As it drives along it's like a printer, pushing the grass in all different directions to make the badge. The flaps underneath are going like the clappers.' Such was the hype around Leicester's pitch art that a concert producer got in touch asking if John could create Phil Collins's face on the Hyde Park lawns. 'He thought it was me doing it with a broom or something. We had some really strange requests.'

The fun came to an end in 2017 when the Premier League released new guidance that forbade anything other than horizontal lines on a pitch. They said that anything more complex hindered assistant referees when adjudging offsides. John joked that he might be permitted to get crafty again now that VAR routinely checks for offsides, but so far the Premier League haven't changed their tune. 'I take pleasure in the fact that people still talk about it,' said John, who was even once recognised as 'the patterns guy' on holiday. 'They think pitches and they think us. Now, from a business perspective, if they think about us I want them to think about the Sports Turf Academy.'

In addition to his business challenges, John is also responsible for a raft of eco projects that the club committed to in order to get permission for the development. 'Anything that's green falls into my lap,' said John, before explaining that he must adhere to a 144-page document on how to manage the land. Failing to do so could see the entire complex shut down. Causing him the most stress were the native great crested newts, a protected species that live in a pond on the golf course. When I told him this wasn't the conversation I expected to have with a football groundsman, he gave me a rueful look. 'If I'm shown to be negligent to the newts, it's an unlimited fine and jail time.'

Occasionally John's old instincts slipped out, like when complaining about players wearing bladed football boots ('it's a load of bollocks, more of a fashion statement than actual necessity'), or lamenting the work ethic of a typical millennial ('All my success has come from long hours, lots of sacrifices, but maybe I'm the fucking mug.

There is a sense of entitlement with the next generation coming through'). But few will disagree that John, with his turf doctors and sports scientists, sustainable practices and business acumen, represents the new era of groundskeeping. I asked him if it spells the end of the grumpy groundsman.

'One thing that I instil in all my staff here, and a lesson I had to learn myself, is we've got to move away from the stigma of being people that just throw their forks at people when they go in the goalmouth. At the end of the day, we are here to facilitate the players. That's our job. I've had full-blown rows with goalkeeping coaches on matchday. I've been told to fuck off. But I've realised that there are better ways to do it. Our industry has moved on so much. The grumpy old groundsman is a label I try to avoid. We're changing that. But it still exists, trust me. There still are forks flying.'

Grass Masters

Despite having over a decade on John, Tony spoke warmly of the man some in the industry have mischievously nicknamed 'John the Legend': 'They back him financially and it's pushing the industry forward. The technology is unbelievable.' At a recent industry awards do, Tony took part in a Q&A where he was asked if he was wary of passing on his knowledge. The insinuation being that if he did so he risked making himself obsolete. He disagreed. 'Somebody trained me up. Why should I not train the next generation? That's what it's about. You've got to have fruition.'

Whether on 1980s cow fields or Premier League carpets, Tony has grown more blades of grass than there are visible stars in the sky. Like a hybrid Grassmaster pitch, he blends tried-and-tested methods with new-age execution. And he has already begun the process of passing that knowledge on, at home and abroad. His attentive French assistants in Paris went on to manage the grounds at Bordeaux, Nice, and Strasbourg, while the grounds teams at West Ham and Charlton are similarly privileged to learn from one of the best in the business. 'All those stadiums are benefitting from somebody being with me for a year,' he said. 'Then whoever they take on, the legacy goes on.'

It's a legacy that all three grounds managers hope will gradually change the perception of the job. In France, Tony bristled at being dismissed as a *jardinier* (gardener) by the office accountant. '"Oh, you just cut grass," they said. I wish!' Today's ground staff are more than red faces with dirty fingernails. They are also experts in agronomy, meteorology, business, and technology.

'I still feel like people think that this is something for the uneducated,' said John. 'There's a misconception that we're all just hairy-arsed groundsmen who just cut grass, are all mucky, and smell like shit. I defy anyone to come to our building and tell me that's the case. It's a genuine career for people. Once people scratch the surface, they see that there's a lot more science to it.'

While Tony nurtures and John innovates, Ben harbours more modest ambitions at Accrington Stanley. When I asked if he might be tempted to take the next step up, perhaps completing a career loop by returning to Wigan, he played down any transfer talk like the pro footballer he once was. The sudden jump from non-league level to professional required that he attain the next level of qualifications and he was studying again for the first time since school, all while juggling the demands of the job with the trickier task of looking after a young family. At least for now he will continue his daily battle with Lancashire's brooding clouds, knowing that he will always have that sunny day at the pinnacle of English football.

'When I went down to Wembley, Karl Standley, – probably one of the best groundsmen in the country – said, "Thank you, Ben, because you've put us on the map again." And if it's just highlighting a bit of what we do then great. Because at the end of the day, if we don't do our job, football matches don't get put on. Maybe people don't see us as that valuable person within the team. But, when you think about it logically, we are.'

12

LION'S DEN: Rugby Medics

*Rugby union is one of the toughest sports
on the planet. Since turning professional in
1995, the players are bigger, the game is faster,
and the collisions are more brutal. Recurring
injuries include breaks, dislocations, and
the condition described as the game's hidden
epidemic, concussion. So when it comes to
treatment – and prevention – it calls for
Britain's best sports medics.*

A Lion's Wail

It took just 41 seconds for Doctor James Robson and
physio Phil Pask to enter the field during the first Test
of the 2005 British and Irish Lions tour of New Zealand.
As the fearsome All Blacks heaved their way towards the
visitors' goal line, over 37,000 fans inside Christchurch's
Lancaster Park screamed in a frenzy. But the two medics
could hear only the desperate howl of a Lion. It came from
captain Brian O'Driscoll.

Nobody else watches a game of rugby like a pitchside medic. If they're ball watching they're not doing their job properly. They need to fight their instincts and develop a visual delay. Like a firefighter watching the smouldering bonfire while the rest of us gawp at the sky. And so while everybody else had eyes on Dan Carter's arrowing kick towards the Lions' corner flag, James and Phil were already by O'Driscoll's side.

They had spotted what the TV cameras had missed. An ugly off-the-ball spear tackle by New Zealand pair Tana Umaga and Keven Mealamu had sent the Irishman tumbling head first towards the pitch. O'Driscoll's reflex was to throw out his right arm. The price for saving his neck was a dislocated shoulder. It was Phil's job to pop it back into place.

'To reduce someone's shoulder in front of thousands of people, with 20 million watching it on telly, in ten seconds. It's quite stressful,' said Phil, the England physio who was on his first Lions tour. He and James would be back on the pitch just minutes later, either side of a hobbling Richard Hill. The 32-year-old flanker's anterior cruciate ligament was no longer in one piece.

It was indicative of a gruelling tour in which the medical team had been bombarded from day one. Only days previously they had treated Lawrence Dallaglio's dislocated and fractured right ankle during the opening warm-up match. 'I almost had post-traumatic stress disorder,' said Phil. He would return for a further three Lions tours.

For James, a man of six Lions excursions and seven World Cups with Scotland, this was nothing new. His reassuring presence was not only familiar to the players but also to the travelling fans. O'Driscoll's replacement in Christchurch was England's Will Greenwood, a player who owed his life to James after swallowing his tongue during the 1997 trip to South Africa. The behind-the-scenes film *Living with Lions* documented Greenwood's 17 unconscious minutes and the rapid response that turned the amiable GP into a cult hero. But the acclaim doesn't sit too comfortably with a man as modest as he is passionate. 'It's not about you, it's about the protection of the player,' said James, while tucking into a sausage roll on a lunch break at his Dundee home. His energetic patrolling of touchlines has become a common sight in over 250 Test matches, and an impressive one too given his ability to keep pace with elite athletes 30 years his junior.

Take George North's memorable try against Australia in 2013. As the pulsating winger reached the 22m line, a bald-spotted figure in a green shirt and yellow armband could be seen just off the pitch, out-sprinting the touch judge. It was James, who then proceeded to pump a blue-gloved fist into the air. Having worked in rugby since 1991, the Cumbrian-born doc is still consumed by the thrill of top-level sport. 'The toughest part is not getting carried away with the emotion of the day and staying calm enough to do your job,' he said. 'After the game, you can get involved and you can celebrate. Occasionally I do put the fist up if we've scored because you can't take that element away.'

Although out of shot on the opposite touchline, Phil was also giving chase that day. And for good reason. North had passed a late fitness test on his hamstring and the medical team were nervous about whether it would hold out. 'You've always got your heart in your mouth when a player goes back, particularly after a soft-tissue injury like a hamstring. Because when you cross the white line, anything goes. You can't replicate in rehab and training what goes on in a game,' said Phil, whose 150 appearances in Northampton Saints' back row gives his medical expertise an added air of authority.

He had worked tirelessly with North over two weeks in a bid to get the Welshman ready for the first Test in Brisbane. 'He made a remarkable recovery and we got him fit, but well within what I'd expect in terms of a timeline. So we put him in,' remembered Phil. 'And of course, he got an interception and had to run 60m to score, with Israel Folau chasing him at flat-out pace. You're just waiting for [his hamstring] to ping. And it didn't. That was a heart-stopping moment.'

Getting caught up in the occasion is only to be expected. Just like for the players, being selected for a Lions tour represents the pinnacle of a rugby medic's career. Whether a physician or a physio, if you are on that plane headed south you know that you are deemed to be the best in the business by a coach regarded likewise. And you also know that when treating rugby union's leading titans, a magic sponge is as much use as fairy dust. But it wasn't always the case.

Death of the Rubs Man

The rubs man was usually a genial, veteran ever-present, with water in his pail and lager in his glass. He would be known for his 'good hands', as adept at bandaging a stud wound as he was at repairing the hinges on the clubhouse door. James came into contact with several rubs men when he played for Murrayfield Wanderers while studying at Edinburgh University. Despite training to be a qualified physiotherapist, he held them in high esteem. 'Every club had a rubs man, a traditional guy that was almost a pseudo first aider. I don't want to do them down because some of these guys were marvellous. They had that multi-role.'

After graduating from Edinburgh's Queen Margaret College in 1980, James reckons he was one of the first qualified physios to start working in sport when he was offered the role at district side North and Midlands. 'They had parted company with the rubs man just prior to the last game of the season. He had turned up and had perhaps been imbibing just a little too often. So they gave him the heave-ho, and they were desperately looking for somebody to cover.' James's first game coincided with the final career appearance of former Scotland captain David Leslie.

By that point the physio was also back at university, this time pursuing a six-year medicine degree at Dundee. 'It was never with the idea of actually being full-time in sports medicine. That was unheard of in those days. But I just thought if I was doubly qualified I could offer better service to sportsmen and women.'

Then in 1991, with rugby union still four years away from professionalising, James received a call from the Scottish game's governing body. The Scots were off to North America for three weeks and needed a physio at short notice. James spoke to his NHS superiors and offered to work every weekend so that he could combine his entire annual leave in order to make the trip. On his return, Scotland offered him a role in their World Cup campaign later that year. Thankful that his boss was a rugby fan, James duly accepted. Not only was the post unpaid, but when James eventually became a GP he found himself paying a locum to cover his day job while he got his rugby fix. 'For many of the early adopters of sports medicine roles you either used your holidays or you financed the role yourself. You would have to make sacrifices.'

At around the same time, a 28-year-old Phil was playing for Northampton Saints while paying the bills with a job as a PE teacher. 'We came from an era that to have time to be passionate about your sport, you had to be a teacher, or in the army, or the police force. Because they were the only guys who could get enough time off to do it,' said Phil, a policeman's son raised in a small village near Worksop.

Dissatisfied with teaching, he decided to retrain as a physio. A Saints supporter loaned him a car, while the club paid his expenses and guaranteed him a job at the end of it. They kept their word. But with no dedicated facilities, he would be forced to treat future England stars such as Matt Dawson, Paul Grayson, Nick Beal, and Tim Rodber at the back of the changing rooms on Tuesday and Thursday nights.

Then, on 27 August 1995, the International Rugby Board (now World Rugby) announced that the game was going pro. Salaries were no longer the preserve of the boardroom. The new cash-injected backroom setup was a far cry from what Phil had been used to. 'When I was a player at Northampton Saints, our pitchside physiotherapist was an MFI security guard who'd done a few weekend courses,' said Phil, who still looks physically capable of rucking with the best of them. He then gave a rueful chuckle. 'Of course, I retired from rugby just as the game went professional, so I never made any money out of it as a player.'

For the likes of Phil and James, who have witnessed and worked across both eras, the days of amateur rugby are now unrecognisable, particularly from a clinical perspective. 'In the pre-professional era, if you got a bad knee injury you retired from the game. You'd go back to work because you couldn't afford to get injured again,' said Phil. He told me to dig out old team photos from before 1995, and to note the ever-changing playing squads. 'You'll see different faces each year. Apart from the lucky players like myself who had about nine or ten seasons, there was a massive turnover in players.'

The vast majority of today's injured pros tend to be recycled back into the game following surgery or rehab. 'We know that surgical techniques have improved out of sight and the care of professional athletes is so much better,' said James, adding that players are better conditioned to survive the rigours of the high-impact sport. 'We got an awful lot of muscle tears in the first two or three years of my international career. Those are few and far between now because people are better conditioned. So instead of routine hamstring injuries, you don't see them for vast periods of the season.'

That is also down to a change of emphasis from those who look after them. Medics are no longer simply reacting to injury. They are also preventing them. Back in the early days of professional rugby, British players were like kids at Christmas. For the first time in their lives they were able to give up their graft and be paid for playing the sport they loved. But their boundless gratitude meant there were few expectations or demands. 'They weren't used to having loads of physios and massage therapists, and ice baths and facilities for recovery. We had to cobble it all together, begging, stealing, and borrowing to start with. Using local gyms, spas, and bringing in people for free,' remembered Phil.

Instead, the bar would be raised by the game's imports. When Aussie flanker Mark Connors joined the Saints in 2002, Phil remembered seeing a lot of him. 'He was presenting to treatment a lot. And it wasn't because he was injured. It was because his expectation was that we'd do screening and maintenance, not just treat the injured players.' It was a common trend among the overseas players, and the habit soon spread to the natives. 'The English players started to pick up on that. That's where it started,' said Phil. 'And now it's an expectation across the board that we screen to the nth degree. We have massive individual development programmes and treatment programmes for each player.'

At international level England coach Clive Woodward wasn't only on the same page, he was writing new chapters. He insisted on specialists in every area of the game. In came scrum coaches, line-out maestros, kicking connoisseurs, strength and conditioning trainers, and a fully fledged medical team. Phil, who had been a volunteer physio with England since 1997, would be Woodward's senior physiotherapist. 'We suddenly had a staff of about 30. We had Pennyhill Park to train in, a designated training centre. We stayed at top hotels with recovery facilities, pools, and saunas. We travelled first class. All the stresses and strains were taken off the players by having a management team that was large enough to absorb it all.'

England won the World Cup in 2003 and Woodward's bold blueprint became rugby's bible. Meanwhile, the rubs man went the way of the pig's bladder, replaced by something more sophisticated and better suited to the modern game.

Tackling a Pandemic

On the final Lions tour of rugby's amateur era, to New Zealand in 1993, James Robson was one of only five backroom staff. There was manager Geoff Cooke, head coach Ian McGeechan, assistant Dick Best, physio Kevin 'Smurf' Murphy, and Doctor Robson. The five of them supported 36 players over eight weeks.

Contrast that with the 2021 trip to South Africa where the medical team alone outnumbered the entire supporting cast of 1993. Two doctors, two physios, and two soft-tissue therapists reported to the head of medical, Prabhat 'Prav' Mathema. A former physio at Queens Park Rangers FC and Wasps RFC before joining up with Wales, Prav's first Lions call-up was alongside Phil and James in 2009. His fourth excursion would be his first in charge.

Held in the epicentre of an active pandemic, it would present a challenge that none of his predecessors had ever dealt with before. 'It was the hardest thing I've done in my career. Absolutely no shadow of a doubt. And that was because of Covid,' Prav told me, just a month after returning to the UK. 'We were playing multiple teams, in the global hotbed of Covid. We had to manage multiple positive cases. All while running a medical team on a Lions tour. Which is tough.'

Prav's clinical responsibilities as Wales's medical manager are combined with a governance role, allowing him to influence health and safety changes in the sport. It put him well placed to act as chair of the tour's medical advisory group, working with virologists and authorities from both sides to craft a strict set of protocols. Games were to be played behind closed doors. Players were to remain in tightly controlled bubbles. And sealed red zones were put in place at stadia, airports, and hospitals. Entry was only permitted to those who had been tested within 24 hours.

But no bubble is impenetrable. On the day that over 21,000 Covid cases were recorded in South Africa, and just two hours before they were set to play their third warm-up game, the British and Irish Lions announced that a player had tested positive. Fourteen close contacts, including nine players, were forced into isolation. As some in the media called for the players to return home, the remainder of the tour was plunged into doubt.

'The challenge that you have is when one person in a closed group gets it, it's highly likely it's going to spread,' said Prav. 'But when we did get the positive, it was an incredible experience. Because the whole team came together straight away.' With the meticulous precision of a decorated drill sergeant, Prav put his fallback plans into practice. It began with a message to the entire party. 'This is not a joke! Everybody go to your room and isolate,' it read. His opening caveat hinted that Prav was fond of a wind-up. He didn't deny it. But the disadvantage of having a sense of humour is that he had to send twice the number of texts. 'I'm a bit of a joker sometimes. And the first thing that came back was, "Ah, you're joking." I said, "No, I'm not joking. Go to your room now and isolate." We mobilised very quickly.'

A South African laboratory partner arrived to set up a makeshift PCR station, and one by one the players were called down for testing like jittery talent show contestants. 'We had to essentially get all of those results turned around in time to allow us to play in the evening,' said Prav. Packaged meals were sent to each player's room, and kick-off was delayed. When a clean sweep of negative tests came back, the game received the go-ahead. The Lions beat the Sharks 54-7. 'We had this mantra, "chaos, change, and adapt". We got through it without any further infection through the whole squad, which was incredible.'

Although the Test series ended in a disappointing 2-1 defeat, that it went ahead at all represented a medical and epidemiological success for Prav and his team. 'I know, [the result] was disappointing. But I think everybody involved should be proud,' he said. I wondered if he had ever envisaged, back when he was training as a physio, that he would one day be coordinating a pandemic response. 'No chance,' he said. 'Talk about being out of your comfort zone.'

'Tis But a Scratch

If Prav and his team felt more at home strapping knees than swabbing nebs, it certainly showed in the treatment room. When it came to the decisive third Test in Cape Town, head coach Warren Gatland found himself with a welcome selection headache. 'Going into the final Test match, Warren and the coaches had every single person fit and available, which is unheard of on Lions tours. So we were very fortunate from that perspective,' said Prav, modestly crediting it to luck.

Given that the Daft Punk song 'Harder, Better, Faster, Stronger' could have been written as an ode to the transformation of the professional rugby player, the fact there wasn't a single Lion on the treatment table after 640 minutes and six weeks of attrition was a remarkable anomaly and a testament to their head of medical's ideology. 'An ethos that I've had through my whole career is about preservation versus preparation,' said Prav. Sit a player out for too long and he'll be short of match fitness. But allow him to train at full pelt and there's every chance he'll hear the hum of an MRI scanner before he does the buzz of a crowd. Delicately judging those intensity levels is like pouring vodka in a Bloody Mary. Too much, no good. Too little, no point. 'It's making sure that the balance is spot on so that ultimately we can give the coaches the guys they need to get the job done on a weekend.'

Strong communication and UN levels of diplomacy are handy skills to possess when it comes to this juggling act. Being a rugby medic regularly means playing the bad guy, delivering news that neither the player nor the coach wants to hear. Rugby has for years been renowned for its unflinching combatants who take a masochistic pride in playing through the pain barrier.

A story told by one of Phil's former Northampton team-mates sums this attitude up more than any other. Wayne 'Buck' Shelford made his New Zealand debut against France in 1986. That the game became known as the 'Battle of Nantes' gives an indication as to what is to come, but any males with a squeamish disposition may wish to skip the next paragraph.

After 15 minutes against a fired-up French side, Shelford took a kick to the face at the bottom of a ruck. Three of his teeth found a new home on the Stade de la Beaujoire turf, but worse was to come. Just before half-time he took a blow on the forehead from meaty French prop Jean-Pierre Garuet-Lempirou and was knocked out cold for two minutes. Yet the man who would go on to captain his country still emerged for the second half. Ten minutes in, an errant boot from hooker Daniel Dubroca struck him in the groin. Despite having only water to soothe the area, Shelford played out the remaining half an hour. His disappointment at a 16-3 defeat was nothing compared to what he would discover in the changing room. As Buck removed his shorts and stood up, his horrified team-mates alerted him to the bloody sight between his legs. One of his testicles hung by a thread, having been ripped from his scrotum (don't say I didn't warn you). When talking about the incident decades later, a resolute Shelford said, 'These sort of things do happen. And you've just got to play on.'

Reasoning with athletes who share the mindset of Monty Python's Black Knight can't be easy. 'Footballers spend 90 minutes trying to fake injury, our boys spend 80 minutes trying to show they haven't got injured,' is how Phil summed it up. As a boyhood Sheffield Wednesday fan who dreamed of turning out for the Owls before setting his sights on rugby, the Yorkshireman is only half joking. But comparing gravity-friendly soccer players unfavourably with their robust egg-chucking peers remains a common jibe in rugby clubs.

As someone who has worked in both sports, Prav isn't as comfortable with the stereotypes. 'That's just athletes in general. You get that wide spectrum of people that you need to push, and people that you need to pull back.' And while it might be those kicking the round ball who have, perhaps unfairly, earned the sicknote reputation, it's those throwing the oval one who present the most diverse collection of ailments. 'You see a significant amount of lower-limb injuries in football,' said Prav. 'But in rugby, it's a total body sport. You get injuries from top to toe. So you have to be across a number of aspects of clinical care. When I started out at London Wasps it was eye-opening to see how different the injuries were. You're talking collisions with G-forces akin to car crashes.'

Yet as it heads towards its fourth decade as a professional sport, medics are seeing signs that rugby is being weaned off the to-the-death legacy of the amateur era. Rachel Scurfield, lead doctor at Newcastle Falcons, has seen a gradual shift in attitudes during her nine years at the north-east club. She told me that, in the machismo environment of rugby union, players are starting to let their guards down, although not with everyone. 'The players use me as a buffer. I am the go-between that gets shouted at by both sides. The player says "I'm fine to play" to the coaches. Then he'll come to me and say, "I don't want to be in contact training. I won't be ready."'

As the Falcons' mental health lead, Rachel encourages injured players to be more honest about their condition and concerns. 'I'll say to them, "Do you want to be seen as somebody who's invincible and ready to go? Or do you want to be someone who's actually admitting that you're injured, getting better, and making sure you're fully ready to come back?"'

While there is a societal trend for improving individual wellbeing, it's not the only reason behind this attitude change. Although James has noticed it, he reckons the reasons are more performance-led. 'If you'd asked me ten years ago, I would have said the difference between rugby and other sports is that your problem with rugby is getting people *not* to play. We've got guys with dislocated thumbs on the pitch saying "just strap me up and get on with it".'

But with the stakes, including financial incentives, higher than ever, winning has become a squad endeavour. 'They're more honest. They know that if they stay on at 90 per cent, there's a guy on the bench at 100 per cent,' said James, before reciting rationale that he has uttered many times to athletes who didn't want to hear it. 'It's not themselves they're doing a disservice to, but their team-mate. That team environment is paramount. It's not about 15 guys. It's about getting through 80 minutes with 23 players. So get yourself off, man.' At least at the top level, it is no longer seen as big, nor clever, to soldier on.

The tone change of James's last line hinted at the stern bedside manner needed in order to be listened to. Prav affirmed that, like a head coach, a medic without the players' respect is a medic without a mandate. Phil was confident that his playing experience brought with it the gravitas required. But Rachel, like the other half a dozen female medics in Premiership rugby, was well aware that she had a decades-old, testosterone barrier to surmount. 'You have to have huge confidence in your ability,' she said. 'They will eat you alive if not. If you waiver you've had it.'

Pinch Points

Rachel has been a rugby fanatic her whole life. As a toddler, she stood pitchside watching her PE teacher dad running games between Newcastle schools. Her brothers played too, and she has no doubt she would have joined them had it been more common for girls to do so at the time. 'It's probably good otherwise I would be very broken now,' she told me, a few days after returning from the Falcons' bruising February trip to Bristol Bears.

When she attended medical school in Leeds, she drew curious looks from fellow students when she told them she didn't like hospitals. Working in sport was always the aim. After completing a master's degree in sports medicine her opportunity came in 2004, in the humble surroundings of rugby union's fourth tier. Rachel spent ten seasons volunteering as the doctor for Northumberland club Tynedale RFC, turning up at every home match and training session and becoming a popular face among its rugby-mad farming community. Then she was poached by Newcastle in 2012, moving from treating players who could drive tractors to those who were built like one. 'It used to be that you had your little scrum-half, your big fat prop, and your really tall lock. And now they're all just giants. They're all over 100kg.'

It wasn't just the players who looked different. The fact they weren't sloshing around on pitches resembling a ploughman's field also made an impact in the treatment room, especially when a new synthetic pitch was installed at the Falcons' Kingston Park stadium in 2014. 'We were much faster, the ball was in play more, there were fewer knock-ons, and it was an easier surface to play on,' said Rachel. 'The boys can get up to top speed, they're not churning away in the mud. So they can train harder, and play harder. That definitely increased the number of injuries.'

It took some time for her to adapt to the sheer physicality of top-flight rugby and the formidable pain thresholds of her new patients. 'To begin with, I sometimes felt that I wasn't on the same wavelength of how severe an injury a player can have and yet appear to be absolutely normal.' Players would tell Rachel they were 'a bit sore', only for her to later discover that their injuries were worse than first assumed. 'You'd get the scan and oh my God, he's broken this, he's ruptured this, he's torn that. He's going to be out for at least six months. And I've not prepared them for that. I've done a disservice by saying it didn't look too bad.'

Rachel's concern for managing the expectations of a diagnosis aligns with a renewed focus on player mental health. 'The hardest part is the emotional attachment. You feel their pain when they've just got back from one injury, and then something goes and they're out again for three months or a season. It's brutal. The psychological impact of injury by far outweighs the physical.'

Despite the clear physical improvements in these players and the advancements in prevention techniques, there remains an element of helplessness when it comes to injury. James emphasised that while today's athletes can spend hours in the gym toning up muscle, there are parts of the body that remain entirely in the hands of genetics. 'You can strengthen muscle. You can't necessarily strengthen the tendon or ligament. So you're seeing very highly tuned physical specimens but the pinch points are the joints.'

Estimating the duration an injured player will be on the sidelines is a part of the job that few medics relish. At England, Phil and his colleagues were notorious for their go-to catchphrases when fielding the dreaded question from coaches. 'They used to take the mickey out of me because it was "four to six weeks" for any injury we ever had. Or "I'll know better in 24–48 hours". I learned that quite early. We knew how to handle coaches,' he said, keen to remind me that he's worked under the likes of Wayne Smith, Eddie Jones, Warren Gatland, and Ian McGeechan.

Friction between coaches and medics can occur. It is the natural by-product when one role prioritises winning at all costs and the other puts a player's welfare above all else. If a doctor says the scrum-half will need three months to recover, the response from many coaches will be to push for two. It is one of the reasons why treatment table guesstimates have been replaced by target-based schedules. 'We don't do timelines anymore,' said Phil. 'We do criteria-driven rehab. It is basically you can't run until you can walk. You can't do zigzags until you can run in a straight line. No contact until you can run at 75 per cent of your pace. And unless you hit the marker, you don't get back to play. The coaches know that. That might be in three weeks and it might take two months.'

By eliminating subjective predictions and putting the onus on the player to prove their readiness for return, debates between medics and coaches are less likely to occur. Though, as Rachel described, it's not always the case. 'At Tynedale injuries were accepted. But at the Falcons it's almost, "Why are they injured?" The coaches almost look at you as if you're trying to sabotage them,' said Rachel, who made no secret about where her priorities lay. 'Player welfare is my ultimate. I always say to them, "I'm looking after you now. And long-term."'

Coming to a Head

The long-term medical impact of playing the game remains the most contentious and emotive subject in rugby. The concern is that stronger players and faster surfaces result in more collisions. And it's backed up by the data. According to World Rugby stats, there was an average of 257 tackles per game at the 2019 World Cup. That's compared to 113 in the 1993 edition, the last before the sport turned pro. Then consider that professional players now engage in full-contact training nearly every day, have a higher rate of recovery, and enjoy longer careers. It all makes for a potentially damaging combination.

In December 2020, England World Cup winner Steve Thompson revealed that he had been diagnosed with early-onset dementia. Having lifted the Webb Ellis Cup only 17 years earlier, the 42-year-old said that he was no longer able to remember much of his time in Australia. He and seven other players launched a lawsuit against rugby's governing bodies. Since then, they have been joined by over 150 more. The players not only share similar diagnoses but they are all part of the same first generation of professional rugby. The sport is desperately trying to change its ways.

Doctors and physios have been the welcome beneficiaries of a notable power shift. Coaches wanting their stars rushed back will no longer be placated. Players will no longer be able to stubbornly take the field against better advice. 'Now, you find that the sway is no longer with the coach. It's with the medic. Whereas many years ago they never even asked the opinion of the medic. That is a sea change,' said James. Rachel has also welcomed the developments. 'Because injuries, mental health, and concussion is now scrutinised so much, that has really empowered me to be able to say, "Look, this is what we have to do to look after them." So that part of the job has got a lot easier over the years.'

Consider the earlier case of Buck Shelford. Its wincing denouement plays up to the romantic notion of rugby players as indestructible warriors. But what often escapes remark in the anecdote is that had today's head injury assessment (HIA) protocols been in place, Shelford would never have been on the pitch to take the stud to his nethers. He would have been removed from play the moment he lost consciousness in the first half. 'In those days,' said Phil, presumably referring to his own playing days, 'it was a badge of honour to play the next week if you'd been knocked out.'

Reassuringly, these badges are no longer in fashion. In 2014, James co-authored a paper titled *Concussion: no longer a laughing matter in sport*, in which he argued for culture change in rugby. Eight years on he believes it has arrived. 'There are certain areas where people could get better. But the awareness of head injury and concussion, its management, and its importance is so much better.' He used the example of players approaching him to air concerns about team-mates, with small tells such as forgetting line-out codes being potential signs of brain injury. 'The education of players and ancillary staff, particularly coaches, has gotten immeasurably higher. And that's a fantastic thing to see.'

Medics themselves will admit when mistakes have been made in the hope that it will lead to better practices in the future. In 2009, James was inundated with complaints by television viewers who had noted that Scotland's Simon Webster had briefly lost consciousness in a coming together with Wales flanker Martyn Williams. Despite being on the scene just six seconds later, James hadn't seen Webster's blackout. Unlike those at home, he had no access to action replays. With the winger talking freely to the doctor and insisting that he was merely winded, he was allowed to play on. He was replaced ten minutes later, walking groggily off the pitch.

In 2015 Wales's George North played the entire Six Nations tie against England despite taking two knocks to the head, the second of which appeared to momentarily knock him out. The reaction in the media was one of disbelief, and it was chief medical manager Prav who fronted up with a mea culpa. 'I'm not ashamed to admit it, we were involved in a very public error. We didn't have direct sight of it. It was actually my side of the pitch as well, but I was obscured by a couple of players. And we assessed him and left him on the field of play,' he told me, unflinching in his self-criticism six years later. 'After the game, we were upstairs in the post-match function and the game was rolling in the background. And the doc and I saw it and we were like, "Oh shit." Clearly, he'd had a loss of consciousness. And that was a very big mistake that we made.'

By the time the World Cup began in England later that year, lessons had been learned. Matchday medics had access to a multitude of camera angles to bolster their review process, while an independent doctor sat in the stands with a better vantage point. Not only can these impartial medics now flag potential head injuries to their pitchside peers, but they also have the unilateral authority to remove any player from the field.

Prav recalled that when he started working with Wales in 2011, the average time medics had to assess an injured player was 74 seconds. As part of today's HIA protocols, that time is now a mandatory off-pitch 12-minute evaluation. 'There are multiple cognitive assessments like immediate memory, delayed memory, balance, neurological examination,' said Prav. 'And they're all matched against your baseline from pre-season.'

In the days following a concussion diagnosis, players must go through a six-step graduated programme before they can even be considered for selection. As with the criteria-led rehabilitation described above, no player recovers from a concussion at the same rate. 'It's an incredibly complex area. And we're far better at managing it than we ever were. But everybody knows that you can't rest on what we've currently got,' said James, who was also up to speed on technological advancements intended to make his job easier in future. These include iPad apps that can measure a player's balance, swab tests that can identify brain injury markers in saliva, and smart gum shields with in-built impact sensors.

The battle to save rugby, and to protect those who play it, goes on. As the research continues and the evidence builds, there is no doubt that much more must be done. And its dedicated medics will play an increasingly influential role in this future. For while progress in this area appears to lean towards objective decision-making, a medic's intuition will never go unheeded. Especially if a suspect player has ticked all boxes with flying colours.

'If you've actually got a sixth sense, and many doctors do, and you're still not happy with this person's condition, then you just keep them off,' said James, just weeks before Scotland's autumn internationals. 'It's quite a difficult decision sometimes, and players won't thank you. But then at the end of the game when they've got a thumping headache and they feel a bit nauseated, they'll come along and say, "Thanks, Doc. I'm pleased you didn't put me back on."'

Making a Difference

When James and Phil rushed to a stricken Brian O'Driscoll in 2005, they didn't wait for any permission to join the fray. There aren't many other sports where a medic can enter the arena while a game is still ongoing (rugby league is another). They are advised only to go on when it is safe to do so and are forbidden from interfering with play. In other words, make your entrance only when the ball has moved on, just as it had done in Christchurch courtesy of Carter's diagonal boot. But in another example of a medic's Hippocratic instinct taking precedence, there have been exceptions.

In the 2010 Six Nations draw between Scotland and England at Murrayfield, James spotted a sickening clash of heads between Ugo Monye and Kelly Brown as Scotland attacked England's try line. As the ball fell from Brown's hands, a melee ensued. Both players were motionless and at risk of being trampled. Despite the game's action continuing exactly where he needed to be, James ran on. It forced the referee to bring the game to a halt, but as Monye left the field in a neck brace and Brown was confirmed as having lost consciousness, James's rogue actions could well have prevented a more serious incident.

'Occasionally, you end up putting your body on the line to protect an injured player,' said James, adding that referees have become sharper at stopping play when a medical incident occurs. 'You've got to be immensely aware because play could quickly come back to you. And players don't stop. If they don't see you, they can go through you. More importantly, if you've got somebody down injured, they could go through them.' Despite the dangers, James spoke glowingly about the privilege of being an active part of the match. 'I've got the best job on matchday because not only can I actually go up and down the pitch with play, but I can also get on if I need to.'

Quite understandably, Rachel wasn't as quick to describe this as a perk. 'I am probably more conscious than anybody because if I get hit by them, I will be broken in two. So I tend not to go on unless [the play] is finished, or is miles away. I've seen so many people get run over. It's very high on my radar that this is dangerous,' she said, remembering one occasion that she wasn't able to live down for weeks. 'I can recall a running-on, running-off scenario. Which I don't want to repeat again. I think they put Benny Hill music to it!'

They may often be the butt of the jokes, but every medic I spoke to mentioned the changing room camaraderie as one of their highlights. As they prowl the touchline for 80 minutes they are closer to the players than any other member of the backroom staff. Often they manage more minutes on the pitch than some of the bench replacements. And given sport's propensity for finding a competitive edge wherever one may present itself, medics can also become a useful strategic tool. A player wanting a breather, or a coach needing to quell opposition momentum, may subtly request for treatment to take longer than it would normally require.

With all that in mind, it's not unusual for some medics to be treated as just another team-mate. Number 24, if you will. But that's not always as fun as it might sound. James was once punched in the changing rooms by a player who thought he was being pranked. 'I know not to spray disinfectant on somebody's cuts without actually telling them,' he said. While James nursed a swollen jaw, the player apologised profusely.

There is also a reason why Rachel, who jokingly described her job as 'like herding cats', turns her phone to silent whenever there is a squad social. She learned the hard way that players seem to think she is on call 24/7. 'I had eight missed calls and ten text messages. "Can you come and help with such-and-such. He's fallen in a bush." And then I got this photograph and there was massive laceration right across his forehead,' she said, casting some doubt as to the real cause of the injury.

There's also the fact that elite sportspeople are bad losers. And when you have to work with dozens of them in the moments after defeat, it's rarely a pleasant experience. 'When you lose, it's the last place on earth you want to be,' said Prav, who quickly contrasted it with the better times. 'Being able to share the 2019 Grand Slam [won by

Wales] with my daughter on the pitch was an incredibly proud moment for me.'

And Rachel was only too happy to make herself available for duty when, working as an independent doctor at the 2015 World Cup, she got word that the New Zealand skipper needed stitches removed from his eyebrow. 'Now I don't usually get [starstruck], but Richie McCaw is a legend isn't he? When I was removing them I said, "Can you just sign this rugby ball?" I felt like a teenage girl.'

Given these experiences of being embedded within the tapestry of the game's most memorable moments, it is easy to see why a medic can sometimes feel like 'one of the boys'. But very occasionally there is an acute reminder that they are anything but. 'The hardest thing for any clinician practitioner is saying that a player's career is over,' said Prav, slowly shaking his head.

On 13 February 2010, Scotland winger Thom Evans ducked into a tackle from Wales full-back Lee Byrne at the Millennium Stadium. Earlier in the first half he had been off the pitch receiving stitches to a cut lip, and dipping into the collision had been his attempt to prevent re-opening the wound. Instead it resulted in exposing the back of his neck. As Evans tumbled to the turf, the ball spilt from his grasp. His reaction was to grab the loose ball but he found himself unable to move his arms. Within seconds James was there, ordering the other medics not to move the player a single millimetre.

Few things can quieten a raucous Cardiff crowd on Six Nations matchday, but the sight of a neck brace and stretcher did just that. As James went about his work in front of 70,000 worried onlookers, Evans's breathing was short and panicky. Still numb, he thought he was going to die in his Scotland shirt.

Suddenly he felt a thrust of pain in his legs and back, which he likened to being hit by a sniper's bullet. Despite being in agony he was refused painkillers in case they prompted him into a movement that would have snapped his spine. At the hospital he underwent emergency surgery. Scans showed two vertebrae so severely damaged that the surgeons needed to operate through the front of his neck, moving aside his vocal cords. Before going under, Evans signed a waiver acknowledging that he had a 50 per cent chance of making it through. The 24-year-old made a full recovery but was forced to retire from the sport.

It took two months for James to fully process the moments of that day. 'The enormity of the ultimate diagnosis, and what we might have done if we'd got it wrong on the pitch, that's when you have a moment's emotional self-doubt. I can remember every day driving to Murrayfield and my thoughts were re-running that scenario. You couldn't get away from it.'

James's calm but swift actions almost certainly prevented permanent paralysis or a worse fate. Like Will Greenwood, Evans is on the record as owing his life to the humble physician. He has since gone on to enjoy a post-rugby career in music and television, alongside his pop star girlfriend, Nicole Scherzinger. James now smiles every time he sees his former patient on TV. 'I love seeing Thom. He's off with Nicole now, having a fantastic life.'

Glancing above his television also reminds James of that distressing day. There, hangs the only piece of sporting memorabilia that the doctor owns. It is Evans's jersey, which was cut off from him in A&E.

'Because every day I thank goodness that we were able to affect what we did. Not only to that individual, but their family and their friends, and what happens for the rest of their lives,' said James, ending our conversation on a hopeful note. 'Medics worldwide do that every day. We don't do it quite so much in sport. But every now and again you think, "Wow, I did make a difference."'

Acknowledgements

I WOULD like to begin by thanking Jane Camillin at Pitch Publishing for her enthusiastic backing of my book idea, not to mention patience in allowing me to see it through. I hope I have repaid your trust and that it has delivered on your expectations.

I am of course immensely grateful to everyone I interviewed during the writing process. Over the course of 16 months I spoke to more than 60 people, of whom over 40 are featured in this book. Your hospitality, generosity of time, and pride in the way you spoke about your work was heart-warming. I hope you enjoyed the read. To those of you who were kind enough to speak to me but – for editorial reasons of space or time – didn't make it on to these pages, it remains my aim to tell your story one day. Watch this space.

I am incredibly fortunate to be surrounded by a squad of family and friends who have supported and encouraged me throughout the making of this book. There are way too many to name you all here and still come in under the contracted word count. But there are some whose contributions I can't go without specifically acknowledging.

I would like to thank Chris Stewart for casting a critical eye over the proposal that got the ball rolling. Also my thanks to Matt Walker, for his integral creative input, John Devlin, for kindly sharing his football kit contacts, and Steven Railston, for his diligent transcription work back when this book was but a twinkle in my eye.

I owe much to Sam Barry and Katie Newton, whose support and belief in this project gave me the confidence to give it a wholehearted crack. Though I never intended to do the same to your furniture (apologies again). To my brother Seb, and my cousin Dom, thanks for your constant offers of help. You do more than you realise by just being there. That goes for all of my best pals. You know who you are. I'm looking forward to catching up with you all after emerging from my cave. Seb, let's get that away trip in the diary. Dom, if this book sells a few copies, I promise to buy you a new toilet seat.

And while a mother's support is a given, it should never be taken for granted. Antoine de Saint-Exupéry wrote, 'Toutes les grandes personnes ont d'abord été des enfants, mais peu d'entre elles s'en souviennent.' All adults were once children but few of them remember it. Mam, your unwavering enthusiasm and infectious positivity proves that you are one of those few. Among everything else you have done for me, thanks to you and to Keith for letting me convert your empty home into a writing sanctuary for those final two weeks before deadline. The silence was a godsend.

Finally, to my wife Melissa. My unsung hero. Not only have you been left to raise our children alone while I tap away in the office until the early hours, but you have also had to put up with me speaking about little else on the rare occasions we enjoy a moment's peace together. I couldn't have done this without you, my love.

I suppose I should thank those two tinkers as well. To Layla and Rosie. Shouting up the stairs after school to tell me you had a cupcake for lunch/found a bug under a rock/have a wobbly tooth does not provide a conducive working environment. But it remains my favourite part of the day. Your dad is sorry for being so grumpy while he was writing his story. And no, it's still not about unicorns, dinosaurs, or Lego.